The Verbum Book of Digital Typography

Also by Linnea Dayton and Michael Gosney
The Verbum Book of Electronic Page Design
M&T Books/Prentice Hall, 1990

The Verbum Book of Digital Painting
(with Paul Goethel)
M&T Books, 1990

The Verbum Book of PostScript Illustration
(with Janet Ashford)
M&T Books/Prentice Hall, 1990

The Verbum Book of Scanned Imagery
(with Phil Inje Chang)
M&T Books, 1991

This book is dedicated to
type designers of yesterday, today and tomorrow,
those who give artful form to the written word.

The Verbum Book of Digital Typography

Michael Gosney ▮ Linnea Dayton ▮ Jennifer Ball

M&T BOOKS

M&T Books

A Division of M&T Publishing, Inc.
501 Galveston Drive
Redwood City, CA 94063

Printed in the United States of America
First Edition published 1991

Library of Congress Cataloging-in-Publication Data

Gosney, Michael, 1954–
The Verbum book of digital typography / Michael Gosney, Linnea Dayton, Jennifer Ball. — 1st ed.
       p. cm. — (The Verbum electronic art and design series)
Includes index.
ISBN 1-55851-092-3: $29.95
       1. Printing, Practical — Layout — Data processing. 2. Type and type-founding — Digital techniques. 3. Electronic publishing. 4. Desktop publishing.
       I. Dayton, Linnea, 1944–   II. Ball, Jennifer.   III. Title.   IV. Series.
Z246.G65 1991
       686.2'2544416 — dc20   91-25010
                                                 CIP

94 93 92 91   4 3 2 1

Produced by The Gosney Company, Inc. and *Verbum* magazine

670 Seventh Avenue, Second Floor
San Diego, CA 92101
(619) 233-9977

Book and cover design: John Odam
Cover illustration: Jack Davis
Back cover illustrations: Louis Fishauf, Tom Gould and David Smith
Production Manager: Martha Siebert
Administrative Manager: Jeanne Juneau
Proofreading, research: Valerie Bayla

Contents

Welcome to the *Verbum Book of Digital Typography*. Like the other books in the *Verbum Electronic Art and Design Series*, this is an art instruction book rather than a technical computer book. This volume focuses on the revolutionary field of digital typography and type design.

The first two chapters of the book give an overview of digital type technology and the innovative personal computer products that bring it to the desktop. The following chapters take you through the step-by-step development of actual design projects by talented artists. Each chapter introduces the designer and project, and re-creates both the artist's creative thought processes and the technical steps as the project developed. At the end of each chapter is a Portfolio of other designs by the artist, with brief descriptions of each.

You'll find sidebars and tips throughout the project chapters. The sidebars provide supportive information on significant subjects. ▮ *Tips are introduced by this vertical symbol, and they appear in italics like this.*

An extensive Gallery of exemplary typographic and font design examples follows the project chapters. These samples are from designers who have had extensive experience with personal computer design systems. We've chosen works that represent not only creative design solutions, but also effective and innovative use of the electronic tools. At the 'end of the book, a Glossary provides terms and definitions, and an Appendix lists useful products and services. Production Notes provides details on the development of the book itself. The Index will help you find specific information.

Origins of digital typography

JACK DAVIS

Where did the digital type world of the '90s come from? Although some early glimpses of it were seen on high-end design workstations in the early 1980s, the primary spark came in 1985 with the synergistic integration of three key products: the Apple Macintosh computer with its graphic user interface (including flexible font-handling capabilities built into the system software); the Apple LaserWriter printer (using Adobe's PostScript page description language) and the Aldus PageMaker desktop publishing program. Suddenly, computer users were designing with type in ways never imagined by graphic designers or typehouse managers.

The initial digital type capabilities were impressive: a variety of "screen fonts," with their companion PostScript printing versions, could be mixed and matched. Adobe licensed the rights for many leading fonts from the major suppliers and began selling font packages by the thousands. The typographer's art, as it had been previously known, was changing again, just as it had when computer phototypesetting replaced cast metal type. This time, typesetting was to come under the direct control of designers and production artists. In PageMaker and other desktop publishing programs, type could be positioned and modified instantaneously, allowing for on-the-spot type design without tedious hand-rendered roughs. And final layout allowed absolute precision with type. Type became one of many elements composing a finished page produced on the computer, which was sent out for "imagesetting" at a local service bureau. Major typesetting houses became imagesetters, and small type firms sold their old phototypesetting systems, bought personal computers and became desktop publishing services.

Once talented designers got involved with the early digital type programs, things evolved rapidly. Page layout programs tried to meet the designers' expectations with more sophisticated built-in type-handling capabilities. A few programs specialized for font design were released, and new typefaces began emerging. PostScript illustration programs such as Adobe Illustrator and Aldus FreeHand brought even more type design power — in the form of color and special effects — to the desktop.

Establishing standards

After several years of rapid evolution, the field of digital typography is established. Hardware and software standards are set. But change is still rapid, and new standards are still coming. For example, Apple's TrueType font format brought new screen font display and printing options to the Macintosh. New versions of the desktop publishing and PostScript illustration programs offer ever-increasing typographic power. But for the most part, digital type tools, even if on different hardware platforms, work in similar fashion. During the next few years, we don't anticipate quantum leaps that will make the existing standards obsolete; rather we expect steady refinements. That's why most of the material in this book will be useful to you for several years to come, regardless of your specific system configuration.

MAX SEABAUGH

What *more* can I do with digital type?

The Verbum Book of Digital Typography introduces the state-of-the-art in digital typography through a variety of font and typographic design projects and samples. But the future state-of-the-art will be even more diversified. For example, sophisticated new illustration and image-manipulation programs, such as Adobe Photoshop on the Macintosh and Aldus PhotoStyler on the IBM, are making the bitmapped or "paint" environment a very important resource. Three-dimensional type rendering is also becoming practical with a host of powerful 3D programs. The synergistic combined use of the aforementioned processes opens many new possibilities for type design in both print and video. In addition, digital typography is important for *interactive multimedia*, the ability to combine and spontaneously access text, graphics, sounds and animations on a personal computer. Type has truly entered many new domains, and we look forward to exciting new design opportunities for written material produced with digital tools.

LOUIS FISHAUF

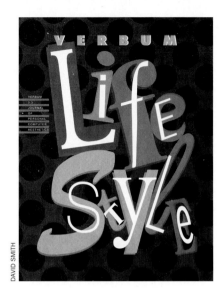

DAVID SMITH

What is *Verbum?*

Verbum, the Journal of Personal Computer Aesthetics, is a magazine dedicated to exploring the aesthetic and human aspects of using microcomputers. Founded in 1986 by a group of artists and writers who had the good fortune to be involved with the early electronic design tools, the journal has tracked the evolution of electronic design and illustration tools, contributing the artist's perspective (and conscience) to an industry that has at times been unbalanced in its commercial and technical emphasis.

Each issue of *Verbum* has served as an example of the latest desktop publishing tools, beginning with the early issue's laser-printed camera-ready art on up to today's digital four-color separations. Through the development of the magazine, we've helped to galvanize the community of advanced artists, programmers and industry visionaries who have pushed the new frontier forward. As an ongoing experiment, *Verbum* has covered not only electronic design, but illustration, fine art, typography, digitized imaging, 3D graphics, animation, music and even the new realm of interactive multimedia. *The Verbum Electronic Art and Design Series* was conceived as a way to bring *Verbum*'s accumulated resources into a practical, instructional context.

Beyond the magazine, *Verbum* has been involved in popularizing PC-assisted art as a fine art form. The *Verbum* team has produced the "Imagine" exhibit of personal computer art since the spring of 1988. Sponsored by Apple Computer, Inc., Letraset U.S.A., SuperMac Technology and other firms, Imagine has been an evolving exhibit featuring the work of over 60 artists from around the world. Major shows have been held in Boston, San Diego and Tokyo, with abbreviated exhibits at conferences in Toronto, Washington, D.C., San Francisco and Los Angeles. As of the fall of 1990, the Verbum Gallery of Digital Art is open in San Diego, showcasing some of the top digital painters from the United States and other countries.

A few acknowledgments

The Verbum Book of Digital Typography and the entire *Verbum* book series have involved the helpful efforts of many people — too many to mention here. But we would like to give special thanks to the contributing artists who committed that most precious resource to the project — time — and to Jason Levine who did preliminary research and writing for several of the project chapters. Also, we would like to thank our literary agent, William Gladstone; our *very* patient editor at M&T Books, Brenda McLaughlin; our service bureau here in San Diego, Central Graphics; and the many software and hardware companies who helped keep us up-to-date on products. Finally, we'd like to thank our *Verbum* readers, who keep inspiring us to push the envelope — just a little further!

An Overview

When we communicate through the written word, our messenger is usually *type* — the collective body of printed letters, numbers and other symbols. Whether a printed page holds several paragraphs of text or just a line or two of headlines, at first glance the typography makes an impression on the reader, even before the words themselves are read. *Typography* can be defined as the composition of printed material from type, the art and technique of such composing, or the arrangement and appearance of material thus composed. *Type design* is the creation of a matching set of characters to be used to accomplish the job of typography.

Well-conceived typography employing well-designed type invites the reader, reflects the designer and illuminates the message. Good typography aids in the understanding of the content. Bad typography can make the reader want to turn the page without reading.

To catch or hold the reader's attention, type relies on some combination of legibility, readability and aesthetic content. *Legibility* is the quality of type that makes it possible to quickly decipher characters, to distinguish a *c* from an *e*, for example, or to recognize a *5* as a *5* and not a *6*. *Readability* is the relative ease with which text set in type can be read — the effortlessness of seeing the words as units, of following a line of type (from left to right across the column in English and other European languages, for example) and of making the leap from the end of one line of type to the beginning of the next. Aesthetic content has more to do with the form of type as art than with its ability to convey information. The typography of *Emigré,* for instance, invites the reader to be more determined about braving typographic frontiers than he or she would typically need to be in order to read a magazine (Figure 1).

Figure 1. Demonstrating the type-as-art philosophy. *Emigré* magazine throws traditional standards out the window in favor of modern aesthetics.

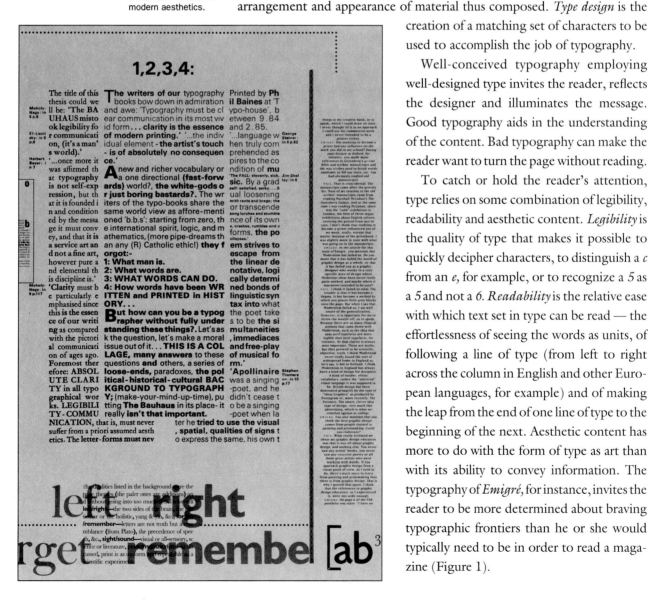

A brief history of type

In the earliest recorded history, the "print" medium consisted of pictographs and hieroglyphics — fairly literal representations of the things whose existence and interactions they recorded. Then, in Phoenicia, around 1600 B.C., a new concept in written communication evolved: using symbols to represent sounds of speech rather than ideas or objects. At first there were symbols only for the sounds we call consonants today. The Greeks added vowels around 1000 B.C. Five hundred years later, the Romans made such a lasting impression on our alphabet that we still incorporate their name in many of our typefaces. Wood-block printing began in China at around A.D. 400. Lower-case letters were apparently Charlemagne's idea in the late eighth century. Type cast in clay and bronze emerged in Asia during the late 11th and early 12th centuries. And history became much more easily documented during the 15th century, when Gutenberg (or possibly one of his contemporaries) invented movable metal type.

The history of type sped up. Soon after the invention of the printing press, type foundries were established and printing presses began publishing. Within 50 years, italic type, Bembo and Garamond — all of which are still actively used today — were designed (Figure 2). The first print shop in America opened in 1638. During the 18th century, the Caslon, Baskerville and Bodoni families of type were introduced (Figure 3). A hundred years later, improvements in printing presses were bringing the cost of printing down. Photography became practical in the mid 1800s, and the halftone process for printing photos followed within the next half century. In the late 1800s, hot metal typesetting and printing had become efficient enough that magazines started to circulate.

Hot metal typesetting dominated the printing and publishing industry until the mid 1960s, when phototypesetting was developed. Using photographic methods and materials, this typesetting technique moves the type characters, which have been recorded on negative film, in front of a light source and exposes their images on photographic paper, which is then processed with photodeveloping chemicals to bring out the type. With the

Bembo
Garamond

Figure 2. Early typefaces. These are Adobe's electronic versions of Bembo (top) and Garamond (bottom), two typefaces that were developed soon after the invention of the Gutenberg printing press.

new process, characters could be set at any distance from each other — without the typesetter having to shave off the sides of metal type blocks to place the characters closer together than usual. Letters could even overlap, which had been impossible with metal type.

In the early 1980s, the microcomputer (or personal computer) became a reasonable investment for offices and homes. And in 1985, Adobe Systems Incorporated released PostScript, a computer language that can describe a page, including its typography, in terms of mathematical equations that can be interpreted by an output device such as a printer (Figure 4). The printer can then print the characters at any resolution (or number of dots per inch) that it's mechanically capable of (Figure 5). The PostScript method of page description, rather than specifying where the printer must place each dot, lets an interpreter in the printer determine the best way it can image the page. The PostScript-based Apple LaserWriter, along with the PageMaker page layout program, provided the basis for typesetting on the desktop. More recent

Figure 3. Eighteenth century typefaces. Caslon, identified by the upper and lower serifs on the *C* and by the angular turn of the top of the *a*, Baskerville, with its vertical weight stress and moderate *x*-height, and Bodoni, known for its un-bracketed serifs and long ascenders and descenders, were designed within 50 years of each other. Here are Adobe's digital versions.

Caslon

New Baskerville

Bodoni

Figure 4. Defining PostScript characters. PostScript fonts are constructed using Bezier curves, whose control points define equations that describe the character outlines. When printed, font outlines are scaled, oriented and filled to generate smooth bitmaps at the resolution of the output device.

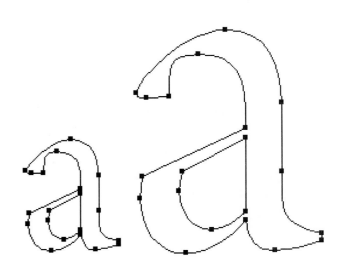

desktop developments have improved the typesetting functions of page layout programs as well as illustration software. And applications created specifically for designing and manipulating type make desktop type even more malleable.

The Adobe Type Manager program for the Mac and for applications running in some operating environments of DOS-based systems such as the IBM PC makes it possible to use printer fonts to create on-screen images of type whose sizes, shapes and spacing are as close as the screen display can make them to the characters as they will finally print (Figure 6). These screen representations are much more refined and accurate than the images created by the standard screen fonts (see "Screen fonts and printer fonts" on page 5).

To design, modify or use type well, it helps to understand what type is and how it communicates. In "Reviewing the basics" (see pages 5–12), designer Tom Gould, whose type design work is also presented in Chapter 7, discusses the basics of desktop typography.

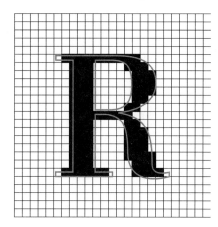

Figure 5. Making the best bitmap. The dot pattern that defines a printed PostScript character is determined by the resolution of the output device. For example, an Apple LaserWriter can print the letter using 300 dots per inch; using the same PostScript information, a Linotronic L-300 imagesetter can print the letter using 2540 dots per inch. Shown here is a comparison between a character at 72 dpi (screen or Image-Writer resolution) and 300 dpi. Constructing the letter at even higher resolutions would create even smoother-looking bitmaps.

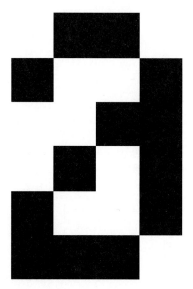

Figure 6. Using ATM. These enlarged screen dumps of a Galliard *a* show the effect of Adobe Type Manager (ATM). The *a* on the left was made without ATM on a Macintosh that had only the 10-point screen font installed in the System and the printer font stored in the System folder. The letter on the right was produced with the same System and screen and printer fonts but with ATM installed and turned on. ATM works by using the resolution-independent printer font information to construct a more accurate on-screen representation of the font.

Reviewing the basics

There are two components that make up type: sticks and everything else. The sticks identify and define the symbols of letters. For example, sticks made by a Number 2 pencil on a yellow copy pad are often used to write a first draft of text. "Everything else" is some kind of attempt to express and improve on those symbols for reasons of aesthetics, science or culture. The aesthetician wants to produce beautiful letterforms; the scientist develops the technology to mass produce those same letterforms, and the culture drives the desire to have complete access to the letterform so that people can mold it as they see fit.

With the stick being the lowest common denominator of type forms, one might be surprised that any self-respecting type house's text-typebook could contain more than 75 variations on the basic stick style. Helvetica alone has at least 90 variations in a standard typebook. It's obvious that the variations possible, presumably desirable and theoretically discernible are enormous. How can this diversity be possible when the identity of letterforms must remain a constant?

The letter's beginnings are prehistoric, while type as we know it came along only a little over four centuries ago. And type is not the only way to produce letterforms even now. People write post-its, letters, grocery lists and recipes by hand, with a variety of tools. Over the years, this combination of hand and

---

**❚ Screen fonts
and printer fonts**

Screen fonts are those files that tell the computer how to form characters for on-screen display. Screen-font-characters are *bitmaps,* formed as patterns of dots at the screen resolution of 72 dots per inch. The desktop icons of screen fonts look like suitcases and are installed in the system through the Font/DA Mover. Programs such as Suitcase and Master Juggler allow you to access screen fonts without installing them in the System Folder, which keeps the System file less cluttered. At least one screen-font size per font is necessary for accurate positioning of characters in illustration and page layout programs. Most image-setting service bureaus distribute screen fonts free of charge or for the cost of a disk.

Printer fonts are files that reside in the printer or that the computer downloads to it when, at printing time, it finds the related screen font in the document it's asked to print. The printer font is a mathematical expression of an outlined shape, so its resolution is device-independent. This means that the higher the resolution the printer has, the better the font will look. Sending a file to the printer without the corresponding printer font in the System folder results in either font substitution (the printer substitutes what it considers to be the most similar font it has available) or a bitmapped (72 dpi) image of the font, depending upon choices made in the software.

tool has determined what we recognize as a letter, whether penciled on a legal pad, cut in stone, molded in lead or digitized on a video display terminal. Letters, as they diverge from the stick, generally trace the mark of the tool and the flexibility of wrist and fingers. Alphabets evolved by trial and error, and survived through demonstrating both efficiency and visual delight.

Two aspects of letter anatomy, variation in thickness and termination of strokes, demonstrate how that anatomy is shaped. The thickness derives from a flat tool, pen or chisel, which, when held at a fairly constant angle, produces a consistent variation in stroke width that depends on the angle of movement (Figure 7). Notice that the fit isn't *too* consistent — and this is where the art comes in. This is also why a letterer's mix-up in these customary thicks and thins produces a disconcerting appearance (Figure 8). The difficulty of maintaining an even base or boundary termination of a letter's stroke produced the serif (Figure 9), a short flick of pen or chisel to provide a base and to define a contour for individual letters and words, much as the light blue lines of a legal pad confine and control the sprawl of hasty writing.

So the letter evolved in all its variety: Sans Serif or Gothic, Roman, Uncial, Slab Serif, Modern, Script, Italic, Calligraphic and on and on (Figure 10). Does the practice of typography then consist of picking the right typeface out of this lush collection?

It's a start.

Letters and spaces Consider the letterform, with all its inside and outside contours to think about, 26 basic letters plus numerals, punctuation and other symbols (Figure 11). Don't forget capitals and lower case! In English we have *A, I* and — poetically — *O* to form words by themselves. Any other words must use two or more letters in combination, so we have to consider the spaces between letters as part of the equation.

Figure 7. Thicks and thins. A chisel-pointed tool, maintaining a constant angle, gave type its original thick and thin characteristics.

Figure 8. A letterer's mixup. Switching sides for customary thicks and thins produces a disconcerting appearance. The "A" on the left is correct, while the "A" on the right has been reversed.

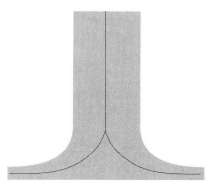

Figure 9. The reason for serifs. The serif provides a finish and gives structure to the type stroke.

But then we usually need more than one word to convey our meaning, so there's space between words as well to think about. Words become lines, lines columns, columns pages, pages spreads, then articles or chapters, and finally complete publications or books. All of these depend upon some variation on sticks and the permutations and combinations of relationships between them.

Using type Some designers feel that type should be transparent; that if it's noticeable, it's wrong. Without completely subscribing to this exclusion, we can conclude that certain defaults are helpful to a designer unless there's a good reason to do something else ("Everybody's doing it" is *not* a good reason.) Those defaults would be white paper; one typeface; legible, black, undistorted type; and a simple, logical format. In other words, learn the basics and the possibilities of simplicity before attempting to push the envelope. And have a reason for doing what you do, especially if you have to explain what you do to someone else in order to get it onto paper.

Mathematically, there might be more ways to misuse type than there are available typefaces. It follows that an understanding of type is more important than access to all the hot new exotics rolling off the font mills and to all the bending, squeezing and extruding software one can buy .

Resident faces Most people with access to a computer and a printer have access to certain fonts: Times, Helvetica, (Helvetica Narrow, a computer-generated squashed Helvetica), Courier and Symbol. Upscale printers may add Avant Garde, Bookman, New Century Schoolbook, Palatino, Zapf Chancery and Zapf Dingbats (Figure 12).

ITC Avant Garde is hard-core stick, derived from ruler and compass, but if you look closely you can see subtle variations in line weights that aid legibility and minimize ink traps where lines join. It was also designed with many variation characters and joined characters (ligatures), which have led many would-be designers astray, usually because they were insufficiently acquainted with the classic rules, or because they subscribed to the idea that if a little bit of design is good, then a lot must be better.

Figure 10. Identifying faces. This bumper sticker plays on the fact that *G* is one of the most distinctive letters in a typeface. Shown left to right are Bookman, Souvenir, Helvetica, Times, Avant Garde, Palatino, Optima and New Century Schoolbook.

HONK IF YOU LOVE GGGGGGG's

Helvetica is basic stick, but elegantly detailed, with thinned strokes in the classic positions for ease of reading. It's been a workhorse for many years, and only the most jaded designers will find it unusable now and for the future.

So much for the sticks; now for everything else. Times Roman, another workhorse, has a voluptuous collection of curves and a suave italic. Drawbacks are a slight heaviness in the text weight and an unlovely bold (Figure 13). Times Semibold is a much preferable version.

New Century Schoolbook, Palatino and Bookman continue a spectrum from modern to traditional. Schoolbook is quite plain, Palatino is very usable except for a rather crabbed italic, and Bookman is a little quaint, with a horizontal bias that likes more room than is often available.

No script has ever seemed to me to work as type. Zapf Chancery is the best of a flawed lot of script faces trying to be useful as type. It seems to remain a specialty face for certificates and such. Some of the Zapf Dingbats characters are indispensable (Figure 14).

Courier is roundly disliked by computer graphics people, probably because it's usually seen when a mistake has been made in font availability or when limitations in printer memory are encountered. It's also a hangover from typewriter technology, and there's not much that can be done with it because of the monospace letterforms.

Figure 11. Anatomy of type. Though many more terms can be used to define typographic components, these are the most basic.

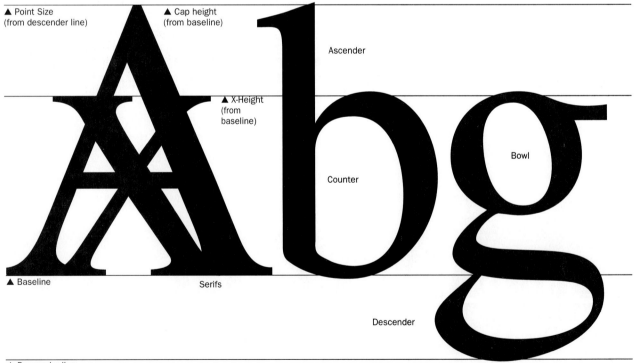

▲ Point Size (from descender line)

▲ Cap height (from baseline)

Ascender

▲ X-Height (from baseline)

Bowl

Counter

▲ Baseline

Serifs

Descender

▲ Descender line

Setting serif faces Serif faces tend to lead the pack when it comes to body setting, whether because the thicks and thins plus serifs really do aid readability, as partisans claim, or because we have been trained to read them faster due to their ubiquity.

A rule of thumb for sizing type is "Spec the type you like, and then make it a size smaller." It's a little simplistic, and styles have changed in 30 years, but I've noticed that I've been more often in trouble with type too big — almost never because it was too small. Nine to 12 points is the usual size for text. Here's a line of 10-point Times:

Lorem ipsum dolor sit amet, consectetuer adipiscing elit sed.

That was default spacing — we can, using typical page layout programs, change the spacing:

Lorem ipsum dolor sit amet, consectetuer adipiscing elit sed.

Lorem ipsum dolor sit amet, consectetuer adipiscing elit sed.

Lorem ipsum dolor sit amet, consectetuer adipiscing elit sed.

Lorem ipsum dolor sit amet, consectetuer adipiscing elit sed.

Lorem ipsum dolor sit amet, consectetuer adipiscing elit sed.

Times
Helvetica
Helvetica Narrow
Courier
Σψμβολ

Palatino
Bookman
Avant Garde
New Century Schoolbook
Zapf Chancery
✻❀❑✷ ❖✸■✳❁❀▼▲

Figure 12. LaserWriter fonts. The first tier of fonts (Times, Helvetica, Helvetica Narow, Courier and Symbol) are resident in the Apple Laser-Writer Plus. The next tier (Palatino, Bookman, Avant Garde, New Century Schoolbook, Zapf Chancery and Zapf Dingbats) are resident in the rest of the Apple LaserWriter line.

Investors Report
San Diego Gas & Electric　*Spring 1990*

Proxy Statement and Notice of Annual Meeting 1990

San Diego Gas & Electric

SDG&E

Figure 13. Using Times for titles. Above is a newsletter heading and at left, a publication cover, both using Times Italic, slightly condensed.

Now let's try adding some more lines of text. This paragraph is the "Auto" leading default for PageMaker — 10/12:
Lorem ipsum dolor sit amet, consectetuer adipiscing elit sed diam nonummy nibh euismod. Tincidunt ut laoreet dolore magna aliquam erat volutpat. Ut wisi enim ad minim veniam, quis nostrud exerci tation ullamcorper suscipit lobortis nisl ut aliquip ex ea commodo consequat. Duis autem vel eum iriure dolor in hendrerit in vulputate velit esse.

Setting it solid, with no lead (10/10) results in the following:
Lorem ipsum dolor sit amet, consectetuer adipiscing elit sed diam nonummy nibh euismod. Tincidunt ut laoreet dolore magna aliquam erat volutpat. Ut wisi enim ad minim veniam, quis nostrud exerci tation ullamcorper suscipit lobortis nisl ut aliquip ex ea commodo consequat. Duis autem vel eum iriure dolor in hendrerit in vulputate velit esse.

With 1 point of leading (10/11), it looks like this:
Lorem ipsum dolor sit amet, consectetuer adipiscing elit sed diam nonummy nibh euismod. Tincidunt ut laoreet dolore magna aliquam erat volutpat. Ut wisi enim ad minim veniam, quis nostrud exerci tation ullamcorper suscipit lobortis nisl ut aliquip ex ea commodo consequat. Duis autem vel eum iriure dolor in hendrerit in vulputate velit esse.

With 4 points of leading (10/14), this way:
Lorem ipsum dolor sit amet, consectetuer adipiscing elit sed diam nonummy nibh euismod. Tincidunt ut laoreet dolore magna aliquam erat volutpat. Ut wisi enim ad minim veniam, quis nostrud exerci tation ullamcorper suscipit lobortis nisl ut aliquip ex ea commodo consequat. Duis autem vel eum iriure dolor in hendrerit in vulputate velit esse.

And with 6 points (10/16), like this:
Lorem ipsum dolor sit amet, consectetuer adipiscing elit sed diam nonummy nibh euismod. Tincidunt ut laoreet dolore magna aliquam erat volutpat. Ut wisi enim ad minim veniam, quis nostrud exerci tation ullamcorper suscipit lobortis nisl ut aliquip ex ea commodo consequat. Duis autem vel eum iriure dolor in hendrerit in vulputate velit esse.

Type size and leading have predictable effects on each other. One variable in typefaces that affects leading is the height proportion of lower case to caps, called *x-height*. In large x-height faces, the lower case is larger in proportion to the cap height (Figure 15). Not all faces are visually the same size at the same point sizes, and small x-height faces can be set more solidly (meaning tighter leading) than large x-height faces. Also, in the previous leading example, notice how the apparent size of the type changes as leading changes. Which is easier to read? ▪ *You can do copyfitting (making a given amount of text fit a given space) more easily by fiddling with leading than with type size, since larger type often just fills in the paragraph's last lines before adding new lines, and making type big is often dangerous.*

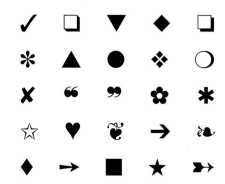

Figure 14. Twenty-five good dingbats. Zapf Dingbats, one of the fonts resident in the LaserWriter series, is a collection of premade symbols, a few of which are shown here.

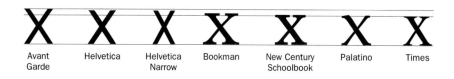

Avant Garde   Helvetica   Helvetica Narrow   Bookman   New Century Schoolbook   Palatino   Times

Figure 15. Comparing x-heights. Not all faces are visually the same size at the same point size. Small x-height faces can be set more solidly (with tighter leading) than large x-height faces. The examples here are all 48-point.

Now, keeping the leading constant at 10/12 and applying no tracking, let's try changing the line lengths. What does line length have to do with readability? A rule of thumb for line length is that 40 to 60 characters per line is considered optimal. Some authorities say 60 to 70, but those studies were done before the postliterate generation came along:

Lorem ipsum dolor sit amet, consectetuer adipiscing elit sed diam nonummy nibh euismod. Tincidunt ut laoreet dolore magna aliquam erat volutpat. Ut wisi enim ad minim veniam, quis nostrud exerci tation ullamcorper suscipit lobortis nisl ut aliquip ex ea commodo consequat. Duis autem vel eum iriure dolor in hendrerit in vulputate velit esse.

Lorem ipsum dolor sit amet, consectetuer adipiscing elit sed diam nonummy nibh euismod. Tincidunt ut laoreet dolore magna aliquam erat volutpat. Ut wisienim ad minim veniam, quis nostrud exerci tation ullamcorper suscipit lobortis nisl ut aliquip ex ea commodo consequat. Duis autem vel eum iriure dolor in hendrerit in vulputate velit esse.

So far we've used flush left, ragged right alignment, which gives us even color spacing in each line. Typographers use the word *color* to describe the overall evenness of tone in a block of type. Even color is a desired quality for a block of text. Other factors to consider when setting type are that flush left, ragged right text is easier to read than justified text, in which the type is spaced across the line so that both the left and right margins are straight. Justified text set too narrow can lead to some very awkward results (as shown at left).

This kind of textual distortion applies not only to straight, full columns of type but also to all those sophisticated text wraps that our software makes so easy.

Lorem ipsum dolor sit amet, consectetuer adipiscing elit sed diam nonummy nibh euismod. Tincidunt ut laoreet dolore magna aliquam erat volutpat.

Using sans serif faces Problems of distortion are usually worse when sans serifs are pushed out of shape than when serif faces are. The geometry of the letterform is much more critical in a face like Helvetica, and even when undistorted it requires a different approach to spacing than does Times. Here are 10-point Helvetica samples similar to the ones we did with Times (starting on page 9):

Lorem ipsum dolor sit amet, consectetuer adipiscing elit sed.
Lorem ipsum dolor sit amet, consectetuer adipiscing elit sed.
Lorem ipsum dolor sit amet, consectetuer adipiscing elit sed.
Lorem ipsum dolor sit amet, consectetuer adipiscing elit sed.
Lorem ipsum dolor sit amet, consectetuer adipiscing elit sed.

Set 10/12 (auto):
Lorem ipsum dolor sit amet, consectetuer adipiscing elit sed diam
nonummy nibh euismod. Tincidunt ut laoreet dolore magna aliquam
erat volutpat. Ut wisi enim ad minim veniam, quis nostrud exerci tation
ullamcorper suscipit lobortis nisl ut aliquip ex ea commodo consequat.

Set 10/10:
Lorem ipsum dolor sit amet, consectetuer adipiscing elit sed diam
nonummy nibh euismod. Tincidunt ut laoreet dolore magna aliquam
erat volutpat. Ut wisi enim ad minim veniam, quis nostrud exerci tation
ullamcorper suscipit lobortis nisl ut aliquip ex ea commodo consequat.

Set 10/11:
Lorem ipsum dolor sit amet, consectetuer adipiscing elit sed diam
nonummy nibh euismod. Tincidunt ut laoreet dolore magna aliquam
erat volutpat. Ut wisi enim ad minim veniam, quis nostrud exerci tation
ullamcorper suscipit lobortis nisl ut aliquip ex ea commodo consequat.

Set (10/14):
Lorem ipsum dolor sit amet, consectetuer adipiscing elit sed diam
nonummy nibh euismod. Tincidunt ut laoreet dolore magna aliquam
erat volutpat. Ut wisi enim ad minim veniam, quis nostrud exerci tation
ullamcorper suscipit lobortis nisl ut aliquip ex ea commodo consequat.

Helvetica's larger x-height suggests loose leading and spacing in body text, but the open counters (inner spaces) also allow tight leading, especially in large sizes (and for small amounts of text). Really large Helvetica, with hairline spacing between letters, works very well.

In order to get a feel for type and its optimal settings, consider setting up style sheets with the kinds of variations seen here, and then flow in each typeface and print out the results. This exercise will teach you more than the one-line alphabets in type catalogs. Once these experiments are absorbed and some experience with using these faces efficiently has been gained, *then* think about branching out into the jungly thickets of type. *T.G.*

Type horizons

With the history and the basics of type briefly covered, we can look at the developments of the present and the future. The evolution of type didn't stop with the development of PostScript. In addition to Adobe's original Type 1 fonts, as they were called, other vendors developed Type 3 fonts, typefaces that worked with PostScript software and output devices but that didn't incorporate all the refinements of PostScript type design (called *hints*) that Adobe was at that point keeping secret (Figure 16). In late summer of 1989, the Type 1 technology became available to other type developers, one of whom "cracked" the code at about the same time Adobe released it. Type manipulation programs that made it possible to control type as objects — to change type from characters that could only be typed from the keyboard into outlines that could be modified or filled with patterns, for example — at first operated on Type 3 fonts only. But by the spring of 1990, the software was able to manipulate Type 1 characters as well.

As this book goes to press, another advance in desktop type is on the horizon. Apple's TrueType fonts, as well as improvements in PostScript, will allow a greater (perhaps almost continuously variable) selection of type styles, weights and sizes from one set of outline descriptions per type family. Apparently, the TrueType and PostScript technologies will be compatible, and both will be supported by the companies that develop digital type. One trend in desktop type seems to be continual improvement and increasing compatibility in type technology.

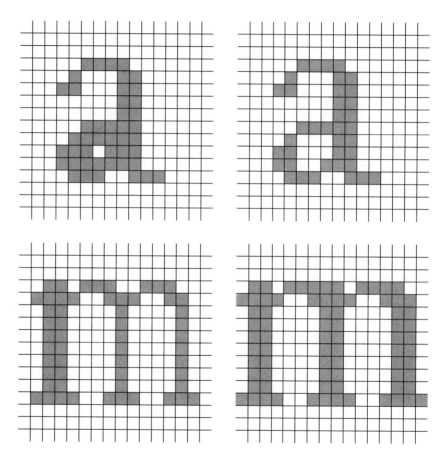

Figure 16. Including hints. Adobe's hinting technology helps keep characters looking good when type is scaled to small sizes at low resolution (such as the 300 dpi of typical laser printers). For instance, it keeps counters from closing up and maintains consistent stroke weights within letters. Hinted versions of the characters are shown here on the right, unhinted versions on the left.

CHAPTER 2

Applications

I n less than a decade, type on the microcomputer advanced from the "typesetting" done by the first word processing programs to sophisticated, true typesetting functions, type design, conversion between different kinds of electronic type systems, modification of letterforms and even automatic conversion of type characters to outlines that can be treated with all the electronic embellishments available for line art. The few faces designed for the first laser printers have been joined by thousands more (Figure 1), which has in turn led to the development of software for managing this wealth of faces. We find these type-making and type-handling capabilities distributed among several kinds of software packages:

- The fonts themselves have a great deal of typesetting information built-in and available for use by page layout and illustration programs.

- Systems for accurate display of type (such as Adobe Type Manager and TrueType, the Apple font technology built into System 7) show size, form and placement of characters that are very similar to what the final printed version will look like. That makes it possible to make precise and reliable design decisions by looking at the on-screen display.

- The more typefaces that are accumulated on a computer system, the more time it takes for type-using applications (such as page layout and illustration programs) to keep track of them. Having a large number of fonts can slow the process of opening an application on-screen, for example, and can also make scrolling lists of fonts a very long and unwieldy process. Programs have been developed to deal with both sorts of problems.

- Programs specifically designed for creating fonts let the artist design letterforms, specify how much space to put around each character (above, below and to each side) and even determine pair kerning (the way individual pairs of letters will fit together when type is set).

- Font conversion programs allow Type 1 and Type 3 fonts (see "Type horizons" in Chapter 1) to be interconverted, so they can be used with programs that can take advantage of features of one kind of font or the other. In addition, there are applications that can convert True-Type (Apple's outline type format) to the standard PostScript format and vice versa.

Figure 1. New developments in type. Tekton, an Adobe Original typeface, brings type design full circle, as electronic type mimics hand-drawn lettering. Created by David Siegel, who modelled it on the lettering of Seattle architect Frank Ching, Tekton was designed with drafting applications in mind. However, it's widely used by computer-based designers who want to add a "human touch."

A high-quality fountain pen has an indefinite life-span. Well maintained, it could pass from generation to generation of regular use.

— *Life-Spans, or How Long Things Last* by Frank Kendig and Richard Hutton

- Typically, page layout programs can take advantage of the kerning infor-mation built into fonts. (That's why text set in a page layout program usually looks better than type set in a word processor.) They can also modify pair kerning and tracking (the overall tightening or loosening of spacing in type set in a particular face) and can condense or expand character width or height. Most page layout programs can also apply limited special effects to type — for example, rotating, drop shadowing and reversing (white type on a black background).

- PostScript illustration programs provide some of the same typesetting functions described for page layout programs, although they generally have less extensive facilities for setting large amounts of text. In addition, though, they can vary the color and thickness of the stroke (the outline that defines a character) and fill it with flat color or with a pattern. They can fit text to a path created with the program's drawing tools or make it fill a shape. They can also change type to outlines that can then be modified or used as masks to allow other artwork to show through.

- Before type-to-outline conversion functions and special effects were built into PostScript illustration programs, specialized programs were devel-oped to convert type into art. There are also programs that do the opposite, converting art into type, so that logos or other often-used symbols can be typed from the keyboard. Even with the special effects now built into PostScript illustration software, type special effects programs can be very useful for those who work mostly with page layout programs rather than illustration software. Their special effects functions can also be easier to use than illustration programs.

- Type converted to outlines has made its way into clip art, predrawn artwork supplied on disk. Artists, designers and desktop publishers can include the type clip art in illustrations and page layouts.

- Some painting (or bitmapped) programs now come equipped with func-tions that integrate smooth-looking type into their illustrations. Though the type eventually loses its object-oriented PostScript character and be-comes part of the "painting," these programs can create some spectacular special effects for type.

Fonts

Many of the first fonts for desktop systems were conversions of faces designed for metal type or phototypesetting. And the conversion process continues as old favorites are made available for the desktop. Extended character sets that include fractions, ligatures and special symbols have been developed for some faces. In addition, new, modern faces have been designed, including some conceived especially for output at the relatively low resolution of the standard laser printer and even for on-screen display and interactive presentations (Figure 2).

abcdefghijklmnopqrstuvwxyz
ABCDEFGHIJKLMNOPQRSTUVWXYZ
1234567890!@#$%^&*()?
Modula

abcdefghijklmnopqrstuvwxyz
ABCDEFGHIJKLMNOPQRSTUVWXYZ
1234567890!@#$%^&*()?
Modula Serif

abcdefghijklmnopqrstuvwxyz
ABCDEFGHIJKLMNOPQRSTUVWXYZ
1234567890!@#$%^&*()?
Modula Bold

abcdefghijklmnopqrstuvwxyz
abcdefghijklmnopqrstuvwxyz
1234567890!@#$%^&*()?
Modula Serif Bold

abcdefghijklmnopqrstuvwxyz
ABCDEFGHIJKLMNOPQRSTUVWXYZ
123456789!@#$%^&*()?0
Modula Black

abcdefghijklmnopqrstuvwxyz
ABCDEFGHIJKLMNOPQRSTUVWXYZ
1234567890!@#$%^&*()?
Modula Serif Black

Figure 2. Designed for low resolution. The Modula family of typefaces from Emigré is among those designed to look good at screen resolution (72 dots per inch) or printed on a laser printer (300 dpi).

Several traditional and electronic typehouses in addition to Adobe Systems, Inc. produce PostScript fonts. (Many of them are listed in the Appendix of this book.) And the leading digital type manufacturers also produce TrueType editions.

Organizers and managers

Font/DA Mover, a utility that has been supplied with Macintosh computers, and **Font Porter,** a similar program included with Adobe Illustrator 3.0, can open files (such as the System file or files identified by suitcase icons) that contain fonts or desk accessories (DAs), so that the fonts or DAs can be deleted or copied from one file to another (Figure 3). ▮ *Macintosh System 7 makes it possible to open and copy font and DA files without the Font/DA Mover utility required for earlier systems.*

Suitcase II and **Font/DA Juggler Plus** are designed to make fonts (and desk accessories) available all the time, without their having to be installed in the System file, where they occupy memory and can slow down the operation of programs that use type. With these applications, fonts are grouped in files that can be opened by Font/DA Mover and used just as if they had been installed in the System. Font files can be designated to be opened automatically at startup, and other font files can be opened or closed while an application is in use (see "A look at Suitcase II" on page 155).

Font Harmony is a utility supplied with Suitcase II that resolves font number conflicts by looking at all the installed font suitcases and all the fonts in the System file and then renumbering if an ID number is shared by two or more

Figure 3. Moving fonts. Font/DA Mover (shown here) has been the standard method for copying screen fonts from one file to another. With System 7 screen fonts can be transferred by dragging their icons from folder to folder like many other icons.

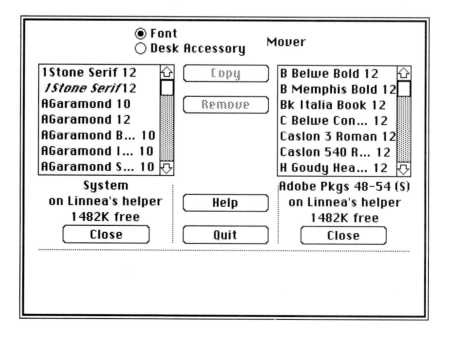

fonts. Most page layout and PostScript illustration programs now refer to fonts by name rather than by number, but many word processors and other programs still use the numbers.

Adobe Type Manager (or **ATM**) lets users get PostScript-quality type on-screen and from non-PostScript printers. By accessing the PostScript printer font outline, ATM creates smooth-looking text at any size the artist specifies (see Figure 6 in Chapter 1). Parameters for ATM are set in the Control Panel (Figure 4). ∎ *ATM is an INIT—a program that the System looks at before it does much else and then doesn't re-examine until the next time the computer starts up. So, in order for ATM to work, the computer has to be restarted after ATM is installed and turned on.*

ATM makes it possible to eliminate from the System file — and therefore from the computer's RAM — or from screen-font storage on a hard disk, all but one size screen (or bitmap) font. ∎ *It's necessary to keep one size because the screen font file contains not only the bitmap representation of the file for on-screen display and construction of type on non-PostScript printers, but also the font metrics information — character width and pair kerning values, expressed as proportions of an em space — needed by typesetting programs and by the printer or other output device.*

Like ATM, **Freedom of Press** makes it possible to output PostScript type on non-PostScript printers. It works by intercepting the information normally sent to a PostScript printer and *rasterizing* the type outlines — converting

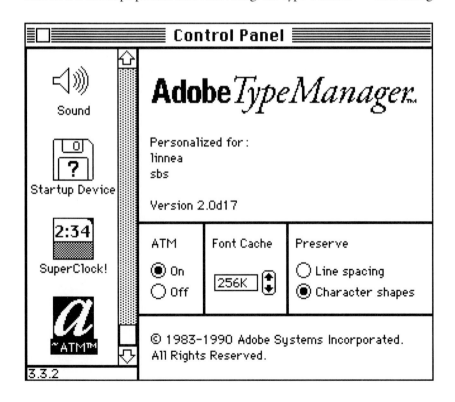

Figure 4. Managing fonts. Adobe Type Manager can be turned on and off in the Control Panel. Increasing the size of the font cache allocates more memory for font outlines, which allows ATM to run faster. Choosing Character Shapes rather than the default Line Spacing optimizes the shapes of individual characters, even if lines of type must be rebroken or leading adjusted to do so.

them to bitmapped information at the resolution of the output device. The program can print to more than 50 different output devices, including laser, inkjet, 24-wire dot matrix and color thermal printers, as well as film recorders. Freedom of Press comes with 35 printer fonts (the standard fonts found on the LaserWriter Plus). A Light version of the program includes fewer fonts and prints from fewer printers, and a Professional version supports more output formats and more fonts and can scale and rotate type.

Adobe Type Reunion, another INIT, is a font-menu aid that groups all the styles of a particular font under the font's name. Bodoni, for example, is listed in the font menu with an arrow that points to specific font weights (Figure 5). This simplifies the font menu by shortening it and also makes it easier to choose a font because names are listed in a logical (alphabetical) order by family.

Fontina is another INIT that improves font menus. When it rearranges the menu to group related fonts, Fontina fills the entire screen, if necessary, with multicolumn menus (rather than a scrolling list) that show every font at a glance.

Figure 5. Reuniting families. Type Reunion simplifies font menus by listing all family weights under the family name.

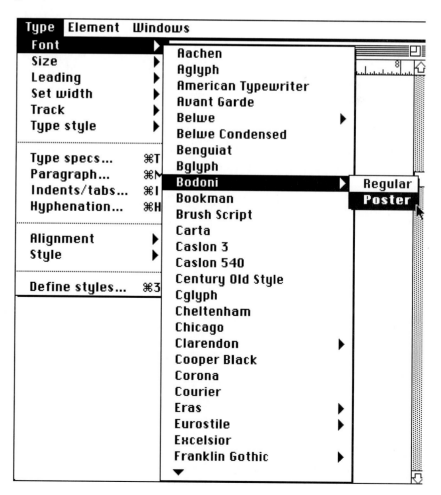

MenuFonts displays fonts in their own faces in on-screen menus. The utility can also be configured to show a submenu of point sizes for a selected font in that font's face. These features can be helpful for designers who aren't familiar with large numbers of fonts.

With **FontShare,** a font-server program, all Macintoshes on a network can share the same set of printer fonts. Every Mac has its own set of screen fonts, however.

Octavo TypeChart and **SPECtacular** are programs for producing customized type catalogs automatically (Figure 6). Spec sheets that show text and headlines set in several sizes and with varied leading are supplied as electronic files on disk, ready for the designer to select a typeface from his or her collection and print out the pages. Octavo TypeChart includes preformatted catalog pages for an overview of the font, headlines, text, Shift-Option characters and styles. SPECtacular templates include full alphabets, sample text, E-charts, and charts of character locations and average number of characters per pica, as well as pica rulers and compass/protractors. Both programs allow the user to modify existing templates and create new ones.

Figure 6. Printing a custom type catalog. Pages generated by Octavo TypeChart (shown here) and SPECtacular show samples of the fonts you specify.

Font creators

Fontographer is a graphics program specialized for creating fonts (Figure 7). The tools (for example, Bezier curves, autotrace and a bitmap editor) that Fontographer uses to create object-oriented (or vector) printer fonts and bitmapped screen fonts are similar to those of other PostScript illustration programs. Unique to this and other font-creation programs, however, are the ability to set side bearings (the white space that cushions a character on either side) and kerning pairs (specific pairs such as *To* and *AV* that require special spacing adjustment to look good when they occur together) and the ability to save the graphic information as a Type 1 font (with hints for modification of characters at small sizes and low resolution and the ability to work with Adobe Type Manager to produce an accurate on-screen display), a Type 3

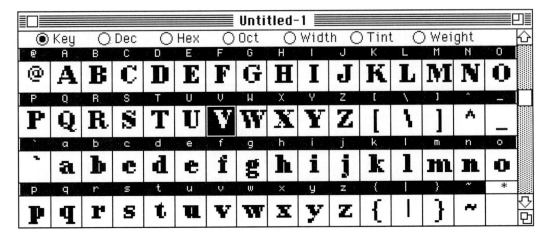

Figure 7. Fontographer's keyboard arrangement. Double-clicking on the particular character's slot opens up a drawing area where the character can be designed or altered.

font or as encapsulated PostScript illustrations. Fontographer can also import and build into fonts PostScript outlines created in other drawing programs.

In addition, Fontographer can make a composite font (a font that references another font and adds any changes the user has made), a composite character (a character that references another character or part of a character, which is a useful function for creating a series of complex characters with many features in common) and libraries (source files that can be attached to a font for accessing symbols or characters that are common to several fonts).

Fontastic Plus creates new bitmap fonts or edits existing ones. It can be used to optimize the screen fonts generated by Fontographer.

FontStudio lets artists create new typefaces or modify existing fonts. Besides importing and opening existing fonts, FontStudio can open MacPaint, PICT and TIFF files as templates for tracing. Adobe Illustrator 88 files can be copied (by holding down the Option key to record the PostScript information and choosing Copy from Illustrator's Edit menu) and then pasted into character slots in FontStudio. In addition to PostScript drawing and editing tools such as the pen, scissors, measuring tool, magnifying glass and reflection, rotating, scaling and shearing tools, FontStudio has a paint bucket function for automatically filling the outline so the character can be previewed on-screen (Figure 8) and an easy-to-use interface for kerning (Figure 9). The program produces Type 1 fonts.

One of FontStudio's specialties is creating type for presentation programs. Antialiasing can be specified to smooth angled and curved strokes by fading

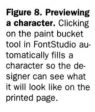

Figure 8. Previewing a character. Clicking on the paint bucket tool in FontStudio automatically fills a character so the designer can see what it will look like on the printed page.

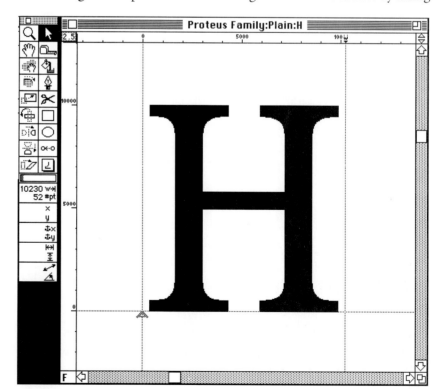

the bitmapped edges so that they blend smoothly with the background. A palette of 256 colors or gray shades can be used.

ATF TypeDesigner is another PostScript font creator. Characters can be drawn freehand or traced over TIFFs imported as templates, and they can be displayed in large type to allow accurate positioning for kerning pairs.

Font converters

Evolution and other font-conversion programs can change Type 3 fonts into Type 1 (so that they can be used with Adobe Type Manager to produce accurate screen displays) or vice versa (which used to be important when font-creation programs could work only with Type 3 fonts). Evolution can also *regularize* type, adjusting lines and curves of the characters slightly for optimal 300 dpi laser printer output. The program can convert Type 3 or Type 1 fonts to editable outlines for use in Adobe Illustrator or Aldus FreeHand — again, more important before both of those drawing programs acquired the ability to do such conversions themselves.

The Art Importer (formerly KeyMaster) can turn logos, symbols or virtually any other artwork that can be saved as an EPS or a PICT file into a font whose characters can then be typed from the keyboard. The program automatically creates screen and PostScript font files from the imported artwork, and the screen fonts can be edited with the program's bitmap editor to improve their appearance on-screen.

Metamorphosis Professional, besides converting Type 3 fonts to Type 1, and Type 1 fonts to editable outlines, can also convert TrueType fonts to Type

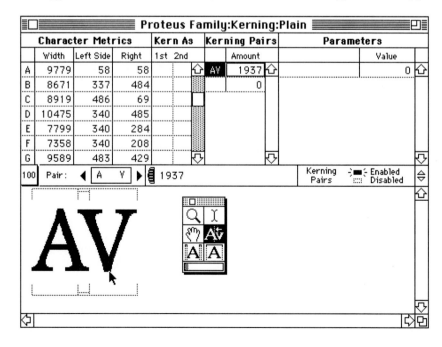

Figure 9. Intuitive kerning commands. A special FontStudio tool palette appears when the kerning window is opened, allowing alteration of kerning, side bearings and the size of the em-square.

1 PostScript (for use on Macintosh, DOS-based or NeXT computers) and vice versa. Other programs that can make the PostScript–TrueType conversions are **FontMonger** and some of the font creator programs such as FontStudio and ATF Type Designer.

Page layout programs

Although it has been known better for its designer-friendly interface than for its type-handling capabilities, the current version of **Aldus PageMaker** provides kerning, justification, hyphenation, preset tracking and style sheets that combine to give the user a great deal of control over type. PageMaker can rotate text in 90-degree increments and can wrap text around graphic objects (Figure 10).

QuarkXPress provides the same kind of tight control over type that it does for other elements. For instance, every text block and graphic element can be rotated to any degree, and text can be kerned and tracked in very fine increments. Type specifications can be changed in the Text Box Specifications dialog box, or just dialed in on the floating measurement palette (Figure 11). A font usage search function can identify any font used for any character in an entire XPress document, including blank spaces. XPress can wrap text around other type blocks as well as graphic elements, and drop caps are easy to set.

Ventura Publisher, a leading page layout program for DOS-based computers such as the IBM PC, has many capabilities not found in other programs. Large drop caps are created by simply entering formatting commands, headlines can span more than one column but still be part of a multicolumn text block, and vertical justification, which matches up the bottoms of columns of text, can be set at either multiples of the leading or in minute increments.

Figure 10. Wrapping text. PageMaker's Text Wrap option, displayed at top, shows the default standoff in inches. After you choose this setting and click OK, a custom wrap can be created by clicking the pointer tool on the dotted line which now surrounds the selected element. This creates another corner point which can be dragged. Holding down the space bar as points are added or moved allows several changes to be made before the screen redraws.

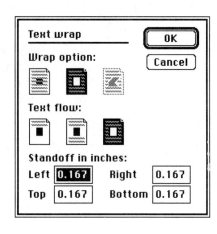

Ventura Publisher uses the concept of "frames" as containers for text and graphics. A frame can contain an entire page or just a small text block or graphic. Text can be flowed from frame to frame. The program provides automatic pair kerning, tracking, letter spacing and widow and orphan control, and it supports style sheets, which are lists of specifications that characterize all the type elements of a document.

PostScript illustration programs

A long-time leader in PostScript illustration, **Adobe Illustrator** is even more powerful with the release of version 3. Text can be entered and edited without the use of a dialog box. Text blocks have no limit on the number of characters they can contain, and they can include any mixture of styles, sizes and faces with advanced typesetting capabilities such as kerning, tracking, vertical shifting, horizontal scaling and more. Best of all, Illustrator now allows text to follow a path (which means it can curve) and to fill the contours of an object (even one defined by an open path). Illustrator's toolbox has pull-

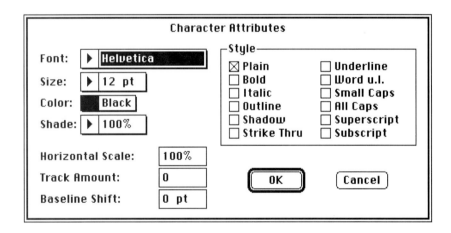

Figure 11. Superior text control. In QuarkXPress, type parameters such as font, size, color, shade, horizontal scaling, tracking or kerning, and style can be changed in Character Attributes or entered on the floating measurement palette found below the document window.

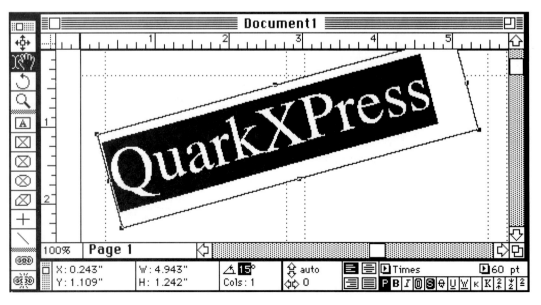

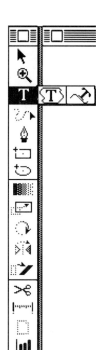

Figure 12. Using the expanded tool set. Adobe Illustrator's three text tools set type in standard block format (left tool icon), inside a specified shape (middle icon) or along a previously drawn and selected path (right icon).

sideways tool selections that become visible as you slide the cursor to the right (Figure 12).

Type can also be entered, selected and then converted to outlines with the Create Outlines command from the Type menu (Figure 13). Like programs designed strictly for type conversion, Illustrator accesses the printer font and makes its outlines available for editing. For this to work, the printer font must be installed and Adobe Type Manager (ATM) needs to be running.

Like other shapes in Illustrator, type converted to outlines can be given a graduated fill by setting up a blend from one shape and color to another and then using the outline to mask the gradation produced by the fill. The fill shows inside the mask only.

Aldus FreeHand has advanced typesetting and manipulation capabilities. The ease of spacing, kerning and baseline shifts helps to make FreeHand very flexible. A menu of special effects can be applied to text (Figure 14). Text joined to a path, which can be done very easily by selecting text and path and pressing Command-J for Join, can still be edited. FreeHand 3 includes the ability to join type automatically to both the top and bottom curves of an ellipse and to fit text to a path and then convert it to outlines for filling and other editing. Type conversion works for both Type 1 fonts and Type 3 fonts created with Fontographer.

When type is converted to outlines, the type as a whole becomes a composite path, which can be filled with a single fill and which allows a background placed behind the composite element to show through the counters and the spaces between letters. Selecting the composite outline and choosing Split Element from the Element menu makes each character a composite path: Now characters can be filled separately, and counters still serve as "windows" to the background. Selecting a character and choosing

Figure 13. Creating font outlines. Editable outlines of type can be made in Adobe Illustrator. After entering the text and then selecting the pointer arrow, choose Create Outlines from the Type menu to convert the character into a manipulatable Bézier outline.

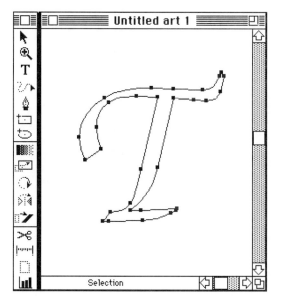

Split Element again makes separate elements of the character's outline and any counters or other included shapes (Figure 15).

Though FreeHand has a blending function very similar to Illustrator's blend tool, it also has a fill specification called Graduated, which is quicker and less confusing than Illustrator's equivalent function. A Graduated fill allows the artist to specify the beginning and ending colors as well as the direction and "speed" of the graduation.

Corel Draw's text handling encompasses kerning, word spacing, letterspacing and applying fills and strokes. WFN BOSS, a font conversion program included with Corel Draw, converts printer fonts into a Corel Draw format so that the character outlines can be edited. WFN BOSS works with both Type 1 and Type 3 fonts. Corel Draw files can be exported as WPG, CGM, GEM, EPS, PICT, HPGL, SCODL and DXF.

Micrografx Designer requires over 10 MB of hard disk space to hold both the program and data files, and recommends that the computer have at least 2 MB of RAM. Included in the data files are 1700 clip art images and a desktop slide presentation. In Designer, type can be converted to editable Bézier outlines, and styles, fonts and colors can be within a text string. Although Designer supports masking, it doesn't support kerning, automatic word wrap, text wrap or differing fill and stroke on text. Files can be exported as Adobe Illustrator, DRW, DXF, EPS, HPGL, GEM, PCX, PIC, PICT, PostScript, TIFF, WFM and WPG.

Computer Support Corporation's **Arts and Letters** supports 24-bit color and automatic spot and color separations, imports PostScript, EPS, TIFF, GIF, PCX and TARGA files and provides clipping paths (masking), text along a path, autotrace, dynamic shape transformation and blending. Arts and Letters also comes with 5000 clip-art images and 50 outline fonts. Illustrations can be created in color or in wireframe (keyline) mode. Running under Windows 2.1 or later, Arts and Letters requires 640 K of RAM.

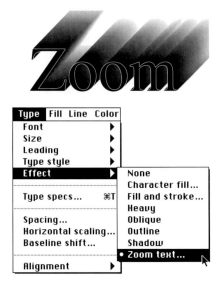

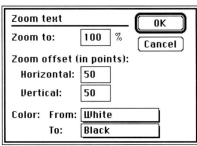

Figure 14. Zooming text. Zoom Text is an unusual effect that can be created automatically in FreeHand. Text graduates from one specified color to another. The offset (origin of the zoom) can also be set.

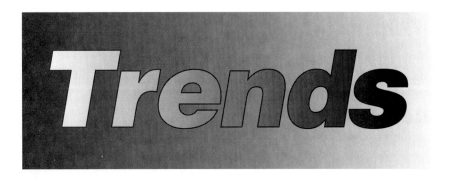

Figure 15. Making composites. The word *Trends*, set in Helvetica Black italic type, was rendered using FreeHand's Convert To Paths command and the resulting compound outline was assigned a graduated fill and placed over a background filled from the opposite direction. Note that "holes" in the composite allow the background to show through.

Figure 16. Creating special effects. Split Reverse is one of many special effects provided by the Smart Art desk accessory. The angle and vertical placement of the split and the density of the fill can be specified for one or several lines of text. The EPS file thus created can be placed over filled shapes created in a page layout or PostScript illustration program, as shown here.

Special effects for type

Smart Art works by intercepting PostScript font information as it's being sent to the printer and adding any of a library of predesigned text and graphics effects (Figure 16). (A PostScript printer must be connected to the computer for this to work.) The program can work with both Type 1 and Type 3 fonts and can save files in EPS, TIFF or PICT format.

TypeAlign is a desk accessory that can rotate type, set it along a curve or distort it in various ways. The product can then be copied and pasted into another document or saved in EPS, PICT or Illustrator 88 format. One method of using TypeAlign is to "photograph" your current document with the camera tool, which creates a template that allows you to fit the type to your original graphic (Figure 17). Alternatively, the template can be drawn and edited within the program with curve, straight line and freehand tools.

Alignment, color, style, size and font can all be controlled in TypeAlign. Once text is entered, spacing can be adjusted between pairs of letters, and if several characters are selected at once, spacing can be changed for the entire selection.

TypeStyler provides a quick way to apply special effects to type. The program has a library of custom shapes and styles that can be applied to entered text (Figure 18). Type, converted to outlines, can be bent, squeezed, stretched, twisted and rotated, and perspective, shadows, shades, patterns and colors can be added. Fills (including a variety of graduated ones), outlines and inlines can also be added. Files can be exported as paint, PICT or EPS files. Such advanced typographic capabilities as kerning, line spacing, word spacing and letter spacing are easy to use. The program even includes a variety of panels

Figure 17. Curved text for any application. TypeAlign lets you "photograph" your current document window (in this example, a Page-Maker file), allowing you to fit type to an already existing curve. After tracing the resultant template with the curve tool, type is entered and can then be copied and pasted into the original document.

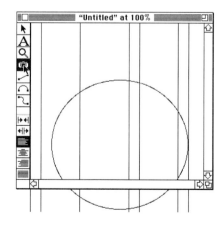

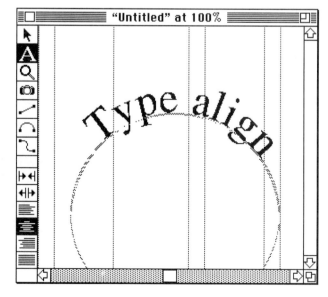

(background shapes such as stars, squares and semicircles) to be added to showcase the text. Some fonts are included with the program, and others can be converted.

Type clip art

Initial Caps is a modular system that includes the outlines for five alphabets of capitals (and 78 additional variety capitals) in encapsulated PostScript format. The package also includes a series of predesigned background tiles (also in EPS format) and six TIFF images to be used as backgrounds or fills for the letter outlines (Figure 19).

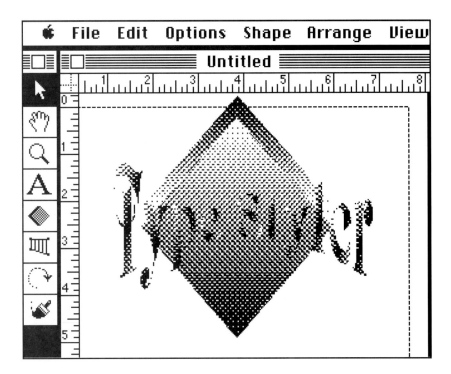

Figure 18. Custom display type. Using an assortment of type effects, Type-Styler can create specialty text for any font that has been converted into its proprietary "Smooth-Font" format, a format that speeds up processing and printing of outline fonts.

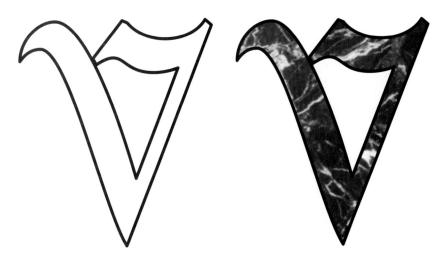

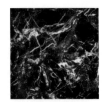

Figure 19. Using "clip type." This *V* is one of the capitals provided in the Initial Caps software package. The PostScript outlines can be filled with TIFF images such as the marble shown here or with EPS background patterns.

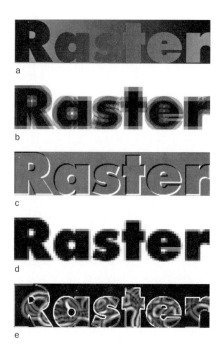

Figure 20. Photoshop effects. Not just a program for retouching scanned images, Photoshop can be used to create interesting type treatments. After the type was entered, the following effects were used: two alternating ramps (a); the Fragment filter (b); a Custom Emboss filter (c); the Mosaic filter (d); and an airbrushed image was copied and pasted inside the letters and then the Find Edges filter was used (e).

Painting programs

As a raster (or bitmap) program, Letraset's **ColorStudio** has many special effects not available in a vector environment. For example, the paint bucket can be used to apply a color spectrum across several elements, such as individual letters of display type. Text can be antialiased, as can any object created from the pen palette. A mask can be displayed in 256 levels of gray, which means that it can vary in opacity, allowing an operation to affect, in differing degrees, whatever is underneath the mask. Color correction can be done globally or to specific areas only.

Shapes is an add-on program included with ColorStudio to provide Post-Script capabilities. Bézier curves, freehand drawing and specialized forms such as stars and curved lines are available on a drawing layer that operates separately from the raster layer of ColorStudio. Once drawn, PostScript elements can be rendered into the raster layer at the resolution of the image, or they can remain in and be printed from the PostScript layer. Type 1 fonts or any font from the LetraFont library can be kerned, stretched, distorted and treated as an object. Any shape can be used to carve a hole in another object allowing the background to be seen. Video titling is possible because of the high-quality antialiasing that occurs when a PostScript object from Shapes is rendered into a ColorStudio image. Complete control of opacity aids in creating special effects. The Shapes 'Tweening command is a blend function that creates intermediate objects that can reflect differences in shape, color and opacity. Illustrations and type outlines from other PostScript drawing programs, such as Illustrator or FreeHand, can be imported into ColorStudio via Shapes.

Though not generally considered a program for creating text, **Adobe Photoshop** has the ability to generate, through filters and effects, some powerful type elements (Figure 20). The type dialog box offers a variety of choices, including antialiasing, a technique available in many raster programs to smooth stairstepping on curves and angles such as those that define type by fading out the edges.

Photoshop can also import Adobe Illustrator–compatible PostScript artwork, including type outlines, which can be antialiased at the time it's rendered into the bitmap of the Photoshop image. Video-specific filters allow Photoshop to be used as a paintbox program for video editing.

C H A P T E R   3

Designing a Typeface

Designer

In 1981 Joe Treacy, independent graphic artist and type designer, walked into the Linotype company with inked drawings for a new typeface and walked out with a contract. Three years later, Bryn Mawr was released as an eight-weight family of typefaces, and it has since become a staple in Linotype's library. It has appeared on ads for airlines and book publishers around the world.

Now using the Macintosh computer and Fontographer software, Treacy has created his own line of original typefaces called Treacyfaces, which include Forever, Habitat, Crossword and Bryn Mawr, and is in the process of creating more.

Project

I wanted to design a sans serif face with characters that were bright, urbane and distinctive, but also had a balance and friendliness about them. I enjoy calligraphy, and I think a calligraphic touch in a typeface design adds a lot of warmth to the face and makes it more approachable.

To design the Forever font, I used Fontographer software on a Mac II with 5 MB of RAM and a 40 MB hard disk. Attached to the Mac was a Radius two-page grayscale monitor. I used a VisionScan scanner to bring preliminary pencil sketches into Fontographer. A LaserWriter IINTX was used for proofing the design in process. Final, high-resolution proofing was done at a service bureau with a Linotronic L-300.

A typeface survey

Different typefaces, when composed into phrases and blocks of copy, seem to convey different attitudes. Type can be complacent or electrifying, stern or genteel. One of my goals in designing a typeface is that it be bright-looking and responsive — not only when it's set as display type, but equally important, when it's used as body copy.

When I set about designing Forever, I looked at a large number of well-designed bold sans serifs, including Futura Extra Bold (one of my favorites), Gill Sans Ultra Bold, Helvetica Black, ITC Franklin Gothic Heavy, News Gothic Bold, Trade Gothic Bold, Frutiger Ultra Black and others. It's an interesting exercise to look at an existing alphabet and try to find fresh ways of viewing the characters. I find it intriguing to attempt to design them differently and to try to make improvements on what has been done before.

The height of the lowercase letters in relation to the height of the caps is generally referred to as the x-height. A large x-height serves to keep the letterforms very open, bright and cheery-looking, even in the italics, where the width of the letterforms is normally less than the width of the roman shapes. Characters like the lowercase *g* really benefit from a large x-height because it allows plenty of room within the design to make the character very full-bodied, even though it exists in a rather condensed space. The openness also makes the lowercase *g* very inviting to read.

Futura Extra Bold

Gill Sans Ultra Bold

Helvetica Black

ITC Franklin Gothic Heavy

News Gothic Bold

Trade Gothic Bold

Frutiger Ultra Black

Part of the preliminary work in designing Forever was to review existing well-designed bold sans serif faces. Adobe's Futura Extra Bold, Gill Sans Ultra Bold, Helvetica Black, ITC's Franklin Gothic Heavy, News Gothic Bold, Trade Gothic Bold and Frutiger Ultra Black fell into that category.

Breaking new ground

After completing my typeface survey, I decided that there were still a number of options available for creating sans serif characters that were exciting and distinctive in design. I would design a sans serif that was slightly more condensed than the time-honored standards.

I would define a bold roman weight first because that was where the concept for the face originally sprang from. I looked at a number of letters that I generally regard as key characters — those used very frequently throughout any set text, whether it's English or another language.

Lowercase *e* is probably the most often repeated character. Other key characters are the lowercase *a*, lowercase *g* and lowercase *s*. I wanted to make sure that these characters were balanced in Forever. This balance and friendliness would come from two factors. The first is a harmony within the letterform that results from the way different curves interact with each other. And the second is a balance of the height and width of the letterforms, which, among other things, affects how well the face migrates from one weight to the next and from the roman to the italic.

I started out by designing with pencil and paper, getting a little closer with each sketch to what I felt was the ideal proportion for a modern bold sans serif with characters that had a friendly attitude and sturdiness about them, particularly in the lowercase. Finally, when I felt I was ready to begin work on the design in earnest, I scanned the characters at a resolution of 200 dpi (dots per inch), pasted them into the background plane of the Fontographer type design program and then proceeded to refine the shapes.

a e s g — Futura Extra Bold

a e s g — Gill Sans Ultra Bold

a e s g — Helvetica Black

a e s g — ITC Franklin Gothic Heavy

a e s g — News Gothic Bold

a e s g — Trade Gothic Bold

a e s g — Frutiger Ultra Black

a e s g — Forever Extrabold

Lowercase *a*, *e* and *s* are some of the most often-repeated characters in any typeface. And *g* is usually the most distinctive (and sometimes the "fussiest") letterform.

The lowercase *g* was among the first characters I designed. As I looked at the various representations of the *g* in different sans serif alphabets, I found that the character's ear has almost always been handled by projecting it out to the right (Figure 1). The intention, I'm sure, was to finish the character on that side and to balance it against the characters that fall to the left and to the right of it.

I saw that if I finished the stroke that defines the upper bowl of the character as a straight-up stroke (and thus terminated the ear upward), it helped achieve a little bit more efficiency in the character overall by allowing me to fit the *g* more closely to the character that followed it on the right. Especially for display applications (larger point sizes), it's very helpful to be able to set the type a little bit tighter. This ability to compact the letters avoids a gap that can occur when you're trying to fit a lowercase *g* against a lowercase letter that naturally curves away from it (Figure 2).

The other thing I tried to do was balance the size and the positioning of the top and bottom bowls of the character, and to design an effective link between them. The lowercase *g* can be a very difficult character to design and balance. I find that often the bowl on top is carefully designed (usually in a vertical orientation) to match the flavor of the rest of the typeface but that the bottom bowl is left to more or less fill out the space allotted to it (between the linking point and the bottom of the em square) as best it can. Many typefaces look as if there wasn't much consideration given to making the top and bottom symmetrical.

ITC Franklin
Gothic Heavy

Helvetica Black

News Gothic Bold

Figure 1. Looking at *g*'s. A common characteristic of the sans serif letter *g* is an ear that extends out to the right. Helvetica Black is an exception.

Forever Extrabold

ITC Franklin Gothic Heavy

Figure 2. Designing the Forever *g*. The "ear" on the Forever Extrabold *g* is an extension of the upright stroke, allowing tighter letterspacing and an efficient use of space. In contrast, the ear on the ITC Franklin Gothic Heavy *g* curves outward, creating a gap between the *g* and the next character.

I think one of the key successes of this particular character in Forever is that the top and the bottom *do* balance. They seem to occupy the same kind of space even though their shapes are different. And the link between the top and bottom bowl is clearly there, but it doesn't draw much attention to itself. It simply does what it needs to do in a rather efficient way, without a lot of excess design (Figure 3). Using the lowercase *g* as a model, I tried to invoke this same kind of efficiency in the other key characters. ▌ *One indication that a character's design is a well-drafted concept is that it makes the transition from a lighter to a heavier weight without a lot of redesigning, and also without becoming extremely horizontal in its overall feeling.*

Softening the terminals

An interesting technique to help soften up the face and make it more friendly in both the small and large sizes was to insert a certain number of rounded corners in the design (Figure 4). Most sans serif terminals tend either to be completely round-cornered or completely sharp-cornered. In smaller sizes, the roundness serves the same purpose as ink traps that are used to keep joining points from plugging up. The roundness introduces white space into the character so that it doesn't block up as quickly as it might otherwise. In larger point sizes, where the rounded terminals become more noticeable, they also become an interesting design feature of the characters. Although the overall design needed the straight, square corners on most terminals in order to remain a sturdy design, introducing these occasional soft spots into the

Figure 3. Balancing the g. Although they are different shapes, the two bowls of the Forever Extrabold *g* align on both the left *and* right sides. In contrast, the ITC Franklin Gothic Heavy *g* has a much wider and more horizontal bottom bowl, giving it a flattened look.

Forever Extrabold

ITC Franklin Gothic Heavy

Figure 4. Building in roundness. The terminal of the lowercase *a* is rounded on the bottom left of the stroke. This is also a feature of the top inside of the ear of the lowercase *g* and also the lowercase *p*. In other characters, such as the *i, j* and *k,* this technique was not repeated because it would have weakened the letterforms.

typeface helped to give it a softer feeling that, in particular, makes the lowercase more easily read, especially in large blocks of type.

Completing the character set

The beauty of doing letterform design on the Macintosh (in fact with almost any work station set up to do letterform design) is that once you've worked out certain basic shapes (and you've found that the concepts for those shapes are sound and that the rhythm works), you can clone the shapes to make various parts of other letterforms. It was relatively easy for me to take the control characters, which most people in the type design world consider to be capital *H*, capital *O*, lowercase *o* and lowercase *n*, and work out the shapes. I then used those as templates for the widths of the other characters in the typeface (Figure 5). It was very simple for me to move ahead, quickly completing the entire lowercase design over the course of a week (Figure 6).

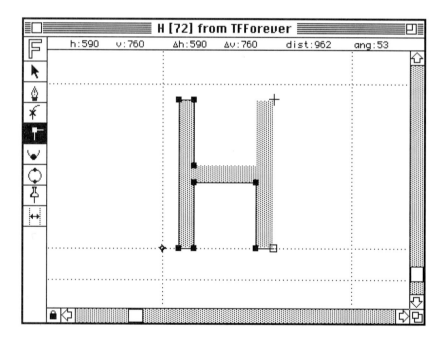

Figure 5. Using control characters. Once the *H, O, o* and *n* were defined, they could be used as templates for starting other characters. In Fontographer, cloning a letterform's characteristics is simply a matter of copying the existing letter and then pasting it into another letter's slot. The slot is then highlighted to show that it has been changed.

Balance

Next I balanced the characters by setting up their side bearings (the designated space on either side of the characters) and by establishing each character's overall position within its space (Figure 7). In the past, striving for balance between the positive and negative shapes has led most typeface designers to design text faces with quite a lot of white space between the characters, because most faces were created to look their best at 12 points. The manufacturers really didn't care much about how they looked when they were scaled to very large point sizes. Before the Macintosh, many systems couldn't set letters more than 2 inches (144 points) high anyway. And even now, most non-PostScript laser typesetting systems have a maximum output size of about 2½ inches on the font's cap height and can't begin to approach the maximum point sizes available by working with the Macintosh and PostScript, where type can easily be set at 3000 points.

Figure 6. Completing the face. The lower case of Forever Extrabold was the first set of characters to be completed.

abcdefgh
ijklmnopq
rstuvwxyz

Figure 7. Balancing the characters. In Fontographer's Metrics window, the side bearings (built-in spaces on each side of the character) can be viewed after they have been established in the Character edit window. The side bearings are represented by the dotted lines on either side of the letter.

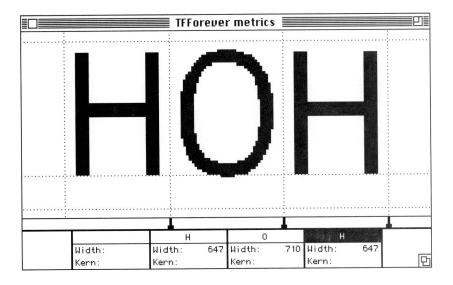

The white space between the characters is certainly just as important as the black strokes that define the characters themselves. In designing a typeface, you want to achieve as much of a balance between those positive and negative areas as you possibly can.

Designing the other weights

Once the extrabold roman was finished to my liking, I looked at other sans serif faces again to determine what kind of weight structures were the most popular in regular (book) weight sans serifs. I finally decided on the weight ratio that you see in Forever (Figure 8). It's fairly similar to that of Helvetica, Futura Book and Gill Sans. I settled on this ratio because it seemed that over the course of the twentieth century, the public has clearly expressed a preference for typefaces that have a weight structure similar to normal book weights or regular sans serif weights.

Designing the "true cut" italic

One of the challenges in any typeface design, and it's particularly true in the case of a sans serif, is what to do with the italic. One obvious direction a designer can choose (as is the case with many modern sans serif faces) is simply to oblique the roman to whatever angle seems to work well and then go in and very subtly reshape the characters to take off the displaced stress that's caused by the mathematical obliquing. I looked at some typefaces, such as ITC Franklin Gothic, Helvetica and others, that do just that. But I decided that I wanted Forever to be more distinctive in the italic, with a calligraphic influence.

Having a preference for calligraphic forms and the warmth that they can bring to typeface designs, I introduced some thick and thin occurrences into the italics for the Regular weight. This made them more interesting, more

Figure 8. Completing the range of weights. Forever is designed in Thin, Extralight, Light, Regular, Medium, Demibold, Bold and Extrabold weights.

PostScript hinting

All PostScript Type 1 and many PostScript Type 3 formatted typefaces incorporate *hints,* or scaling algorithms, that optimize the appearance of printed characters at 300 dpi, especially at sizes less than 9 points. Apple's TrueType, released with System 7.0, also has its own hinting approach. A type designer must pay close attention to proper placement of control points on a character's outline in order to allow the various hinting modules to work properly.

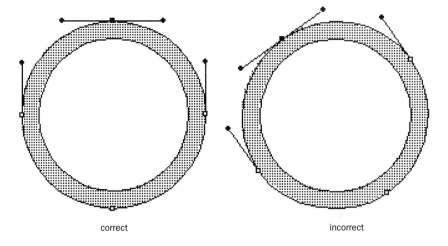

correct   incorrect

obviously italic and unique among modern sans serifs (Figure 9). I then cloned the italicized Regular weight and used it as a background template for the other italics (Figure 10).

Proofing technology

With Fontographer you can proof the character in both outline and solid form, which can sometimes be useful. I proofed the Forever characters in some very large default sizes, around 540 points or so, which allowed me to see the finest details of the curves and corners. Any number of smaller point sizes can be specified as well. Fontographer shows you how the font looks with PostScript hints added if you click on that feature's checkbox in the Font Attributes window (Figure 11). Hints aid letter clarity when a font is printed at low resolutions (see "PostScript hinting" on page 38). ▊ *You can't print test files directly from Fontographer to a Linotronic imagesetter. In order to get high-resolution output, you must pick the font format you prefer in the Font Attributes dialog box, select Generate Fonts from the File menu, and then install the screen (bitmapped) font with a program such as the Font/DA Mover or Suitcase. This allows you to use the font in an illustration or page layout program. When you take your file to a service bureau, be sure to include the printer font (unless it's one the service bureau owns) so the operator can download it to the imagesetter. Fontographer-generated fonts will run on both Adobe and non-Adobe PostScript imagesetters. Since most applications search for fonts by name first, a distinctive name will help you avoid font ID conflicts.*

Kerning pairs

Kerning pairs are any two characters in a typeface that have been given built-in values designating selective spatial adjustment whenever the two letters appear next to each other. Defining kerning pairs in a typeface is very

Figure 9. Designing the italic characters. The rhythm that runs through the italics in Forever results from the modulation of its unusual thick and thin strokes. Compare the "italics" of Helvetica and ITC Franklin Gothic, created by simply slanting the roman characters 12 degrees and then adjusting them to take off the misplaced stress.

It is a newspaper's duty to print the news and raise hell — The Chicago Times
It is a newspaper's duty to print the news and raise hell — The Chicago Times

14-point Helvetica
14-point Helvetica Oblique

It is a newspaper's duty to print the news and raise hell — The Chicago Times
It is a newspaper's duty to print the news and raise hell — The Chicago Times

14-point ITC Franklin Gothic Book
14-point ITC Franklin Gothic Oblique

It is a newspaper's duty to print the news and raise hell — The Chicago Times
It is a newspaper's duty to print the news and raise hell — The Chicago Times

14-point Forever Regular
14-point Forever Italic

important. No matter how much time you spend balancing the characters and balancing their side bearings, you need kerning pairs to make the text look correctly set. The number of kerning pairs depends on the typeface. A typeface that resembles ITC Machine, for example, in which the characters are very similarly box-shaped, may not need very many kerning pairs. However, in just about any design done for the real world of typography, kerning pairs are extremely important (Figure 12). With a little testing, it's actually quite easy to come up with nearly 2000 pairs per typeface weight.

When PostScript fonts first arrived on the scene for the Macintosh, they usually had in the neighborhood of 90 to 120 kerning pairs, if they had any kerning pairs at all. Forever was originally released with 750 kerning pairs, and I later revised each weight to include more than 1700. I found that for another of my designs, TFHabitat (a serifed typeface), 3800 kerning pairs were needed per weight.

More recently, some companies have begun to push the several thousand mark. But you can't assume that a typeface that's offered with several thousand kerning pairs is superior to one that has fewer. In the same way that you would want to scrutinize the design of the typeface for clarity and balance in the letterforms, you should also scrutinize the individual fit of the characters to see that the side bearings, as well as the kerning pairs, have been done properly. A typeface designer is just as likely to make a mistake in defining the kerning pairs as in defining the shapes of the characters themselves.

I like to create the entire typeface family and then go back and establish the kerning pairs after all the weights have been designed. With each weight, the general fitting needs to be redone and the side bearings need to be examined to see if they still work. I generally take a control character like *H* and then apply its side bearing information to more difficult characters. You can establish kerning pairs as you go along, but I think it's better to contain complex procedures. Out of all the possible letter combinations, a designer must decide how many kerning pairs to introduce into the typeface. Kerning pairs pick up the slack where character design ends. In fact, it helps to think of adding kerning pairs as an essential part of the design process, not an optional extension of it.

Figure 10. Completing the italics. After the Regular weight italic font was completed, it was used as a template for constructing the other italic weights.

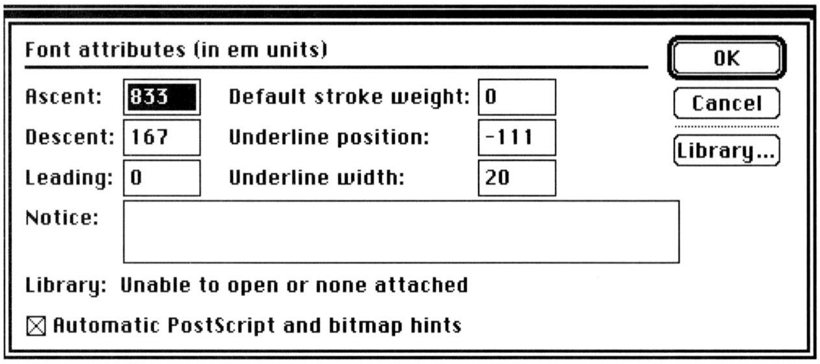

Figure 11. Using the Font Attributes dialog box. Checking Automatic PostScript And Bitmap Hints will improve the typeface's legibility at low resolution in smaller point sizes. (Shown here are Fontographer's default settings.)

Font ID number conflicts

Originally, there were only 256 slots for screen font ID numbers (what the computer and printer use to determine the identity of a specific font). Since there are now over 2500 different fonts available from various sources, the limit of 256 posed a problem for everyone involved.

NFNT

NFNT (for "New Font") was developed to allow up to 32,767 unique ID numbers. Versions 3.8 and newer of the Font/DA Mover (a utility for moving screen fonts between files) recognize NFNT. Older versions do not.

Identification by name

Most PostScript illustration and page layout programs now "call" fonts by name rather than by number, which also helps avoid font numbering conflicts. However, Microsoft Word, for example, still uses font numbers to call for printer fonts.

In retrospect

One of the things that I find extremely useful about Fontographer is the ability to immediately make laser printer samples from the file I'm working on. I continually need to see how the design is evolving. This method saves a lot of time over the older way of doing an outline drawing and quickly filling in the outline with a magic marker. Before the advent of digital typography (and felt-tip markers), some type designers chose to cut the characters out of black construction paper with an X-Acto knife to see how they looked in solid form. You can imagine how tedious and meticulous that was. Once the markers came along and people were used to using them, things got a little bit easier. Today, some designers still use markers to create even their finished lettering artwork. But, being able to send your trial drawings to a laser printer allows you to compare a whole tabletop full of design directions immediately. This method is so much more satisfying.

My electronic design process includes comparing a wide range of different weights. I look at the bolder weights and think, "What will happen to these shapes once they became lighter?" Forever makes that transition with very little redesigning of the characters, and I think it's for this reason that the typeface has proven to be popular with many graphic designers.

Figure 12. The need for kerning. A nearly monospaced typeface like ITC Machine needs little kerning because the shapes and sizes of the characters are very similar. But in a more obviously proportionally fitted face like Forever, kerning pairs need to be defined to specify, for example, how closely an *O* tucks next to a *T*.

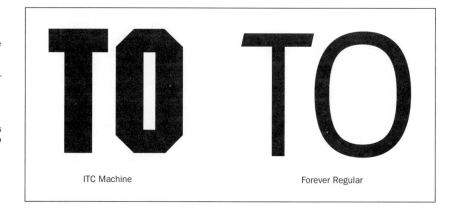

ITC Machine   Forever Regular

PORTFOLIO

JOSEPH MULLIGAN

Joe Treacy

"It's becoming very important to re-evaluate how typefaces are expected to perform these days, when designers are almost as likely to be using a typeface at 1000 points as they are at 12 points, and when both sizes could be composed within a single job and even within a single page. I think that it's incumbent on typeface designers to make the type a little bit more responsive so that the graphic designer doesn't have to spend so much time refitting the characters together at large sizes because they were designed to look their best at 12 points. With the advent of computers, it's now imperative that the characters hold their own at any point size."

TFCrossword™

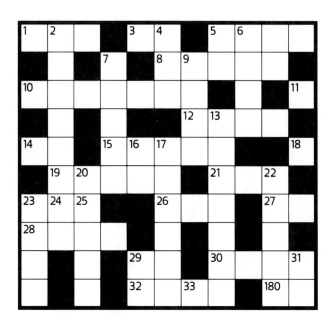

TF Crossword is a monospaced font family consisting of two weights: TF Puzzle and TF Solution. A partial showing of the character set, above, shows the letters and numerals (from the TF Forever typeface) perfectly placed inside their boxes. With this font and a word processing or page layout program, a "solved" or "unsolved" puzzle can be assembled. A framed border was fitted to the puzzle at left in a page layout program. And below, a drawing program was used to skew the puzzle.

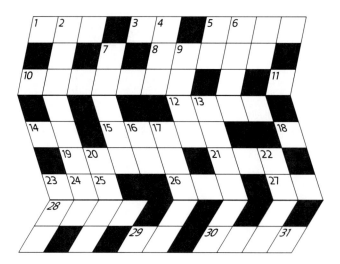

Bryn Mawr Family

ABCDEFGHIJKLMNOPQRSTUVWXYZabcdefghijklmnopqrstuvwxyz&1234567890
ABCDEFGHIJKLMNOPQRSTUVWXYZabcdefghijklmnopqrstuvwxyz&1234567890
ABCDEFGHIJKLMNOPQRSTUVWXYZabcdefghijklmnopqrstuvwxyz&1234567890
ABCDEFGHIJKLMNOPQRSTUVWXYZabcdefghijklmnopqrstuvwxyz&1234567890

Habitat

ABCDEFGHIJKLMNOPQRSTUVWXYZabcdefghijklmnopqrstuvwxyz&1234567890
ABCDEFGHIJKLMNOPQRSTUVWXYZabcdefghijklmnopqrstuvwxyz&1234567890
ABCDEFGHIJKLMNOPQRSTUVWXYZabcdefghijklmnopqrstuvwxyz&1234567890
ABCDEFGHIJKLMNOPQRSTUVWXYZabcdefghijklmnopqrstuvwxyz&1234567890

Habitat Condensed

ABCDEFGHIJKLMNOPQRSTUVWXYZabcdefghijklmnopqrstuvwxyz&1234567890
ABCDEFGHIJKLMNOPQRSTUVWXYZabcdefghijklmnopqrstuvwxyz&1234567890
ABCDEFGHIJKLMNOPQRSTUVWXYZabcdefghijklmnopqrstuvwxyz&1234567890
ABCDEFGHIJKLMNOPQRSTUVWXYZabcdefghijklmnopqrstuvwxyz&1234567890

Bryn Mawr, Habitat and **Habitat Condensed** are among the Treacyfaces type collection for the Macintosh.

C H A P T E R   4

Typefaces Made-to-Order

Artist

Jonathan Hoefler's love for type was already becoming evident at age six, when his most prized possession was a Press-type catalog he unwittingly commandeered from his father's office. Now, professionally involved with type, he has worked with distinguished publication designer Roger Black.

In addition to designing type and designing *with* type, collecting antique type specimen books and being an armchair type historian, Hoefler runs a small design studio in Chelsea, New York, specializing — naturally — in typographic solutions. His type designs have appeared in dozens of magazines, including *Spy, Rolling Stone, Condé Nast Traveler, Sports Illustrated, Entertainment Weekly, 7 Days* and *Newsweek.*

Project

B.W. Honeycutt, *Spy* magazine's art director, approached me about creating two typefaces, Woodtype Antique XXX Condensed and Woodtype Gothic Extended. The magazine had never used Macintoshes before, as their three main fonts

had until then been unavailable for the Mac. By October 1989, Adobe had released Garamond No. 3 and Bitstream had released Metroblack and Alternate Gothic No. 2. Their two additional display fonts (primarily used toward the end of the magazine) were both 19th-century wood types not available in electronic media. At the time, *Spy* was pasting photostats together for every headline.

To make the fonts available from the Mac's keyboard, the artwork for both fonts was drawn in Illustrator 88 and then imported into Fontographer (for Woodtype Antique XXX Condensed) or Font Studio (for Woodtype Gothic Extended). I used an Apple Scanner with a resolution of 75 dpi

at 400 percent scaling to scan the artwork, saved it as a PICT and then used that as a template in Illustrator.

I have a Mac II with 8 MB of RAM and three hard disks: a 144 MB for the System and applications, a 300 MB for fonts and a 45 MB removable cartridge. I also have an Apple 13-inch color monitor and a Sigma Designs' Laser View, which provides 104 dpi display in contrast to most monitors' 72 dpi. I use this special monitor for drawing type. Objects are a little smaller, but you can see curves better. My printer is a LaserWriter IINTX, but all my final proofing is done on a Linotronic L-300.

**PROJECT
OVERVIEW**

Origins

For the bulk of Woodtype Antique XXX Condensed, I scanned and then traced a reproduction of the original type in *American Wood Type: 1828–1900* by Rob Roy Kelly. Some characters that didn't exist in the original font had to be created. For the simple ones (like quotation marks), I drew the art on the Mac. For other, more complex characters (like the question mark), I did rough sketches on paper, which were then scanned into the Mac and traced.

This page from *American Wood Type: 1828–1900* by Rob Roy Kelly shows Woodtype Antique XXX Condensed. This was photocopied, scanned at 75 dpi with an enlargement of 400 percent (the equivalent of scanning at 300 dpi) and then imported as a template into Illustrator 88.

ABCDEFGHIJKLM
NOPQRSTUVWXY
Z1234567890&$

Antique XXX Condensed. First shown by William Page

Some of the characters needed for *Spy* headlines were missing from the original font. For the more complex characters, like the question mark, rough sketches were made and then scanned.

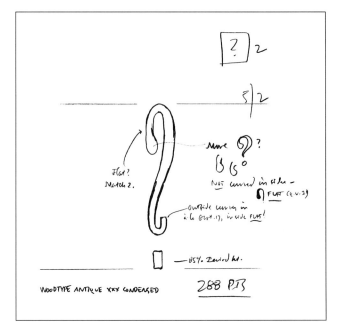

Design decisions

One of the things a designer has to consider is how faithfully to stay with the original design, especially when the original may have had limitations due to its method of production. Are improvements valid, or should the typeface's particular quirks be retained? Antique XXX Condensed is relatively close to its original design. I chose to preserve many idiosyncrasies of the wood type: for instance, because most wood type was cut with a router (a drill-like tool), the characters had rounded rather than sharp interior corners.

In metal type, letters with similar characteristics could be cut with the same punch to insure their congruency; the same tool that created the stems of the *H* could be used to create the stem of the *E*, for example. But in wood type, all letters are cut virtually without guides, so stems are not always of equal weights. This, too, I chose to preserve. *Spy*'s art director had originally chosen a wood type for its clunky feel, and regularizing the stems would have turned the font into a much cleaner, slicker design.

In looking at the interior corners of the capital *E*, *F* and *R*, the effect of the router can be seen in the roundness, not only of the corners, but of the slightly bracketed serifs, which are also present on the *V*.

Wood type letters are usually cut without guides, causing the stems to be of unequal weights. This was an important quality to preserve. In this example, the differences in stem weights can be seen, especially between the *C* and the *O*, and between the legs of the *R* and the *A*.

For both typeface designs, the artwork was drawn in Illustrator. Woodtype Antique XXX Condensed was then imported into Fontographer. Woodtype Gothic Extended was imported into FontStudio. At the time, FontStudio and Fontographer were leapfrogging each other in terms of features. When I re-created the first font, Fontographer wouldn't import from Illustrator; when I did the second, FontStudio wouldn't create Type 1 fonts.

Points and pulls

After importing the scan into Illustrator as a template, I used the pen tool to trace the image. Most drawing in Illustrator is done with the pen tool. All shapes (or *paths*) in Illustrator are composed of lines and curves. All lines and curves are composed of points and pulls, known to the long-winded as *Bezier control points*. Anchor points, which appear as hollow squares, are placed wherever a path takes a turn. Pulls (or direction points), which appear as solid dots, are used to shape curves. A line segment has a point at either end. A curve is a line segment with either one or two pulls describing the curve's shape. The length of the pull affects the depth of the curve: Long pulls mean deep curves, short pulls mean shallow curves, and no pulls means a straight line (Figure 1). As a rule, for drawing type, pulls should always be either horizontal or vertical. There will sometimes be complex curves, such as those defining the bracket of a serif, that just can't be drawn using only vertical and horizontal pulls; so in case of emergency, cheat (Figure 2).

Typographical order

The first letter I drew was the *H*. In general, the *H* has the same mass as the other rectilinear characters, and the stems of the *H* determine the stem weight for the rest of the face. Puny letters, like the *I*, usually compensate for

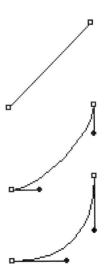

Figure 1. Understanding line and curve segments. A segment with no direction points, or pulls (so-called because pulling on them dictates the degree and angle of the curve), is a straight line. Pulls create the curves, with the length of the pull determining the depth of the curve.

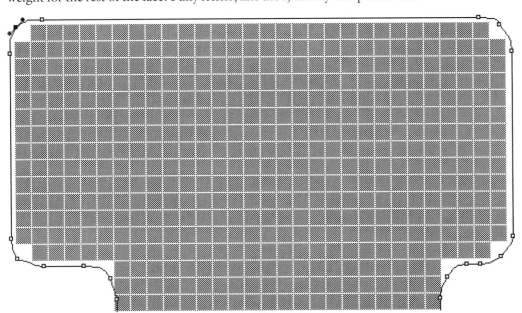

Figure 2. Drawing complex curves. Pulls should be horizontal or vertical if possible. In the case of a complex curve, such as the curve on the upper part of the serif, exceptions to the rule may be observed.

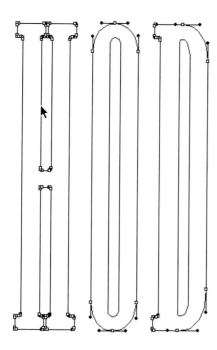

Figure 3. Designing uppercase control characters. The word *HOD* contains the control characters for capital letters. In a face that includes lower case as well, *H, O* and *D* would be augmented with *n, o* and *p*. These characters establish the stem and bowl weights and heights for upper- and lowercase letters, plus the *x*-height and descent.

their weakness with heavier stems, and heftier ones, like the *M*, compensate with thinner stems.

After the *H* came the *O*, which gave me a weight for the bowls and a height for the round letters. (The *O* should be a little heavier and a little taller than the *H*.) And finally the *D*, which combines a stem and a bowl (Figure 3).

After the *H, O* and *D*, we would normally have proceeded to *n, o* and *p*, except in this case, there being no lowercase characters in Woodtype Antique XXX Condensed, we didn't. The characters in *HODnop* (known as the *control characters*) give us stem and bowl weights and heights for upper- and lowercase letters, plus the x-height and the descent. *HODnop* is followed by *Hamburgevons* (no snickering!) which, in upper- and lowercase, gives us all the basic shapes in the alphabet.

By using two open windows, a Preview window and an Artwork And Template Only window, we could see on the screen what the characters would look like when inked, even while they were being drawn (Figure 4). However, screens, like scans, are composed of dots, and thus tend to lose the subtleties of letters. So we applied these three paramount rules for creating fine type on the Mac:

1. Proof drawings on the printer (not the screen).
2. Print characters as large as possible.
3. *Always* refer back to the original art as you draw and proof — scans lie.

Figure 4. Inking on-screen. With two windows open in Illustrator, you can see what the character will look like in both keyline (lines only, along with the template scan) and preview (inked) mode. Final proofing should be done from printer output, however.

Importing artwork

Using MultiFinder (which, in theory, allows several programs to be open at one time, though in reality it can handle only two or three depending upon the size of the programs and the amount of RAM available), you can open both Illustrator and Fontographer at the same time. ▮ *For some programs, the Mac will display a message that says there isn't enough memory to run them but asks if you want to open them anyway. Go ahead. Just save often.*

With both programs open, the artwork for Illustrator was selected, copied (by holding down the Option key to copy the PostScript information as well as the screen representation) and then pasted into Fontographer. The points and pulls changed to depict Fontographer's point structure, which is somewhat similar to Aldus FreeHand's (Figure 5).

Metrics

Once the characters had been brought into Fontographer, we were ready to set the *metrics*. Every character in a font has a *character width* on which the body of the letterform sits. Metrics deal with positioning the body on the character width so it *looks* centered — which is not necessarily the same as *being* centered.

The spaces between the body and the character width are called *side bearings*. Fontographer's Metrics window (accessed with Command-K) allowed us to change the side bearings and move the body of the character left and right. As in drawing, we started with the *H* and moved the *width indicators*, or *T-bars*, that marked the position of each character's width (Figure 6). ▮ *Countless theories abound regarding the setting of metrics for the H. One suggests using the height of the serif as each side bearing. Another recommends setting the side bearings to half the space between the stems. Both are valid theories; do whatever looks best.*

The home stretch

Having set the side bearings of the *H*, we then proceeded to the *O*. The same rationale that makes the *O* taller than the *H* applies to its width, so the *O*'s side bearings should be smaller. The idea is to have every letter look like it's cushioned by the same amount of white space.

The first test of our side bearings was the *D*. Because of its shape, the *D* should have the same left side bearing as the *H* and the same right side bearing as the *O*. To test the side bearings of our character, we can position it between *H*'s and *O*'s to see how it sits.

While the *D* naturally leaned left between *H*'s and right between *O*'s (Figure 7), we had struck a reasonable balance. For the remaining letters with similar stems and bowls, we used the side bearings from the *H* and the *O*. Oddly shaped letters, like the *S,* had to be spaced individually. Some character pairs just wouldn't fit. To create unique kerning pairs, we entered the pair in

a

b

c

Figure 5. Understanding Fontographer's point structure. Unlike Illustrator, Fontographer classifies all points as either corners (a) (where two paths meet and operate independently of one another), tangents (b) (where a line segment smoothly meets a curve), or curves (c) (where a curve meets a curve). This point metaphor is more similar to that of Aldus FreeHand than it is to Illustrator's.

the Metrics window and dragged the right side bearing marker while holding down the Option key (Figure 8).

Generating the new font

Choosing Generate Font from Fontographer's File menu created both the bitmap screen font and the Type 1 PostScript printer font. There are basically two kinds of PostScript fonts. Type 3 fonts are unencrypted, which means they will work on non-PostScript printers (also called PostScript clones) as well as

Figure 6. Setting the side bearings. T-bars (so named because they resemble upside-down *T's*) are used to mark the position of each character's width in the Metrics window. The theory behind side bearings is that, ideally, every letter should be cushioned by the same amount of *visual*, rather than *measured*, white space.

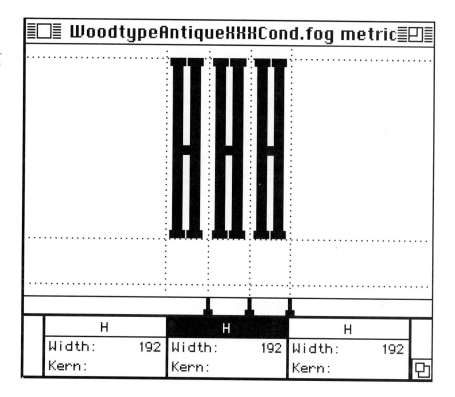

Figure 7. Testing uppercase control characters. The *D*, which shares similar side bearings with the *H* on the left side and the *O* on the right, was combined with the *H* and the *O* in two test strings in order to observe how the characters would sit in relation to each other.

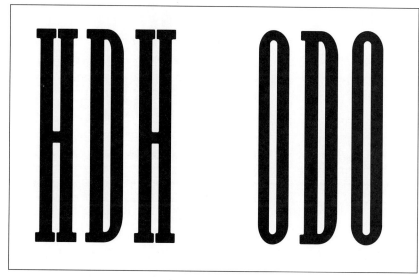

PostScript printers. Type 1 fonts (the kind Adobe has always produced), in addition to being encrypted (meaning they will not print on non-PostScript printers), have *hinting*, a set of mathematical instructions that optimize the font's appearance in small sizes and on low-resolution printers. Originally, Adobe kept the specifications for creating Type 1 fonts secret. Altsys licensed this technology, so that Fontographer could create hinted Type 1 fonts.

The Type 1 hints that Fontographer utilizes primarily control stem weights, ensuring that uniform weights occur on similar stems. For example, with hinting, one side of an *H* will not print one pixel wider than the other side, no matter what the point size. For complete font control, some designers may wish to edit hints directly through the hint-editing module available from Altsys, which combines Nimbus Q (a feature-recognition software) and Altsys-developed software. For most people, however, the hinting currently available in Fontographer is sufficient. It can be supplemented by following a few rules specified by Altsys. These rules are discussed here and summarized in "Rules to aid hinting in Fontographer" on page 54.

The first rule is that characters should always be drawn with the outside path going clockwise and each successive inner path reversing direction. This method requires the program to use a Normal fill technique, not the Even/ Odd fill (Figure 9). Opening the Character information box from the Edit menu displays which fill type has been chosen (Figure 10). Drawing characters counterclockwise causes Fontographer to hint the white space, not the black space. This could create a situation in which the white space between the stems of a *w*, for example, was equal, but the three stems were not.

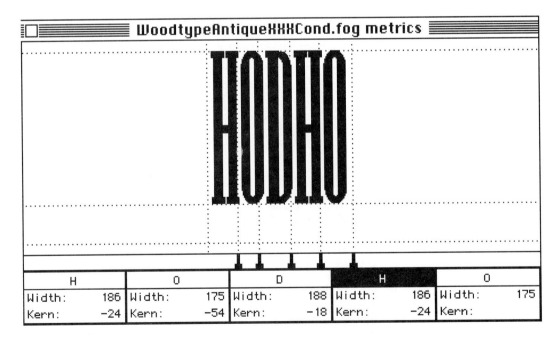

H	O	D	H	O
Width: 186	Width: 175	Width: 188	Width: 186	Width: 175
Kern: -24	Kern: -54	Kern: -18	Kern: -24	Kern:

Figure 8. Kerning characters. Holding down the Option key and dragging the T-bar of the left character made an adjustment that governs the spacing whenever the two characters appear together in the same sequence. Kerning can be set only if there are two or more characters referenced in the Metrics window. The kerning value for the pair shows below the leftmost character of the kerning pair.

The second rule is to draw characters *prenormalized* because no feature normalization is done at print time. This means don't make subtle variations between character strokes (or virtually any character attribute that should be similar) that low-resolution printers can't handle (such as an *I* having a stroke width of 50 em-units and the stems of an *H* being 48 em-units wide). Of course, if your design is intended primarily for high-resolution imagesetters, this rule may not be applicable. In the case of Woodtype Antique XXX Condensed, a typeface originally cut out of wood, I wanted the stem widths to differ and decided to ignore this rule.

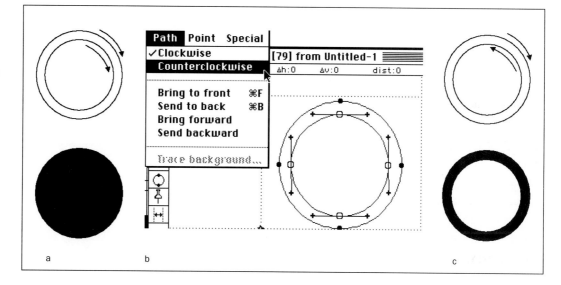

Figure 9. Setting directions. In (a) the arrows show that both inside and outside paths are going in a clockwise direction. With Winding Fill chosen, the character fills completely. Selecting the inside path's points and choosing Counterclockwise from the Path menu (b) results in the letter being filled correctly, as can be seen in (c).

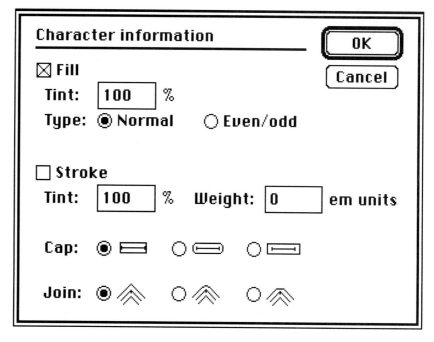

Figure 10. Accessing a character's info. The Character Information dialog box (from Fontographer's Edit menu) has both fill and stroke options. The Fontographer manual recommends that the fill type be Normal as opposed to Even/Odd, so that the hinting will work properly.

Only horizontal and vertical strokes are hinted (though Fontographer recognizes strokes that are within 5 degrees of horizontal or vertical). What this means is that angled strokes, such as those on a *V*, may not maintain uniform weights on low-resolution printers, especially at small point sizes.

Curves are hinted in Fontographer only if the tangent to the curve (the control point or pull) is vertical or horizontal. An *O* is most effectively hinted if its curve points occur at 90-degree increments starting with 12 o'clock. This allows for font compression. If you vary serifs within a character, each point controlling that serif must be registered separately. Creating symmetrical serifs by making corresponding points line up both vertically and horizontally reduces the amount of memory needed to store a font. Of course, there might be times when serif individuality is desired. But keep in mind that it will increase file size and possibly limit hinting.

Working with FontStudio

The Illustrator artwork for Woodtype Gothic Extended was brought into FontStudio via MultiFinder and the clipboard, as I had done with Woodtype Antique XXX Condensed. ▮ *FontStudio imports only the Illustrator path. Patterns, fills and stroke widths are ignored.*

FontStudio's point structure is more similar to Illustrator's than it is to Fontographer's (Figure 11). After importing all the artwork, we could immediately see the outline filled by selecting the paint bucket tool (Figure 12).

Rules to aid hinting in Fontographer

Here are some tips for designing characters that lend themselves to hinting.
1. Use a normal (Winding) fill for the fill type in the Character information dialog box and reverse directions for successive inner paths to create white space inside a black stroke.
2. Limit subtle differences between similar letterforms, because they will not be obvious on low-resolution printers.
3. Keep strokes as close to vertical or horizontal as possible in order to retain uniform weights when printing at low resolutions.
4. Place curve points at 90-degree increments using 12 o'clock as the starting point. Pull Bezier control points (or pulls) to correspond with either a vertical or horizontal plane. This will aid file compression and facilitate hinting.

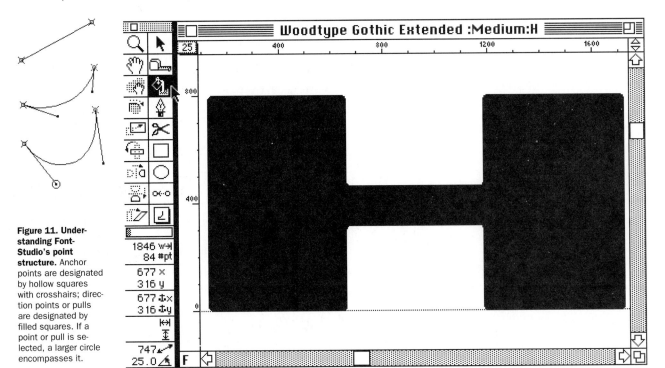

Figure 11. Understanding FontStudio's point structure. Anchor points are designated by hollow squares with crosshairs; direction points or pulls are designated by filled squares. If a point or pull is selected, a larger circle encompasses it.

Figure 12. Previewing a design. In FontStudio you can immediately see the character's outline filled by selecting the paint bucket tool. To return to the outline view, simply click anywhere in the outline editing window

Figure 13. Using the kerning toolbox. Clockwise from top left, the tools available in FontStudio's Metrics window are the magnifier tool, I-beam tool, kerning tool, character width tool, side bearings tool and hand tool.

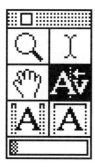

I had already done my designing in Illustrator, so I was ready to tackle the metrics of the typeface. Operating FontStudio's Metrics window is simple. A separate tool palette in this window makes changing a character's width and side bearings and creating kerning pairs very easy (Figure 13). The kerning window is divided into two sections: the Character Metrics area and the Sample Text area. In the Sample Text area, typical strings of letters can be kerned (Figure 14), their character widths can be altered and their side bearings refined. After one kerning pair has been established, those parameters can be used on other kerning pairs as well. Values can be controlled by dragging the letter with the correct tool, by entering the number in the appropriate space or by using the thumbwheel. ▮ *Kerning cannot be set while the character metrics are being changed. First the kerning tool must be selected and the kerning pairs button must be enabled.*

Setting preferences

Under the FontStudio Edit menu, the Set User Preferences dialog box has several categories of preferences to choose from. The categories are General, Color, Outline, Bitmap and Kerning. General handles how many levels of undo are available. ▮ *It's important to remember that several levels of undo will use a lot of RAM and could affect your computer's performance.*

Figure 14. Working with the Kerning window. In the top part of the window is the Character Metrics area; below is the sample text area, where typical strings of letters can be kerned, their character widths can be altered and their side bearings refined.

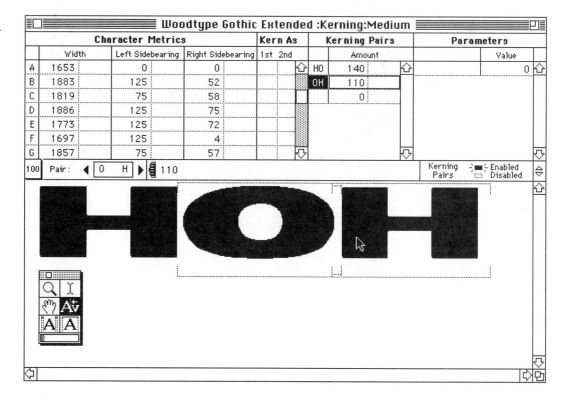

General also controls whether the toolbox and readouts are hidden or visible and whether backups are made when saving. The Color category controls the colors that are displayed for guidelines, gridlines, template layers and so on. Outline affects the way the Outline character-editing window appears — what sample sizes of text are shown, whether guidelines and gridlines are automatically visible and have snap-to capabilities, and what key combinations to use for tools. The Bitmap category has a subset of the Outline preferences. The Kerning category allows the user to change the default settings for the sample text and to define key combinations for the kerning tool palette (Figure 15).

Using and distributing the fonts

Once each font was completed, the screen font could be loaded into the System with Font/DA Mover or accessed through a program like Suitcase (see "A look at Suitcase II" on page 155), Master Juggler or Font/DA Juggler, and the printer font could be placed in the System folder. ▌ *If you're going to distribute a font commercially, register your font family ID number with Apple Computer (see "Registering a font" on this page).*

▌ Registering a font

Apple Computer has established specifications for using font ID numbers. To register a font, contact Apple at this address: Font Registration Program, Developer Technical Support, Apple Computer, Inc., 20525 Mariani Avenue, M/S 75-3A, Cupertino, CA 95014.

Here is the breakdown for the more than 32,000 available font ID numbers:

0–255 .... Original Apple font IDs
256–1023 .... Reserved numbers
1024–3071 .... Public domain
3072–15999 ...... Commercial font vendors
16000–16383 .... Reserved numbers
16384–32255 .... Foreign scripts
32256–32767 .... Special use for developers

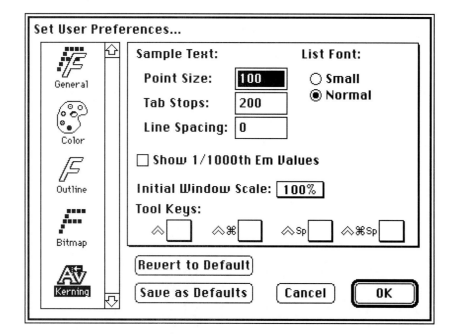

Figure 15. Setting user preferences. Preferences can be set for many functions in FontStudio. Displayed here is the Kerning window preferences set, which allows the user to change the default settings for the sample text as well as define key combinations for the kerning tool palette.

In retrospect

Ed Benguiat, a prolific type designer, once told me that redrawing a typeface gives you license to redesign it. I think there's some truth in that. In re-creating Woodtype Antique XXX Condensed for the computer, one characteristic of wood type I chose to ignore was its visually uneven heights. Traditionally, in typography, round letters are made taller than flat ones so they'll appear optically even. In wood type, however, all letters were cut to the same height, so letters like *C, G, O, Q* and *U* appeared too short because they were exactly the same height as the rest of the face. I didn't feel it would compromise the integrity of the original design to repair this, so I did — by slightly increasing the height of the round letters (Figure 16). The PostScript font looked even, but still had the workmanlike appearance of authentic wood type.

Figure 16. Creating optical consistency. The top example is the original wood type design with vertically consistent heights. This method, which is mathematically correct, ends up making the letters look optically inconsistent. The bottom example is the electronic Woodtype Antique XXX Condensed with the rounded characters made slightly taller to give an even appearance.

PORTFOLIO

A.C. PAUKSIS

Rather than the usual brochure or poster, Hoefler designed a **series of cards** (approximately 4 x 6-inches) as announcements/invitations for the Type 90 conference.

Jonathan Hoefler

"Despite the advantages provided by his movable type, Gutenberg stuck it to his designer contemporaries by limiting them to one typeface. Every mechanical innovation since the 16th century has been perceived by designers as another limitation.

"Computers, especially the Mac, have changed this a little. PostScript, Adobe's digital language that allows type to be stored as geometric blueprints rather than immutable images, has meant indefinitely scalable and sharp type. It's also become a firmer standard than its predecessors, which is why PostScript fonts from Linotype and Monotype are more mutually compatible than metal slugs from Linotype and Monotype machines.

"But most important, the creation of typefaces is no longer the realm of the specialist. The art and the craft of type design are no longer two separate fields, as the tools for designing and producing professional-quality typefaces are merging — and becoming available to the individual designer."

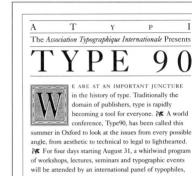

A   T   Y   P   I

The *Association Typographique Internationale* Presents

TYPE 90

WE ARE AT AN IMPORTANT JUNCTURE in the history of type. Traditionally the domain of publishers, type is rapidly becoming a tool for everyone. ❧ A world conference, Type90, has been called this summer in Oxford to look at the issues from every possible angle, from aesthetic to technical to legal to lighthearted. ❧ For four days starting August 31, a whirlwind program of workshops, lectures, seminars and typographic events will be attended by an international panel of typophiles, from eminent type designers Matthew Carter and Adrian Frutiger, to leading graphic designers Neville Brody and Paula Scher, to type historians John Dreyfus and James Mosley, to typographic innovators Peter Karow and Rene Kerfante. ❧ In all, almost one hundred major typographers and designers have been invited to present their work, demonstrate techniques, and steer discussion. Type90 promises to be a truly unforgettable event. ❧

OTHER EVENTS

In addition to the regimen of lectures, workshops, playrooms and Town Meetings, there will be a festival of typographic activity in Oxford this year. In addition to the exhibits by sponsors, we have lined up a number of ANTIQUARIAN BOOKSELLERS *who will have stands featuring new and out-of-print books on typography, bookbinding and design. The* OXFORD GUILD *will also have hand-printed books available, and Ian Mortimer's new boxed portfolio called* ORNAMENTAL TYPES *from the foundry of L. J. Pouchee will be available for inspection.* ☙ *Type90 participants will have the unique opportunity to work in a* LETTERPRESS PRINTING OFFICE *at* READING UNIVERSITY'S *Department of Typography & Graphic Communication.* STAN NELSON *will be on hand to work with those who want to learn to work with metal type.* ☙ *On an epicurean note,* GERARD UNGER *will discuss traditional Dutch* CHOCOLATE ALPHABETS, *and* JEFF LEVEL *will conduct a* TYPE AND WINE TASTING. *Come and help us with this very important research.* ▲▲▲

Type90 conferees are doers in real life, and a passive conference isn't what they want. Supplementing the lectures and town meetings will be a collection of workshops, offering an opportunity to be involved, to talk, and to explore in a more relaxed, social setting. Workshops will include **"Type Design: The Master Class"**, Matthew Carter's celebrated workshop from Type 1987, featuring presentations by Sumner Stone, Günter Gerhard Lange and Gerard Unger. Paula Scher and Louise Fili will lead workshops on developing a **personal design style with type**, and Ronn Campisi and Aurobind Patel will open a discussion of **type in publication design**. Jim Parkinson will lead a workshop on logotype design, and Jonathan Hoefler will work with participants using **type design tools for the Macintosh**. John Benson, Lida Lopes Cardozo and David Kindersley will lead stone-cutting workshops, and John Downer will head a workshop on gold leaf signpainting. ¶ For the type-minded explorer, Type90 will include two playrooms stocked with every new tool for type design, typography and desktop publishing you care to get your hands on.

☞ LECTURES

The core of Type90 will be a series of lectures and specialized 'town meetings,' short presentations followed by open discussions. There will be discussions of type history (including James Mosley's examination of antique ornamented types and John Dreyfus' chronicle of Charles Peignot), a look at the type of today (with presentations by post-modernists Neville Brody and Zuzana Licko) and a look at the type of tomorrow (with Rene Kerfante and Günter Gerhard Lange on the future of type in Europe). Alan Jeeps of the BBC and Fred Smeijers will discuss screen type in "The Good Morning..." and Steven Heller will be leading an informal group on "Truly Disgusting Novelty Faces and How to Use Them." Additional presentations will include typeface protection, type marketing for designers and foundries, and type education.

& TOWN MEETINGS

OXFORD

Home to the English-speaking world's oldest university, the "City of Dreaming Spires" is an intellectual paradise. With more than 900 buildings of historical and architectural importance within one square mile, Oxford's streets, houses, colleges and chapels (enhanced by gardens, croquet lawns and tree-lined walks) capture centuries of English history. There is no one building that dominates Oxford, no famous fortress or cathedral that offers a short-cut view of the city. The best way to get a feel for Oxford is to spend time wandering through the town, slowly fitting it all in.

Type90 has arranged for rooms and meals at the colleges of Christ Church and Corpus Christi, located in central Oxford and near almost all Type90 events. For the best choice of housing, please fill out the reservation card as soon as possible, as hotel space will be extremely limited. PanAm has arranged competitive fares for Type90 attendees. To reach them in the U.S., call (800) 635-8470. Our conference code is CVN10005. Parking in Oxford is extremely limited. British Rail from London's Paddington Station and coach service from Heathrow Airport are quite suitable.

☞ ADOBE
AGFA
APPLE
BERTHOLD
BITSTREAM
HELL
ITC
LETRASET
LINOTYPE
MONOTYPE
URW

SPONSORS

90 TYPE

Not only have these companies provided a great deal of financial support to the conference, they have also bent over backwards to help us form the program and stock the workshops and playrooms.

SERIES DESIGNED BY JONATHAN HOEFLER

SPORTS ILLUSTRATED BANTAMWEIGHT

ABCDEFGHIJKLMNOPQRSTUVWXYZabcdefghijklmnopqrstuvwxyz1234567890.,;:-""""(!&?) ABCDEFGHIJKLMN

SPORTS ILLUSTRATED FEATHERWEIGHT

ABCDEFGHIJKLMNOPQRSTUVWXYZabcdefghijklmnopqrstuvwxyz1234567890.,;:-""""(!&

SPORTS ILLUSTRATED LIGHTWEIGHT

ABCDEFGHIJKLMNOPQRSTUVWXYZabcdefghijklmnopqrstuvwxyz12

SPORTS ILLUSTRATED WELTERWEIGHT

ABCDEFGHIJKLMNOPQRSTUVWXYZabcdefghijklmnopqrstu

SPORTS ILLUSTRATED MIDDLEWEIGHT

ABCDEFGHIJKLMNOPQRSTUVWXYZabcdefghijklmn

SPORTS ILLUSTRATED HEAVYWEIGHT

ABCDEFGHIJKLMNOPQRSTUVWXYZ
abcdefghijklmnopqrstuvwxyz1234

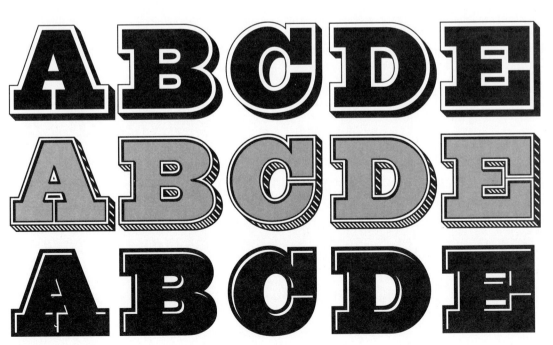

Hoefler designed a series of six **original display faces** for *Sports Illustrated* (above). The faces began with an early 20th-century condensed wood type (traces of which can be seen in the Featherweight), and a sans serif wood type from 1837 known as Gothic, which inspired the Heavyweight.

The skeleton of all three of these **ornamental fonts** designed for *Rolling Stone* magazine is a slab serif design, Egiziano Nero, which appears in the 1920 specimen book of the Nebiolo foundry in Torino, Italy.

CHAPTER 5

Old World Ways, New World Means

Artist

Richard Mitchell, professor of English at Glassboro State College in New Jersey, is the editor and publisher of *The Underground Grammarian*. Published eight times a year, this unusual newsletter employs selected illustrations from Mitchell's series of Typographic Ornaments and other printers' embellishments that he has created or re-created from 19th-century woodcuts. Even the ornaments he has designed himself incorporate the traditional carved block print style.

Project

When I moved my typesetting operation from hand-set to electronic, I had to find a way to move my collection of typographers' ornaments into the digital medium. Using the Apple Scanner and pages from a vintage collection of typographers' catalogs, I scanned individual pieces, brought them into FreeHand (version 2) to use as background templates, traced them by hand and exported them as EPS (encapsulated PostScript) files.

I use a standard Macintosh SE with a 20 MB hard drive and a LaserWriter printer. The SE has a Rapport floppy drive attached to it, which I used to save the finished graphics for the DOS world.

PROJECT OVERVIEW

Ornaments at work

Ornamentation refreshes the eye. Between two columns of type you might drop a little something — not a logo, not clip art, rather an adornment of some sort. I used to do that pretty regularly in *The Underground Grammarian* when I was typesetting it by hand. Now it's much easier to do it on the computer. Sometimes the ornament was appropriate to the text, sometimes it was abstract and nonreferential.

The first ornaments I ever made were border elements created in Fontographer. There's a border strip at the top of every page of *The Grammarian*. Those are standard monotype border elements, set piece-by-piece as though they were type.

Those elements at the top of a page served an important function for printers. As they watched the impressions coming out of the press, they could use the borders to detect inequities in inking. Because that band is regular, everything should ink the same. If something went wrong, the printer would be alerted early and could readjust the inking.

Besides being decorative, border elements serve an important function for printers. As the printer watches a page come out of the press, he or she can quickly detect inking problems based upon coverage in the border element and fix the press before wasting a lot of paper.

---

woman, but because of the easy dismissal of the role of a mother. Neither of our sages looks good in these little stories, and that we are able to see that more clearly now than we might have fifty years ago, is much to the credit of the feminist party.

Here you see a little picture. It is familiar, very familiar. Cut it out and put it in your wallet, or in a locket, as your gender may suggest. Get into your time machine and travel into the distant past of our kind. Go among the painters of the caves. Visit the tamers of horses on the wide steppes. Travel with the herders of the reindeer and the caribou. Seek out the gatherers of nuts and berries in the rain forests and on the high veldt. Don't be afraid of them. They will recognize you, in spite of your outlandish speech and look, as one of them, except in detail. You will show this little picture wherever you go, and all who see it will say, "Oh, yes, we have such a picture too. It is…" And then they will fill in the blanks. Than this picture of a mother and her child, there is no more widespread and universal icon.

Make another such journey, but this time carry with a used Christmas card, on it a crèche, with mother and child, and the gentle beasts, and, a little bit back and off to one side, patient Joseph. Once again the mother and child will be recognized everywhere. And often the beasts as well. "Yes, yes," they will say, "the animals are also hers." Often they will ask, however, "But who is that up there with the mother?" And you will have to explain.

Uh, well, you will have to say, That's sort of the father, not exactly the father, of course, but the one who is, how shall I say,

sort of playing the role of the father, but, of course only that part of the role that comes after the fact of the fathering, you know. Or something like that. You know what I mean, don't you? But they won't.*

We are all so savvy that we all know about fathers and fathering. At the same time, we are all so naïve that we suppose that we know who our fathers are. But we don't. All we have as to the identity of our fathers is testimony, and testimony of a not disinterested party. The whole business of fathers and fathering is not self-evident; it has to be discovered. That, rather than the taming of fire or the coming of writing, may have been the most momentous discovery in the whole history of our species, the discovery that the women didn't bring forth babies all by themselves, but that some man was needed. It may also have been the most direful day in our history, the beginning of war, of property, of government, of bureaucracy, and other plagues and spites beyond counting.

As to all that, of course, your guess is as good as mine, which is, like all guesses, no good at all. But as to something else, we need not guess. It could only have been after that discovery that the idea of "family" came into our lives. Before that, there could only have been something like "the people," which is, in fact, what many so-called primitive tribes frequently call themselves,

*A naughty time-traveler would take the mother-and-child picture and show it to Jesus. His comments would be interesting to hear. The Jews very hot against all hints of female divinity, but so strong is that notion that the Christians have—not wisely, of course, but only inadvertently, and making a virtue of necessity—preserved the worship of the goddess.

10

Typographers' ornaments are a way of refreshing the eye between blocks of text. They can be relevant to the text, or just abstract artistic inserts that let the page breathe. Here is an ornament set into *The Underground Grammarian*.

The originals

The typographers' ornament that I call the Fiddler is the work of one of the most famous typographic ornament creators, Will Bradley. Bradley lived during the late 19th and early 20th centuries and was a printer, a type designer, a typographer and an artist. He spent his whole life in the printing craft and made some of the very best typographical ornaments that there are, including the Fiddler and the Horse (both re-created in my digital collection, EPS Volume 10).

Bradley cut his originals in boxwood, generally using the end of the grain (straight up and down through the tree). With end grain there's no grain direction to fight with, and so cutting mistakes are less likely. The designs were then duplicated with a pantograph (to reduce them) and molds were made. (A pantograph is an instrument for copying on a predeter-mined scale. It consists of four light, rigid bars jointed in parallelogram form.)

The molds were then cast in metal — partly lead, partly antimony, which increased the rigidity of the softer metal. Pure lead was too soft and, after a few impressions, would wear out. Sometimes tin was also added. The typographers often had proprietary formulas for the mixtures that created the best imprints.

Making the transition

I use the same technique for every re-creation: first doing the outline of the entire form, and then going inside each of the sections and doing the inner outline. In essence the outlined form, filled with black, becomes the woodblock; the inside outlines, filled with white, function as the areas that were cut away with the wood-cutter's knife.

Throughout the process of converting an original woodcut to the electronic desktop, one is constantly forced to make decisions about how best to represent accurately what the original artist intended. For example, how do we decide whether a gap showing up in the printed graphic or a fade in a line was intended by the artist? Images may have been printed from a scratched or dented ornament. After all, these molds were originally soft metal; they wore unevenly and they became damaged. I think it's very important to find all of the disorders and fix them up. Sometimes I can whip out my magnifying glass and look at the printed page, and say, "Here. This is where a speck of dust got under the plate. There's a little black dot with a ring around it on the ornament." One has to be careful not to include it in the final piece.

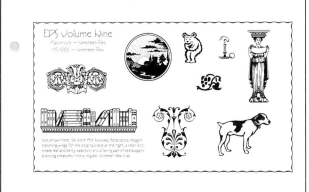
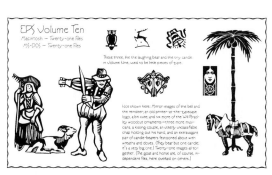

Some of the Typographer's Ornaments (such as Bradley's Horse and the Fiddler) were re-created from prints of the work of early typographers. Others are original artwork, created in a similar style.

The stroke that defines the Fiddler's right leg varies in width. The inside of the leg shows marks that look like they were created with a gouge to provide the shadow effects. Bradley cut away the wood to create the varying stroke widths. The same effect was achieved in FreeHand by drawing a second outline inside the main outline of the leg. When the main outline was filled with black and the inside outline was filled with white, it was as if the wood were being cut away, leaving the gouge marks and different stroke widths in the drawing. The black then looked like a stroke drawn by an artist, rather than by a computer program.

W hen I set out to re-create the Fiddler, I had certain things to think about. Before me on the computer screen was the rough, pixellated version of the ornament, having been scanned and placed in the background layer of FreeHand (Figure 1). On the copystand beside me, I had the original print and my magnifying glass (a six-inch illuminated magnifier). And it was with these tools that I tried to reproduce the strokes of the gouge, those lines that are worn into the white spaces by the point of a sharp instrument (Figure 2). As the carver pushed harder, the gouge got deeper and the opening got wider. It's a very characteristic look of a woodcut and it's important to use one's eyes, look carefully and reproduce it right.

Scanning

When you scan, it's important to make sure that what you're scanning is square. Very often this is a matter of trial and error — scan and rescan until you get the verticals vertical. Set the scanner for black-and-white line drawing, 300 dpi resolution and save the scan in TIFF format. What I look for in a scan is the highest possible contrast without too much destruction of white space. Your image should be as dark as possible, but not to the point where the white space starts eroding away. You're going to need that white space. For example, in these ornaments the white space at the bottom of the knife cuts is very small

Figure 1. Tracing the background layer. Placing an image in the "zero" layer of FreeHand gives it a grayed out, pixelated look, making it easy to distinguish the template from the emerging vector art.

Figure 2. Retaining the marks of the gouge. In the line of the Fiddler's arm, the deep cuts of a woodworking tool can be seen where the artist dug deep to create the folds of the sleeve.

and I wanted to keep it as close to the original as possible. ∎ *If you have a preview option in your scanning software, use it to check the contrast before you complete the scan.*

To provide templates for creating digital type ornaments, we select and scan pieces from our typefounders' catalog collection. Whenever we can, we scan the original at 100 percent. However, with an original that fills half a page, we normally reduce it. Ultimately, size doesn't mean anything, because we're going to redraw this in FreeHand, which, as a PostScript illustration program, allows you to scale your artwork to any size with no loss of information or clarity. But we want an original scan that won't be too jagged when it's enlarged and magnified for tracing.

Bringing the scan into FreeHand

My partner, Terry Donohue (I like to refer to him as my accomplice), and I bring the scanned woodcut into FreeHand with the Place command. If the scan is so large that it's hard to tell where exactly to trace because the pixels are like big blocks, I reduce the magnification in FreeHand by one level. But if the scan is small, I enlarge it so that it's fairly big and easy to work on. While the placed scan is still selected, I hold down the Shift and Option keys, grab a corner with the pointer tool and drag. The TIFF will be enlarged proportionately to the next size that will provide maximum printer resolution. ∎ *The Shift key retains the proportions while enlarging the selected image. The Option key snaps the image into optimal sizes for the chosen printer so that no unusual patterns occur. The higher the printer's resolution, the more sizes there are available.*

Once I have the scan the size I want it, I send it to layer 0, which is FreeHand's Background layer. I deselect the Active check box through Layer Control (Figure 3). This grays the scan and allows me to trace without selecting the scan by mistake. ∎ *Layer Control gives the user the ability to make*

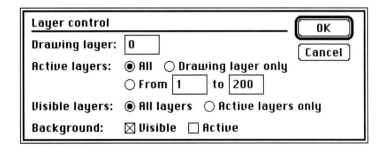

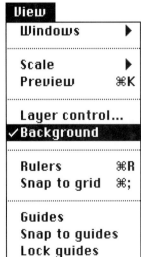

Figure 3. Rendering the background inactive. In the Layer Control dialog box, selecting the Visible option and deselecting Active for the Background layer leaves the background visible but untouchable. Another way to control whether the background appears on-screen is to click Background under the View menu. The checkmark next to Background shows that the background layer is "on," or visible.

any layer, including the Background layer, visible or active by clicking on the
appropriate check boxes. A visible, inactive layer is one that can be seen but is not
accessible for changes of any kind.

Since I use scanned images saved as TIFFs to trace around, I must be in the
Preview mode in order to see the outline of the TIFF. If I go to the keyline
mode (by pressing Command-K), the scanned image completely disappears
and only its bounding box can be seen. Because the Preview mode shows fills
and line weights, I set up a zero-point (0.0) line for tracing. I want the thinnest
line possible (both on-screen and on paper) because I'm drawing an outline.
Even a .5-point line gains thickness on a curve if printed at 300 dpi.

One more thing I do before I begin to trace is to set up a macro key
(MacroMaker or any other macro program will work) to toggle back and forth
between showing the background template and making it disappear (see
"MacroMaker" at the bottom of this page). It's important to be able to look
at your artwork without any obstructions, such as the template. Other
recommended macros are ones that toggle between filling objects with black
and rendering them as purely line art.

Re-creating the original

Now, with the original next to me as a reference and the scanned image in the
background of the FreeHand document, I'm ready to go to work. I do all my
drawing and tracing work on layer 100. I also do most of my work at 400 per-

---

MacroMaker

A A macro is a small program that
lets you activate a series of key-
board- or mouse-controlled
steps by pressing a single key or
key combination. MacroMaker is one of a
number of programs that let you define
macros. A good rule of thumb for when to
create a macro is to ask, "How often do I
use this procedure?" If the answer is "often
enough so I find it annoying," a macro is
probably in order. The MacroMaker program included in the software supplied
with the Macintosh computer is found on
Macintosh Utilities Disk 2 and should be
placed in the System folder. Restart the
computer in order to see the MacroMaker
icon on the menu bar.

Using MacroMaker
To record a routine, pull down the menu
from the MacroMaker icon and select Start
Recording. Now proceed with the routine.
Once the routine is completed (for ex-

ample, selecting Background from
FreeHand's View menu), select Stop Recording from the MacroMaker menu. A
MacroMaker window will appear (it looks
like a cassette). Enter a name for the macro
(for example "Background"). Select the
Keystroke and enter a key combination
that will be used to invoke the macro (for
example, Option-B). Click on the "Store"
button, and the macro is now ready for use.

Invoking the macro
When you want to use the macro, simply
type the saved Keystroke (for example,
Option-B) and the recorded routine will be
activated.

Deleting a macro
If you no longer want to retain a macro,
choose Open MacroMaker from the
MacroMaker menu, select the macro to be
deleted and click the Erase button.

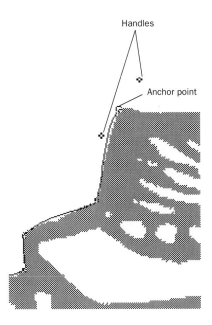

Handles

Anchor point

Figure 4. Adjusting the handles. The two flower-shaped objects are the handles, and they determine the shape of the curve. The round circle is the anchor point, and, like a thumb tack, it stays there no matter how much the handles are dragged. The anchor point moves only if it's selected and dragged.

cent screen magnification. That allows me to get a good sense of the shape of the ornament without being overwhelmed by the dots and jaggies of the scan.

I almost always use the curve tool when I trace. Only when there is truly a sharp point, a sharp turn or a square corner do I use the corner tool. It's very rare that I need to draw straight lines anyway, and where curves come to some kind of a corner, I can still manage that corner with the curve tool. ▌ *The combination tool can be used to place both curve and corner points. For a curve point, drag the tool, for a corner point, simply click.*

First, I hand-trace the outside of the entire form. With the Fiddler I started at the top of the bow. Because there's a clear corner there, it was a good place to start. I work on one line segment at a time, one point at a time, placing a point anywhere the line changes direction. Before I go on to the next point, I adjust the line by holding down the Command key so that the curve tool changes temporarily to the pointer tool. Using the handles or even the anchor point itself (Figure 4), I adjust the line to follow the overall line of the scan as closely as possible. I don't place the next point until I feel I've done the best adjusting I can on the current one. (If you wait until later, you find yourself with a mess, because the handles can be going every which way.)

For example, look closely at the place where the line goes from the body of the violin to the brim of the hat (Figure 5). It's not a simple curve from the violin to the left edge of the brim. It curves slightly to the east and north, but then the line, just for a short space, goes due east, then north, then due west and then north before it starts to rise north and east again. There needs to be a point at each of those direction changes, and the line should be adjusted to follow the scan and, more important, the original. Having the original to refer to so that you can watch for those things is essential.

Figure 5. Following the meandering line. A line that seems simple on casual observation actually changes direction many times.

At the end of the fiddle the pegs at the top are drawn one way and the pegs at the bottom are drawn another (Figure 6). There's a slight break in the bottom pair. Here I made a "judgment call"; I asked myself, "Is this an accidental dent in the ornament?" I decided it was intentional. After re-creating so many of these ornaments, I could say, "This is the kind of thing Bradley might do." The variation between sets of pegs adds interest.

Notice, too, that on the right bottom peg he's got a little squiggle that comes out and goes back. I drew it using the freehand tool while looking at the original, not the scan. I use the freehand tool to follow more complex lines. It's notorious for putting in a point wherever there's the slightest jiggle of the mouse, but I managed to draw this one with only seven points. ∎ *Under the Preferences menu, the Snap-to-Point distance can be set to any value between 1 and 5 pixels. This setting affects the way the freehand tool draws a path. A small Snap-to-Point distance creates a path more consistent with the path drawn by the user but with many points. A larger Snap-to-Point distance constrains the path somewhat, which results in a line that's somewhat smoother but with fewer points, which is an advantage when the document is sent to print.*

Getting the look

One of the characteristics of programs like FreeHand, Illustrator or any vector drawing program is that when you print out a line it's absolutely uniform in thickness. Now, when an artist takes a pen in hand, or a pencil or a brush, and draws on canvas or paper, the stroke is not the same throughout. It changes — often because the artist wanted it to change. It gets thinner and thicker; the line itself has form. Artists often use line thickness to suggest shading. Where the line gets thicker, you imagine more rotundity there.

One way to get around this limitation in PostScript illustration is not to draw the lines at all, but rather to outline the negative space and fill it with white. Once I have the main outline of a figure, I make sure the path is closed

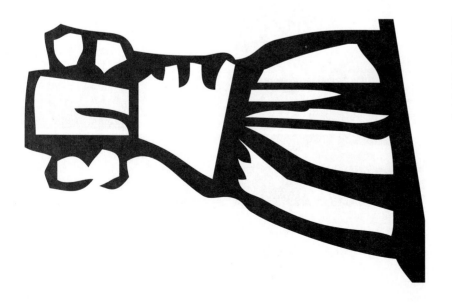

Figure 6. Making judgment calls. It was decided that the differences between the top and bottom pegs of the violin were intended by the original designer, so they were retained in the digitized version.

(Figure 7) and fill it with black (Figure 8). ∎ *A way to ensure that your path is closed is to open the Element Info dialog box of the selected path (by pressing Command-I or holding down the Option key and double-clicking on the selected path) and see whether there's a checkmark in the Closed box. If there isn't, clicking on the box will close the object. FreeHand closes the path by drawing a straight line between its two ends. Always carefully view an object that has been closed this way to make sure that the closure looks right.*

If the filled outline looks correct, I go back to a fill of "none" (by way of a macro keystroke) and then begin to outline the negative space (white space inside the drawing), using the scan as the template. For the Fiddler, I outlined the negative space using both the curve tool and the freehand tool. The curve tool was used for the longer sweeps, the freehand tool for the gouges. When I'm using the freehand tool, I push down firmly onto the mouse. It gives me more control. And unlike the way I use the curve tool, drawing one point at a time and adjusting each one before going on to the next, I make one long trace of the gouge marks with the freehand tool before going back and adjusting. After using the freehand tool, I often remove some of the extraneous points. (This is easily done by selecting the point with the pointer

Figure 7. Closing a path. Element info (Command-I) under the Element menu allows the user to close a path; however, the path will be closed by the most direct route, not always the artistic choice. Unlike Illustrator, a FreeHand path cannot be filled until it is closed.

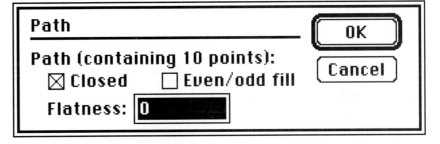

Figure 8. Filling with black. Once the outside outline of the Fiddler was completed and closed, it was filled with black. Creating white shapes for the negative spaces would then produce a thick-and-thin, "hand-crafted" look for the lines of the ornament.

tool and striking the Delete key.) Occasionally, I add points if they're needed in order to be as true to the original as possible (Figure 9).

When the inner outline was completed, I made sure the path was closed and then filled it with white. I selected the outer form, filled it with black and then looked at the drawing carefully, comparing it with the printed original.

In the face, I added another layer of black when I did the eyes, nose and lips (Figure 10): The inside outline of the whole face area was filled with white. Then I traced the facial features and filled them with black. So we had three levels of objects, all stacked up on layer 100. ∎ *FreeHand puts the most recent addition to a drawing on the top level.*

When I'm utterly, finally finished, I always group the elements (Command-G). ∎ *Grouping prevents any changes other than scaling, skewing, rotating or reflecting, so it keeps accidents from changing the drawing.*

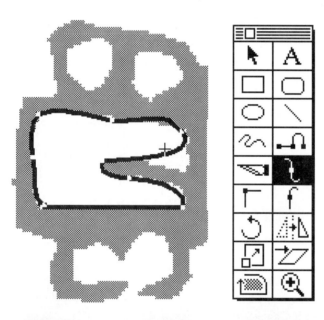

Figure 9. Inserting a curve point. With the path selected, the crosshair of the curve tool was positioned over the path where the new point was to be inserted and the mouse was clicked. Dragging the new point with the pointer tool and making adjustments with the handles made the line conform to the template's curve.

Figure 10. Whittling away the face. In order to create the facial features, the negative space of the face had to be defined and then the features were added on top and filled with black.

At this point I scale the image down, using the Shift key to retain the correct proportions. For the sake of uniformity among ornaments, my rule of thumb is that the finished piece must be somewhere between 1 and 3 inches. A great big EPS and a small EPS are the same thing. A person purchasing one of my volumes can scale a piece from it with no loss of information or distortion of line. After all, it's not area that's being described in PostScript, it's the relations — the lines, curves and fills. When I've resized it, I use the Export command from the File menu to save it as an EPS file (Figure 11).

Complexity takes time

The Fiddler took me three or four hours to trace. Some take a much longer time. For example, a simple leaf-and-berry tailpiece took me a few days because the scan was so poor and it was a very complex form with all its curves and detail. Ornaments like this are deceptive in that they appear symmetrical but in fact are not, so each side has to be done separately, or at least cloned and then altered. Continuous reference to the original was required, as well as very careful adjusting.

In retrospect

If I were doing this today, I'd work on a large-screen monitor instead of on a small screen. I think that a large screen is useful for this kind of meticulous work. In fact, I use a Radius two-page monitor today. In drawing these ornaments, I "bounce around" a lot — I start to work on the hat, and then I have to bounce down to the arm. And in FreeHand the screen redrawing takes a while. So, the bigger the screen, the better — no question.

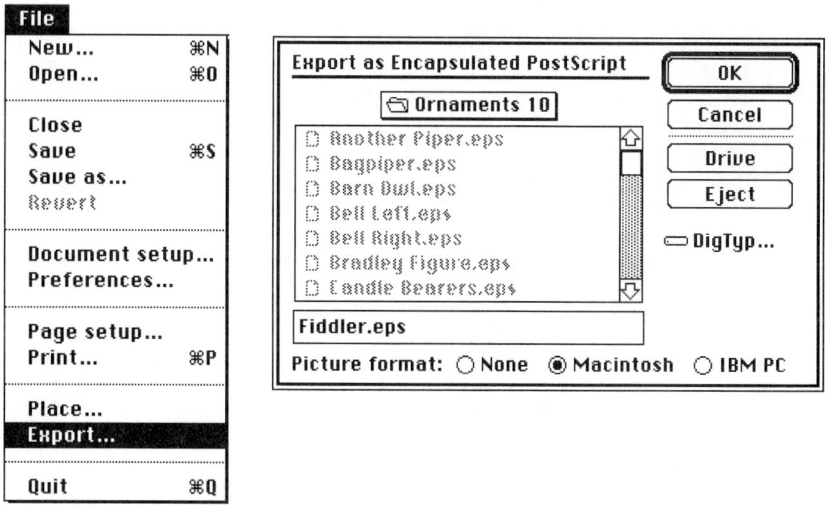

Figure 11. Exporting the file. From the File menu, choosing Export brings up a dialog box where the EPS (Encapsulated PostScript) file must be named. A PICT preview can be chosen for either Macintosh or DOS computers.

Richard Mitchell

"There was a time when making typographers' ornaments was an art. You had to be a true artist to do them well. I fear that we're losing a sense of typography and artistry in this modern age. However, it's also not good for an artist to relive another epoch. An artist has to find his or her own style.

"Typographers' ornaments are important in helping compose the page. They should harmonize with the typefaces. The clip art that I've seen doesn't serve the same function. I find that work created on the computer, especially typefaces, often turns to ice on the page. No human hands have touched the drawings. All the blood and character have been removed and instead we have mass production. We need to regain a sense of style."

Mitchell has included
a variety of styles and
periods in each vol-
ume of **Typographer's
Ornaments.** Shown
here are more selec-
tions from Volume
Ten, which includes
the Fiddler and the
Horse.

CHAPTER 6

Illustrating With Type

Artist

David Smith breaks the conventional boundaries that separate typography from illustration by combining his love for type with a desire to experiment. He has created a portfolio of colorful and witty illustrations that use type in unusual ways. As a representative for Apple Computer, Smith travels to Japan to meet with some of Japan's top designers and illustrators. There he demonstrates his eclectic design philosophy in an endeavor to help develop the graphics market in Japan.

Project

The assignment was a cover for *Verbum* magazine. This particular issue of *Verbum* was to explore how the personal computer affects the life-styles of creative users, and how the artists in turn express those life-styles in their art. So I created a cover illustration to express that kind of exchange. Even though the major components are typographic, I consider the cover, overall, an illustration. I didn't do any hand sketches; I just created the work on a blank screen, letting it grow into what eventually became the *Verbum 3.3* cover.

I used a Mac II with 5 MB of RAM and 40 MB of internal hard disk storage, a 13-inch Apple color monitor and a 19-inch Radius color monitor. The software I used included Adobe Illustrator 88, Streamline and SmartArt. The magazine cover was separated and output on a Linotronic L-300 at 2540 dpi.

**PROJECT
OVERVIEW**

Choosing characters

For the "Life Style" cover for *Verbum* magazine, I chose a variety of PostScript fonts to be converted to outlines. I picked typefaces that attracted me. I didn't care whether the faces usually looked good together because I was going to mold each letter to fit whatever plan formulated in my head, letting the elements take shape on-screen.

Modifying letterforms

The computer has given the artist complete access to the letterform, allowing one to do some exciting things. Before I had SmartArt and Streamline (and now Illustrator 3.0), I used to draw my letterforms from scratch in Illustrator, which took a great deal of time.

Once the letters are created, the fun begins — they can be stretched and filled and distorted, rotated, tilted, pushed up against each other — basically, you can wreak havoc with traditional typography.

I began to build the words "Life Style," adding more letters until I had the faces I wanted. My first draft didn't include the set of white letters. Those occured to me later as a way to brighten up the whole illustration.

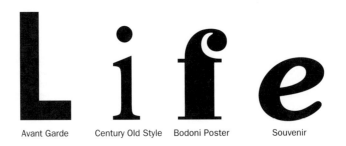

Avant Garde   Century Old Style   Bodoni Poster   Souvenir

Brush Script   Century Old Style   Avant Garde   Brush Script   Century Old Style

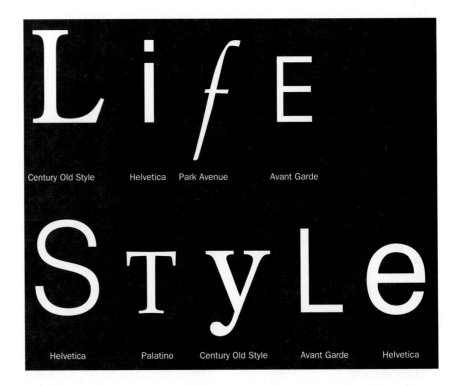

Century Old Style   Helvetica   Park Avenue   Avant Garde

Helvetica   Palatino   Century Old Style   Avant Garde   Helvetica

The original "Life Style" letters (top) were chosen from Adobe typefaces. More choices were made when the white letters (bottom) were added later. Some of the characters were stretched or otherwise modified after they were converted to outlines.

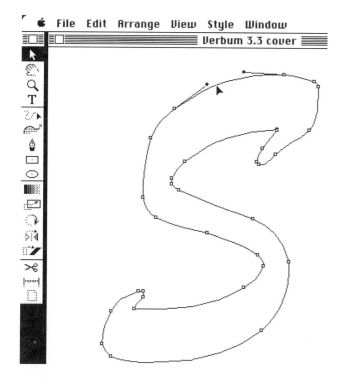

SmartArt, a program that intercepts Post-Script information sent to the printer and can save it in a PICT or TIFF format, and Streamline, a program that can then convert the PICT or TIFF file into editable outlines, were used to create a variety of letterforms. This was the first step in creating the *Verbum 3.3* cover.

Type

Style...	⌘T
Font	▶
Size	▶
Leading	▶
Alignment	▶
Spacing Options...	⌘⇧O
Tracking...	⌘⇧K
Link	⌘⇧G
Unlink	⌘⇧U
Make Text Wrap	
Release Text Wrap	

Create Outlines

An automatic conversion feature was added to Illustrator in version 3.0. Conversion of type to a manipulable outline is accomplished by selecting the type and choosing Create Outlines from the Type menu — a much simpler process than using SmartArt and Streamline.

A custom background pattern was developed in Illustrator. A pattern from Adobe Collector's Edition II (a) was recolored (b), enlarged (c) and further adjusted (d). Then the new pattern was assigned a name and saved.

a

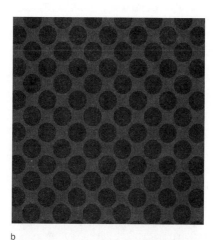

b

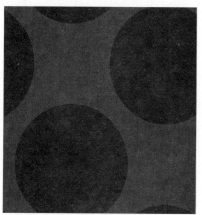

c

d

T he first step in designing the *Verbum* "Life Style" cover was to create the font outlines with the SmartArt desk accessory and the Streamline program. SmartArt intercepts the PostScript font information as it's being sent to the printer and sends it to the screen instead. Streamline can then convert the screen image (via a high-quality autotrace) into an editable PostScript outline. The outline can be manipulated in Illustrator 88. (Illustrator 3.0, which has incorporated the SmartArt function, can automatically convert type into outlines.)

Once the font outlines were brought into Illustrator (when you open Illustrator, select New under the File menu, find your outline and then choose Open or double-click on the outline), I realized that I needed a frame for the design. I drew a rectangle the size of the magazine cover by holding down the Option key, clicking the rectangle tool and, when the dialog box appeared, specifying 8½ x 11 inches. ∎ *If your default is set to points or centimeters, you can change this by choosing Preferences from the Edit menu (Command-K).*

I then sent the rectangle to the back (Command-hyphen) and locked it in place (Command-L). I used the rectangle as an area to play in. I mocked up the little horizontal bars that are on the left side of the page. I knew those had to appear at the same location on every issue, so I took measurements from an old cover and set the bars in and locked them in place.

Figure 1. Interconnecting the pieces. A mockup of the *Verbum* magazine cover was created, and the letterform outlines for the words "Life Style" were stretched, bent and condensed to fit together in a lively way.

Next I started mixing, matching and selecting different letters from different typefaces I had converted to outlines — Park Avenue, Bodoni, Brush Script, Century Old Style and more — until I had the words "Life Style." I felt the letters should be interconnected like puzzle pieces — carefully touching and balanced against each other. The fun for me would be in the stretching and bending and condensing things to fit and work together (Figure 1). In the final cover, each composite letter is three pieces: the main large letter, a drop shadow of the large letter and the smaller white letter superimposed on top.

Manipulating a letter

I selected the letterform *L* with the pointer tool, moved one or two points to change its shape slightly, and then chose the scaling tool from the tool palette. ▌ *This process is true throughout Illustrator. You must always select the object first (in order to communicate to the computer what it is you wish to perform the action on) and then select the tool.*

The scaling tool lets you change the size of the object you've selected. I clicked the tool at a point on the letter outline where I wanted the scaling to originate — in this instance, the middle left-hand side. This is called the point of origin and, during the scaling process, it locks the object down at that point.

I then moved the cursor to the right of the letterform, clicked and began to drag to the right and up to enlarge the *L* (Figure 2). ▌ *The farther the pointer*

Figure 2. Manual scaling. Once the letterform was selected, the scale tool was used to place a point of origin (the "+" on the far left). Clicking and dragging changes the plus into an arrow. The original letter remained visible as a reference until the mouse button was let go, and then the original disappeared, leaving only the scaled version. To copy the modified character, the Option key was clicked and then held down while dragging the arrowhead.

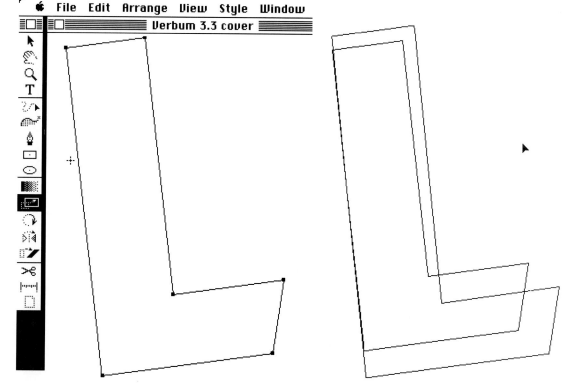

is from the point of origin, the finer the control of the scaling operation. Scaling can also be done numerically by holding the Option key down while clicking (or, in Illustrator 3.0, by selecting the "+" version of the tool from the tool palette). A Scale window will appear. Clicking on Copy will leave the original alone and scale a clone.

The letter *f* (from Bodoni) already had a wide, broad look to it, but I wanted it even wider and broader. I stretched it much more horizontally once I got it to the overall size I was looking for. I created all the letters in this way, moving them, rotating them, reducing and enlarging them, until I finally achieved a balance and cohesiveness that I liked.

One other thing I did was split the letters that had inside spaces — the *e* and the *l*. I did this so that the background, once I decided what it was to be, would show through. The only way to get an inside counter to have a fill of none, and consequently show whatever is behind it, was to topologically create an object that has the outside on the inside. For example, an *O* would have to topologically change to a *C* with its ends overlapping in order to have the background show through the inside space of the *O* (Figure 3). ▌ *Illustrator 3.0, FreeHand 3.0 and some other PostScript illustration programs provided commands for making "compound" paths that let the background show through an inside space.*

Figure 3. Achieving an inside fill of None. In order to get a true fill of None inside an enclosed area, the area had to be topologically altered so that the inside of the area was connected to the outside. In Illustrator 88 this was done by simply cutting both sides of the inside and outside path and then rejoining them so that the outside path was linked to the inside path.

Adding drop shadows

Satisfied with my assortment of letters, I began refining my work. I realized that I wanted a drop shadow on each of the letters, so I clicked on one of the letters with the pointer tool, held down the Option key and dragged to move right or left, whichever direction seemed appropriate. This created a copy of the letter. Once I had the drop shadow where I wanted it, I sent it behind the original letter (Figure 4). ▪ *To enter Move values numerically, select the object to be moved with the pointer tool, then hold down the Option key while clicking on the pointer tool in the tool box. A Move window will appear allowing the user to type in numbers for whatever units have been selected in the Preferences window under the Edit menu. The direction of an angled move can be specified in degrees.*

Figure 4. Creating drop shadows. Each letter was cloned and the clone was sent behind its original letter to form a drop shadow.

Choosing colors

I began by picking bright, saturated colors. The only rule I used for selecting the colors was that I didn't want similar colors next to one another. Nothing would go from blue to green to yellow — no rainbow effect. I wanted the color choice to add to the feeling of animation and edginess that I was shooting for — red next to green, yellow next to gray, or purple next to orange.

With the Illustrator software, Adobe includes Pantone Matching System (PMS) colors for both coated and uncoated papers. I opened the PMS file while my "Life Style" file was open. This made all the colors available in the "Life Style" file when the Custom button was selected in the Paint dialog box (Figure 5).

With my Radius monitor, I chose the PMS colors I wanted. I knew from experience that my Radius monitor matched printed Pantone samples pretty

Figure 5. Selecting Pantone colors. In order to make PMS colors available, Illustrator's PMS file must be open at the same time as the illustration file. Clicking on Custom Color in the Paint window will show the PMS colors in a scroll box. The chosen color(s) will appear in the color swatches at the right of the Fill or Stroke box.

well. After I had picked the colors for the originals, I chose the deeper colors for the drop shadows. The red happened to go to purple in my head, some of the purple went to dark blue, the green went to darker green, the yellow went to orange and so on.

Brightening the illustration

A very late decision in the design was the addition of white letters. I thought the cover needed to be brightened up a bit, and the white letters would do just that. So I went back and created some more outlines. The red *L* in "Life" is a sans serif *L*, so I chose a serif face to lay on top of it. I wanted the white letters to interlock with the letters they belonged to, yet remain independent. This relationship can be seen in the way the white Park Avenue *f* fits on top of the Bodoni *f*, for example (Figure 6). When I filled the new outlines with white, everything brightened up.

The white letters have a different association to each other and to the piece. In the word "Life," each is solely related to the letter it's in and independent of everything else. They're not resting on any other color except that of their designated letter. With the word "Style," I laid the white letters slightly differently — they escaped the bounds of their original characters. "Style" was the more active part of the title, and I made it more jumpy and "jivey."

▍Trapping type

To print yellow type, for example, on a black background, the type must be "knocked out," leaving a "hole" in the black ink where the paper is exposed and can be printed with the yellow ink. But ideally the edges of the yellow type will overlap the surrounding black very slightly, preventing the white paper from showing through any gap that might be created between the yellow and the black when the piece is printed.

Trapping spot colors
In Illustrator, FreeHand and several other PostScript graphics programs, a line is constructed along a "path" that defines the center of the line. A 2-point line, for example, spreads 1 point on each side of the central path. Strokes of letters are constructed in the same way. In a letter with a 4-point stroke, the stroke extends 2 points into the fill area of the letter and 2 points outward.

Overprinting causes inks to print on top of each other rather than knocking out. Many PostScript programs allow the artist to control the fill and stroke of type inde-

pendently. Knocking out the fill area of a letter (so that its color shows clearly) and overprinting the stroke (so that the colored ink extends slightly into the surrounding color) provides the trap necessary to prevent white gaps in printing (a).

When you trap spot colors, be sure to use a stroke of the lighter color, because using the darker color can make the type look thicker or thinner. In the case of dark type on a light background, this means overprinting a stroke of the background color (b).

Trapping process colors
To trap type in process color printing, in which each color is formed by printing a mix of tiny dots of one or more of the four process colors, other trapping techniques can be used. For example, if the type and the background share at least one of the process colors in their makeup, that color will cover any gap that might develop in printing. The small sliver of color thus created is far less obvious than it would be if it were white.

a

b

Figure 6. Interlocking letters. A Park Avenue *f* fits tightly inside a Bodoni *f*. The white letters were added to animate the illustration as well as lighten the overall tone.

Placing the logo

I designed the *Verbum* logotype as well. (For each issue of the magazine the logotype is created differently to match the cover illustration.) I selected the text tool and clicked on the spot where I wanted to start the logo. This opened up the Type window. I scrolled until Futura Extra Bold came up, and then selected it. In the box below, I typed in the word VERBUM in caps (Figure 7). ▮ *Illustrator 3.0 lets you type in place on the illustration, rather than entering text through a dialog box.*

I set the size and leading, left alignment, and then clicked on the OK button and took a look at it before going into letter spacing. Returning to the Type window (Command-T), I kept increasing the Size, Leading and Spacing numbers until they looked right. The final number was 42.0924 points.

Next I chose PMS 376 CV from the Paint window for the fill and stroke, and previewed it to see how it looked. I overprinted the stroke of each colored letter so that the letter would trap (see "Trapping type" on page 82). Then it was time to create the drop shadow effect on the logo. Using the pointer tool, I selected the text by clicking on the left alignment point. ▮ *Illustrator provides a shortcut to getting to the pointer tool. Hold the Command key down and no matter what tool is currently selected, it will turn into the pointer.*

▮ *The alignment point — it looks like a little* x — *is the easiest place to select your text. Its position corresponds to the chosen text alignment. That is, it's at the left end of the baseline for left-aligned text, in the center of the baseline for centered text and at the right for right-justified text. You can also select text by clicking on its invisible baseline.*

I then held down the Option and Shift keys and moved the copy to the right until it looked correct. ▮ *The Shift key constrains the movements to 0, 45 or 90 degrees. The Option key makes a copy.*

I filled the copy with white from the Paint window. Then I sent it behind and previewed it.

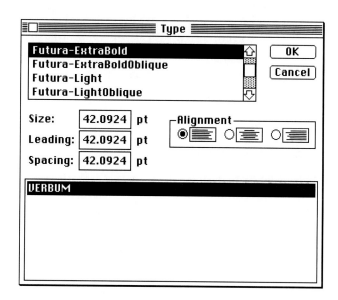

Figure 7. Setting the type. In Illustrator 88, clicking once with the text tool brings up the Type window. Here the text is entered, the typeface chosen, the alignment set and values for the size, leading and spacing are specified. In Illustrator 3.0, text can be typed directly on the illustration.

Adding a background

While I was creating the letterforms, I didn't know what I was going to put behind them. I had laid them all on white. Now it was time to deal with what to put in the background.

I started with a pattern from Adobe Collector's Edition II, which consists of eight disks of patterns (about 400 patterns in all) drawn in Illustrator. I could have created my own patterns, (see "Drawing and using patterns" on page 85), but I decided to start with a "packaged" one and modify it.

I selected the rectangle I had created to represent the overall size of the magazine cover and filled it with a pattern. I did this by clicking on the Pattern button in the Fill section of the Paint window (the patterns file must be open, similar to the way the PMS colors file works, in order for the Pattern button to be selectable.) I chose a dot pattern — sort of an oversized halftone dot screen. When I previewed the file, there were black dots everywhere, filling the rectangle. The basic pattern was correct, but I wanted a few changes.

I went into the Pattern menu, selected that pattern, pasted it back out, changed the coloration so that it was an 80 percent gray background with a black dot, and then established this as a new pattern. (Illustrator forces you to give your new pattern a new name so you can't accidentally delete your old pattern.) Then I went back to the Paint window and assigned this new pattern to the background rectangle of my "Life Style" file.

Now I had small black dots on a gray background. I brought up the Transform Pattern Style window, which is accessed by clicking on Transform in the Pattern dialog box. In this window you can move, scale, rotate and shear your pattern (Figure 8). I enlarged it by 620 percent so I ended up with a huge

Figure 8. Transforming the pattern. From the Paint window, clicking on the Pattern button, selecting a pattern and then clicking on Transform brings up the Transform Pattern Style window. In this window the pattern can be moved, scaled, rotated, reflected or sheared.

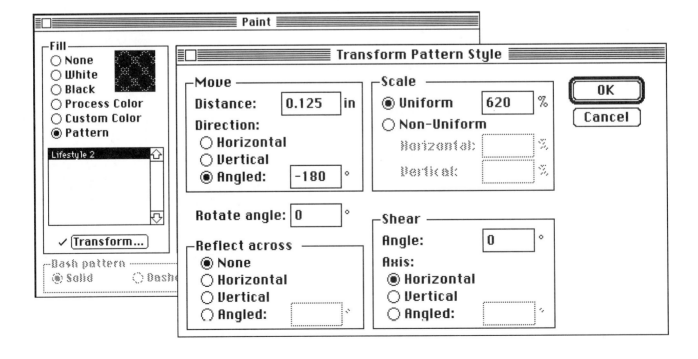

halftone dot screen. I also moved the pattern (by selecting an angled direction in the Move section) within the rectangle so that the dots clipped about equally on the top and bottom, as well as right and left. ▋ *A minus number in the Move section causes a reverse move.*

In retrospect

I enjoyed fitting things together so that the letters danced off one another and expressed the words "Life Style." Although they seem to be moving, the characters are rooted because they are all resting on each other at some point. Some hang from each other — for example, the *E* in "Style" is sort of hooked on the end of the script *l*. And the serif *e* in "Life" is snugly placed in between the *f* in "Life" and the *l* in "Style." I wanted the letters to be interrelated. If they weren't at different angles, they would probably be very tightly kerned. Actually, this arrangement was an exercise in kerning to the utmost degree.

▌ Drawing and using patterns

To create a pattern, follow these steps:
1. Draw a square using a stroke of None (a). (Use the rectangle tool while holding down the Shift key.)
2. Ungroup the square and delete the center point (b). The square's fill will show up in the pattern, so select None if you want no fill.
3. Draw the pattern. Anything that extends outside of the square will be cropped (c).
4. Make sure that the square is sent to the back, and then Select All and Copy.
5. Open the Pattern window under the Style menu.
6. Click on New. The pattern you've selected and copied to the clipboard will show up on the bottom right (d).
7. Enter a name (or leave the default) and click OK.

To modify an existing pattern, open the Pattern window. Select the pattern to modify. Click on Paste. The pattern will be pasted to the Illustrator page, where you can change it. Then follow steps **4** through **7** above.

To use a new or modified pattern, select an object and go to the Paint dialog box. In the Fill box choose Pattern. The name of the new pattern will show up below, ready to be selected to fill the object (e).

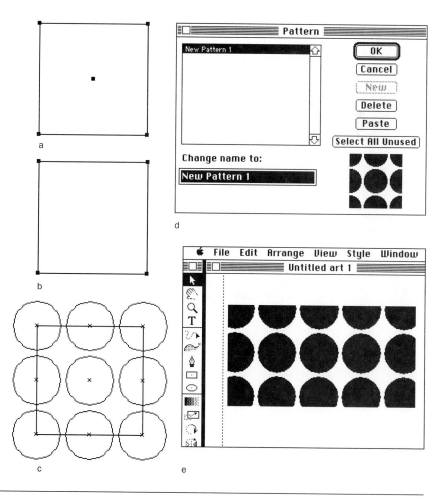

a

b

c

d

e

PORTFOLIO

David Smith

"I like to cross typographic boundaries. The computer unleashes so many possibilities, but it's up to the artist to explore the many choices available. I thought creating the Verbum cover was quite a playful and interesting experiment — intermixing different types of letterforms, as well as different sizes and shapes. I had a great time doing it."

Turnkey DTP! was done in Adobe Illustrator 88 as the cover illustration for an issue of the Japanese version of *Publish* magazine. Type was combined with elements drawn with the pen tool.

This cover **illustration** for the June, 1989 issue of *Publish* Japan was constructed in Adobe Illustrator with the pen tool to show various output options (bitmapped, smoothed and Post-Script, for example) available for type from the desktop.

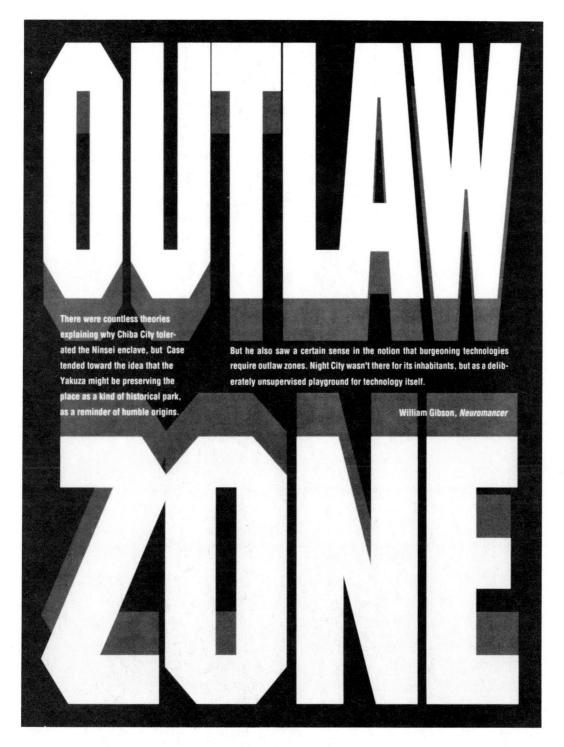

OUTLAW
ZONE

There were countless theories explaining why Chiba City tolerated the Ninsei enclave, but Case tended toward the idea that the Yakuza might be preserving the place as a kind of historical park, as a reminder of humble origins.

But he also saw a certain sense in the notion that burgeoning technologies require outlaw zones. Night City wasn't there for its inhabitants, but as a deliberately unsupervised playground for technology itself.

William Gibson, *Neuromancer*

Outlaw Zone, designed as part of an Apple Computer, Inc. in-house publication called "Click & Drag," was set in Adobe's Machine typeface, which was modified by compressing the type horizontally in Adobe Illustrator 88.

CHAPTER 7

Blending Tradition with Innovation

Artist

Tom Gould studied graphic design at San Diego State University and worked in several studios in the San Diego area before becoming art director of *Psychology Today* magazine from 1968 to 1975. He has worked as a freelance designer since then, concentrating on publication design. His work has included annual reports, textbooks and a two-year stint as art director of *San Diego Home and Garden* magazine.

Project

I was asked to develop promotional materials for a Festival of Italian Arts to be held at an upscale shopping/restaurant complex. The title of the project was *Arté Italiana.* I began thinking about the long history of Italy's art and how to compress these centuries and at the same time reflect the new (possibly ephemeral or obscure) aspects of contemporary Italian design in one symbol for use on posters, mailers, possibly t-shirts and banners.

I worked in black-and-white on a two-page monochrome monitor which is attached to a Mac II with 2 MB of RAM and a 60 MB hard disk. Once I had a design down, I switched to an Apple color monitor to assign colors. I used a LaserWriter for proofs.

Starting with thumbnails

For the first thumbnail sketches, I tried assembling some elements of Italianism: motifs from Rome, the Renaissance and the Baroque period, with an eye to rendering them with a contemporary feel. I looked through art history books, the stage designs of neo-romantic Eugene Berman, our own vacation snapshots and magazines with Italian design features. The Italian flag also suggested itself as a motif. I wanted a festive, cheerful feeling, with some possibilities for color, although, as often happens with a multicolored logo, someone invariably needs to reproduce it in monochrome and you have to make sure that the colorful design has the same impact with only one color.

These thumbnail sketches represent the stream-of-consciousness design process I went through in trying to amass a variety of images to symbolically suggest the subject matter.

Arté Italiana

An obvious problem that had to be resolved was making the very short word, *Arté,* and the very long word, *Italiana,* work together as a whole.

Working in PostScript

Once I had done some "thinking on paper," I started exploring the design possibilities in FreeHand. I can't say enough about the elegance of this program for working out ideas, even suggesting them as I go along. The typographic tools and the ability to work in Preview mode make it almost a digital scratch pad for the developmental stage of a project. Because of this, I often end up with overly complex files. So I generally redo the finished piece for ease of reproduction. This also facilitates making changes later if modifications are needed.

ARTE
ITALIANA
A CELEBRATION
OF ITALIAN ARTS

FreeHand allows you to work in the preview mode (as opposed to the keyline mode, which only shows object outlines without shading or color) and quickly create "roughs" — such as this early experiment — that are virtually finished designs.

One of the first difficulties in designing the logotype lay in the words themselves — *Arté Italiana*. What to do with a short and a long word together? I started with the thought of using the word *Italiana* as a compressed mass of tight caps, maybe with the flag colors — green, white and red — integrated. White type won't show against a white background, so a panel of some kind would make that work; black was the obvious choice for contrast.

For my first idea, I used Century Old Style, tightened and stretched to what I thought were the limits of good taste. ∎ *Condensing type in FreeHand is easily done by grouping the text (Command-G) and then pulling on one of the handles inward horizontally to compress the text or pulling a handle vertically to stretch it.*

I then made the letters *ITA* green, *LIA* white and *NA* red by highlighting each group of letters in the text box and pulling down the Color menu, hoping that with creative kerning the three-letter combinations with narrow *I*'s and somewhat narrow *T* and *L* would visually equal the *NA* (Figure 1). ∎ *To kern in FreeHand, place the cursor between the two letters of a pair and press Command-Delete to subtract .01 em or Shift-Command-Delete to add the same amount. A box at the upper left of the window, below the menu bar, displays the distance kerned.*

Once I had the Century Old Style colored, I put the text in a black panel — a little dull, so I skewed it vertically to allow the colored letters to stick out (Figure 2). I had a bold Stone Serif *ARTÉ* sitting on the pasteboard waiting for a way to use it to suggest itself, so I used Stone Serif for the subtitle as a contrast to the chunkier Century Old Style. The skewed black rectangle gave me the idea to reverse out part of the subtitle and use Paste Inside to insert a white clone of the black type into the panel. I then sent the black type to the

ITALIANA

Figure 1. Designing the long word. The letters were stretched vertically, compressed horizontally and assigned the colors of the Italian flag.

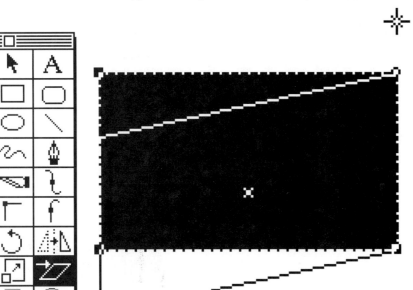

Figure 2. Using FreeHand's skew tool. Taking a rectangular shape and skewing it in Free-Hand is simply a matter of placing the skewing tool on one handle of the selected object and dragging in the direction the object is to be skewed. Using the Shift key while skewing constrains two sides to 0, 45 or 90 degrees. For mathematically controlled skewing, holding down the Option key and clicking on a handle brings up a skewing dialog box.

back (see "Pasting type inside" on this page). It also struck me that the sharp black-and-white contrast suggested contemporary Italian design.

I tried some arched and stone-cut relief-looking treatments with the *ARTÉ*, but felt they were too heavy. I had a Baroque sunburst in my thumbnails and thought it might be fun to wrap the *ARTÉ* around the sun. I had wanted to get in some fluttery elements, so I put in some ribbons to see how they might do. Now I had one idea to submit to the client (see page 91).

Tracing DaVinci

In looking at this first attempt, I decided that it was a little busy and wouldn't be effective without colors. I considered what might be done with a popular icon (in the cultural sense, rather than the Macintosh usage) such as Michelangelo's David, anything Venetian, a Corinthian column, the Mona Lisa. I tried tricking her out with some designer sunglasses. I made a few tracings over a reproduction with the idea of reducing her to a line art logotype and adding some graphic patterns behind her. The problem would be to maintain recognizability and still get goofy.

Pasting type inside

The Paste Inside or similar masking function found in many PostScript drawing programs can be used to create a variety of effects. Here it's used in FreeHand 2.0 to show a change of color as the type intersects a background. This effect can be used with any colors or shapes. But it's important to note that several Paste Insides in an illustration will noticeably slow printing.

1. Type your text across a skewed rectangle and color it black (a).

2. Clone the text (Command-=) and color the clone white (b).

3. Cut the white text to the clipboard (Command-X).

4. Select the skewed black rectangle and choose Paste Inside from the Edit menu (c).

5. Bring the rectangle to the front (Command-F). The intersection of the white text and the black rectangle will cause the white text to be visible (d).

6. To change the text, select the item it's pasted into, choose Cut Contents from the Edit menu and the text will be cut and then pasted to the page, where it can be edited and then pasted inside again.

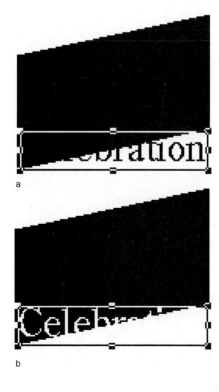

a

b

c

d

I scanned the reproduction and sent it to layer 0. ∎ *Layer 0 is FreeHand's background layer and serves as a nonprinting template. Using Layer Control from the View menu, the designer can choose to make layer 0 visible or invisible as well as active (able to be changed) or inactive.*

Next I started tracing the scan with the curve tool. The hair was created by drawing an initial line, then cloning (Command-=) and adjusting the points (Figure 3). The glasses were made by drawing an outer white circle with a 2-point black stroke and then scaling a clone and filling it with black, no stroke (Figure 4). ∎ *Clicking the scaling tool on the selected object while holding the Option key brings up a Scale dialog box, where the point of origin can be specified to be the center of the object.*

Using the Image dialog box (I selected my scan and chose Element Info from the Element menu), I clicked on Screened and chose the line screen

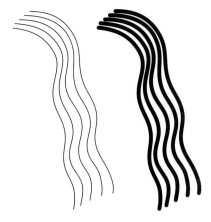

Figure 3. Repeating an element. A single strand of hair was drawn, given a thickness and round ends and cloned several times. Each copy was modified slightly.

Aligning type to a curve

Curved type is one of the hardest things to do with traditional typesetting. On the computer, it's one of the easiest. The following steps illustrate how to set curved type in FreeHand.

1. Type your text.
2. Draw a curve with the curve or combination tool (a).
3. Select the text and the curve by holding down the Shift key while touching on both items (b).
4. When both are selected, choose Join Elements from the Element menu (Command-J).
5. The text should now follow the curve of the line and the line should be invisible (c).
6. To unattach, select the type and choose Split Element from the Element menu. The text and the curve will again become separate elements.
7. While the type is attached, changes can still be made using the Text Along A Path dialog box, which is accessed, once the type is selected, by choosing Element Info from the Element menu, or by typing Command-I (d).
8. Choosing Skew Vertically results in text aligned to the curve at the baseline, but standing upright (e).

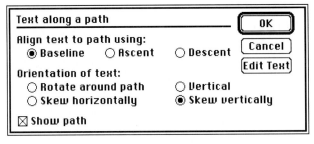

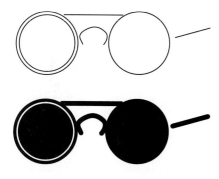

Figure 4. Drawing concentric elements. To center the lenses within the rims of the sunglasses, the rims were first drawn with a 2-point stroke and white fill, then these circles were cloned, and finally the clones were scaled using the Scale dialog box, so that the scaling wouldn't move the clones, and assigned a black fill and no stroke.

rather than the dot screen. I then pasted the scan inside an ellipse that cropped out everything but her nose and mouth (Figure 5). The misty background of the DaVinci painting was suggested by a graduated fill that was set in the Halftone Screen dialog box to 0 degrees, 15-line screen ruling (Figure 6).

Next I dealt with the type treatment. *ARTÉ* was still in Stone, but now I added an effect of Heavy (with the text selected, I chose Effect from the Type menu), letterspaced it (with the text selected, I chose Spacing from the Type menu and entered a number) and aligned it with the top of the panel (broken by Ms. Lisa's head to tie things together). The type at the bottom was joined with a path to suggest the neckline of her dress (see "Aligning type to a curve" on page 94), and the subhead "A Celebration of Italian Arts" was set in Stone Sans, grouped and then slightly stretched vertically (Figure 7).

Blending traditional and modern

I was intrigued by the idea of incorporating the flag into the design, so I came up with another drawing that played upon the Italian emblem: The green and red bars of the flag, blurred together in the middle and overprinted by a workmanlike, black type headline (Figure 8). Wow! This is the kind of design

Figure 5. Defining Mona's face. The scan that had served as a tracing template was cut to the clipboard and pasted inside an ellipse so that only the mouth and nose could be seen.

Figure 6. Controlling an individual object's halftone screen. When an object is selected, choosing Halftone Screen from the Attributes menu displays a dialog box, which controls an object's screen.

that pops up when the process really gets rolling. But a member of the committee felt that it was insulting to the national flag of Italy. Not an argument to win, and certainly not with the standard designer rationalizations for doing what the designer likes. International diplomacy aside, the design would have required three colors to function correctly.

Back to the motherboard

I continued to experiment. Short word, long word, hmmm . . . I've tried the massed caps and do like that, so far. One thing that four-letter words can do (for the designer) is allow considerable warping of the letterforms without losing readability. There's enough context to carry the meaning through. Each letter can carry some symbolic meaning — maybe work through four periods of Italian design (Figure 9).

Since the *A* was the most malleable, I made it Memphis-style: anything goes. Fifties organic design meets Art Deco meets prole tackiness. For now, some squiggles loosely angled across (Pasted Inside the triangle) and a circle (black line, white fill) for the crosspiece and opening of the *A*.

The *R* was roughed in with the freehand tool as a 4-point black line with rounded ends. ∎ *The Basic line dialog box under the Line menu (choose Line and then New) allows several choices for line endings and connections.*

The *T* was constructed with corner and curve points. I used a Bodoni *T* as a template for tracing, to set an anchoring "real" typeface in the middle of the messiness.

I thought maybe alternating squares would read as an *E*. Still a little hard to read — maybe some light squares to fill out the corners. Too heavy and primitive. Several variations of combinations of squares later, I settled on three-by-three squares for the strokes and two-by-three squares for the sections of the vertical stroke between the crosspieces — fairly classic block-

Figure 7. Combining the elements. Line art, type and a screened scan were combined in a Mona Lisa approach to the logo.

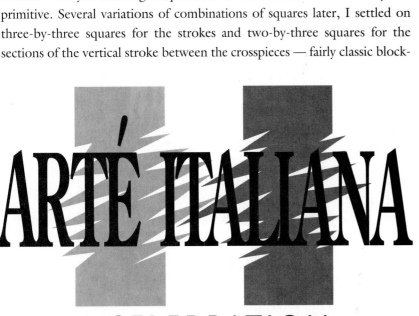

Figure 8. Using the flag as a motif. With the Italian national symbol as a jumping-off point, a modern design was created that reflected not only Italian heritage but also contemporary design in Italy.

Figure 9. Creating letters that function independently and together. Though the individual letters reflect different styles and eras, the gestalt of the design allows the disparate parts to be read as a whole.

letter proportions (Figure 10). The Distribute and Align commands made these variations very quick to try out. I sheared the letter to the right rather than rotating it. The accent was scribbled — six or seven lines, round-ended, made by zigzagging the corner point tool.

Rethinking the letters

Now to look at it for a while. The top is too jumpy, says I. Square everything up. The *A* could be a bit more spotty, I thought, in the Memphis tradition, so I constructed what I call a "skid mat," primarily using the Clone and Duplicate commands (see "Creating a 'skid mat'" on page 98) and pasted it inside the triangle (Figure 11). ■ *Using the Duplicate command from the Edit menu (or Command-D) offsets a copy. The distance and direction that the copy is then dragged with the pointer tool sets the default for subsequent copies created with the Duplicate command. Each time the pointer tool is used to drag the object, a new default is created.*

The *R* was uninteresting — maybe something Deco or Futurismo. (Futurism was an Italian art movement that started around 1910 and was devoted to speed.) A Deco-ish *R* made of circles almost worked, but the "squint test" told me that a straight bottom would convey the letterform better (Figure 12).

Figure 10. Creating a rakish *E*. Using Distribute and Align commands and then grouping everything and italicizing it with the skewing tool produced the sheared checkerboard pattern.

Figure 11. Constructing a Memphis *A*. A triangle with a horizontal base and a texture pasted inside shaped the next version of the *A*. An inverted triangle, cloned, resized, colored white and overlaid replaced the circle used in the previous version.

Figure 12. Adding elements of futurism. Pinstriping the R gave it a speedy, futuristic look.

Designing for hinting

The top half of the word *ITALIANA* would overlie a black panel (Figure 13), and this would provide a base for the cacophony above. I placed the text so that it would intersect at the cross-strokes of the *A*'s, creating a nice division. One thing I had to watch was the typeface's hinting (programming code designed to make the face legible at smaller point sizes; see "PostScript hinting" in Chapter 3). The smaller the size, the lower the cross-stroke drops to avoid filling in the space above. So each output size has to be adjusted to make sure that the bottom of the black rectangle is centered along the cross-strokes. A couple of circles (white line, black fill) soften the end of the panel and add a classical touch.

The type was cloned, made white and pasted inside the panel (see "Pasting type inside" on page 93). The original black type was sent to the back. I decided a drop shadow might add some interest and hold the type together,

Figure 13. Providing a solid base. The word *ITALIANA* serves as an element of classical Italy, to provide a platform for the eclectic *ARTÉ*.

Creating a "skid mat"

A pattern reminiscent of the rubber bumps of a non-skid surface can be constructed in FreeHand as follows.
1. Draw a short, round-capped line (a).
2. Power-duplicate it using Command-D and Group the elements (b).
3. Clone the line you've created (Command-=) and offset the clone by half a line segment (c).
4. Clone the double line and then move it (Command-M) five times (d).
5. Group the drawing, clone it and rotate the clone 90 degrees (e).
6. Group the drawing, color it 10 percent gray, clone it, move it slightly and color the clone 20 percent gray and send it to the back (f).
7. Group the drawing and rotate it 45 degrees (g).
8. Place it in front of the object you want to fill (h).
9. Finally, paste it inside (i).

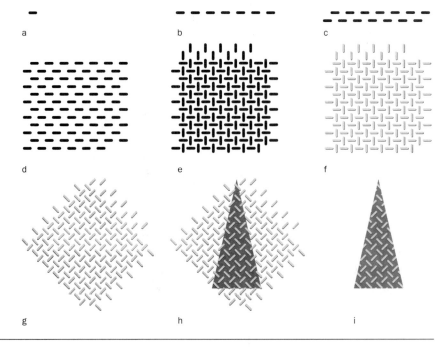

so that was achieved by cloning the type and offsetting it 2 points horizontally and −2 points vertically. ■ *These coordinates can be entered numerically in the Move dialog box found under the Edit menu (Command-M).*

I then changed the type to 20 percent black. I had to Cut Contents on the white type to remove it from the panel, give it its own cloned shadow, group the two and repaste inside.

Taking another look

After the logo had been put on the shelf for a while, I decided to give it some more attention. The skewed *E* had been intended to fill in some negative space under the *T,* but a more relaxed attitude, including reducing the size of the four letters relative to *ITALIANA,* now seemed appropriate. I also felt that the background color in the *E* was superfluous (Figure 14).

The *A* was too busy, so I redid it to suit me instead of trying to follow the Memphis look slavishly. I created a saw-tooth to emphasize the right side of the *A,* just like the classical thick stroke in a regular typeface. The angled fill put weight where the lower left serif would have been, the circle (echoing the two at the sides of the panel below, actually one of them cloned with colors changed) looked like fun, and with all the subliminal cues to the *A* letterform in place, something more abstract could work here.

With the opportunity to do some more work on the logo, I wanted to take the futurist *R* idea further. The basic curve and triangle shape were retained, but now were simply filled with a graduated fill from white at the left to black

Figure 14. Making adjustments. A circle once again replaced the triangle to define the crossbar of a saw-toothed *A,* and the *E* was recolored and straightened.

at the right. I then went to the Special menu under Element and changed the halftone screen to Line, 0 degrees, 10 lines per inch, which resulted in a saw-toothed, speed-lined effect (Figure 15). ▌ *Using the line screen means that lines-per-inch remains constant, no matter how you scale the art. In the case of a PageMaker output, that means the original art in FreeHand has to be changed, exported and relinked to PageMaker with a new screen frequency every time that the art is rescaled.*

Now that a finished version of the logo was at hand, I made about 100 little brush strokes for the accent over the *E* on a sheet of coarse text paper, selected three to scan as line art, tried them in place on the screen and settled on one.

Color to black-and-white

The current version of the logo was in color: purple saw-tooth with orange fill and blue-green circle, yellow center for the *A;* yellow-to-blue fill for the *R;* black *T;* and the *E* was papal purple with a red accent mark. *ITALIANA* had a matching red drop shadow, and the two dots were blue.

The next step was to develop a line art black-and-white version for simple one-color printing. The *A* was given a zigzag white line to separate the two halves, and the circle got an extra outline in white (Figure 16). Converting the red drop shadow on *ITALIANA* was tricky: the white top half of the type was filled white and stroked .5-point white with its shadow filled black and stroked 1-point white; the black bottom half was filled black and stroked .75-point white with its shadow filled black and stroked 1-point white. This was a series

Figure 15. Making further adjustments. The *R* was assigned a coarse halftone line screen at 0 degrees. A hand-painted stroke was scanned for the accent over the *E.*

of trial-and-error experiments on the LaserWriter and one on the Linotronic before these combinations yielded the visual effect desired, and then some superfluous white lines were inked over on master art, which would then be statted to sizes desired. Sometimes it just isn't economical to use the computer all the way to the bitter end.

In retrospect

When I had completed the design (see page 89), the whole project was postponed two months, so everything stopped. As I write this chapter, I'm considering going back to the squiggles in the *A* (see Figure 9). Pre-Macintosh, I would have had so much time, and probably photostat money, invested in the skid-mat fill that nothing could make me give it up, not even a *scuderia* of Italian gunboats.

One wonderful thing we can do with our computers is twist and tweak type beyond all recognition. Aside from the question of whether it's advisable or ethical to distort the work of some of our best and most knowledgeable designers, the type often comes out ugly. Mathematically, there might be more ways to misuse type than there are available typefaces. It follows that an understanding of type is more important than access to all the hot new exotics rolling off the font mills and to all the bending, squeezing and extruding software we can get our hands on. Some designers feel that type should be transparent — unnoticed by the reader. I would not completely subscribe to this philosophy, but I would urge designers to learn the basics and the advantages of simplicity before attempting to push the envelope.

Figure 16. Defining a black-and-white version. Contrasts were more sharply defined in the one-color version of the logo.

PORTFOLIO

Tom Gould

"Type has an abstract aesthetic all its own — letterforms can be as beautiful in themselves as a flower or cloud or fender or wave. Our eyes and kinesthetic senses respond to something an anonymous scribe created with primitive tools and practiced skills 1800 years ago, but the meanings in the combinations of letters — the words — speak to us as well. Type must be read, either easily or with a bit of seductive struggle. Type and its meaning comprise a partnership. The typographer should no more wish to be oblivious to the copy to be set, or to work with bad copy, than a carpenter would wish to work with green, warped wood."

In this **logo design** for some friends, Franklin Gothic bold contrasts with the elegant Goudy italic, setting off the terrific reversed ampersand.

In these **posters** for a campaign against cutting public library funding, Franklin Gothic bold contrasts with the spikey texture of close-set Century Old Style. The words and letters say it all, appropriately. Note the hanging initial quotation marks, which keep the letters aligned left.

My library was dukedom large enough.
WILLIAM SHAKESPEARE 1564–1612 *THE TEMPEST*
▲▲▲▲▲

He who destroys a good book kills reason itself.
JOHN MILTON 1608–1674 *AREOPAGITICA*
▲▲▲▲▲

No barrier of the senses shuts me out from the sweet, gracious discourse of my book friends.
HELEN KELLER 1880–1968 *THE STORY OF MY LIFE*
▲▲▲▲▲

Libraries are not made; they grow.
AUGUSTINE BIRRELL 1850–1933 *OBITER DICTA*
▲▲▲▲▲

Some books are undeservedly forgotten; none are undeservedly remembered.
W.H. AUDEN 1907–1973 *THE DYERS HAND*
▲▲▲▲▲

We shouldn't teach great books; we should teach a love of reading.
B. F. SKINNER 1904– *QUOTE*
▲▲▲▲▲

The library budget will be cut by 62%.
SAN DIEGO CITY MANAGER 1990– *CITY BUDGET*

Save the Library
It only makes sense.

Call or write your council person:
DISTRICT **1:** ABBE WOLFSHEIMER 236-6611 **2:** RON ROBERTS 236-6622 **3:** JOHN HARTLEY 235-6633 **4:** WES PRATT 236-6644 **5:** LINDA BERNHARDT 236-6655 **6:** BRUCE HENDERSON 236-6616 **7:** JUDY MCCARTY 236-6677 **8:** BOB FILNER 236-6688   MAYOR MAUREEN O'CONNOR 236-6630 202 C STREET, SAN DIEGO CA 92101

"Daddy, Why Is Grass Green?"

☐ **A.** Chlorophyll produces carbohydrates by the process of photosynthesis.
☐ **B.** Ask your mother.
☐ **C.** Look it up.

(Better be ready with A or B, if the City Manager cuts Library funding.)

Save the Library
It only makes sense.

Call or write: DISTRICT **1:** ABBE WOLFSHEIMER 236-6611 **2:** RON ROBERTS 236-6622 **3:** JOHN HARTLEY 235-6633 **4:** WES PRATT 236-6644 **5:** LINDA BERNHARDT 236-6655 **6:** BRUCE HENDERSON 236-6616 **7:** JUDY MCCARTY 236-6677 **8:** BOB FILNER 236-6688 MAYOR MAUREEN O'CONNOR 236-6630 202 C STREET, SAN DIEGO CA 92101

"Mommy, Why Is the Sky Blue?"

☐ **A.** High-frequency blue light is scattered by oxygen and nitrogen molecules.
☐ **B.** Ask your father.
☐ **C.** Look it up.

(Better be ready with A or B, if the City Manager cuts Library funding.)

Save the Library
It only makes sense.

Call or write: DISTRICT **1:** ABBE WOLFSHEIMER 236-6611 **2:** RON ROBERTS 236-6622 **3:** JOHN HARTLEY 235-6633 **4:** WES PRATT 236-6644 **5:** LINDA BERNHARDT 236-6655 **6:** BRUCE HENDERSON 236-6616 **7:** JUDY MCCARTY 236-6677 **8:** BOB FILNER 236-6688 MAYOR MAUREEN O'CONNOR 236-6630 202 C STREET, SAN DIEGO CA 92101

*Please join us for a monumental
gathering of former Frye & Smith
employees:* **Friday, August 31, 1990**
*This gala event will be hosted by
Dale and Doreen Stauffer on
the premises of TypeLink,Inc.
at* **1929 Hancock Street, San Diego,**
*California 92110. Festivities will get
underway at 6 PM and go on until the
last horn blows.* **Food, drink and music**
*(by Bob and Delores Pell), a special
unveiling of TypeLink's new delivery
service, and many other surprises are
on tap for the evening. Please make
every attempt to attend and renew old
acquaintances with all your "mover
and shaker" counterparts who once
matriculated at Frye & Smith.* **RSVP**
Dale Stauffer '78 or Larry Brass '76
619 299 8411

Design: Tom Gould '67

*Please join us for a monumental
gathering of former Frye & Smith
employees:* **Friday, September 21, 1990**
*This gala event will be hosted by
Dale and Doreen Stauffer on
the premises of TypeLink,Inc.
at* **1929 Hancock Street, San Diego,**
*California 92110. Festivities will get
underway at 6 PM and go on until the
last horn blows.* **Food and drink,**
*a special unveiling of TypeLink's new
delivery service, and many other surprises
are on tap for the evening. This fun-filled
event will be followed by a* **Saturday picnic**
*starting at noon at De Anza Cove, hosted
by Bob Sheehan '90 and Sal Taranga '90.
Details will be announced at the party.
Please make every attempt to attend and
renew old acquaintances with all your
"mover and shaker" counterparts who
once matriculated at Frye & Smith.* **RSVP**
Dale Stauffer '78 or Larry Brass '76
619 299 8411

Design: Tom Gould '67
Printing by L&L Printers

All the World's a Screen, and We But Scrolling Players

These two designs for **invitations** to a company reunion include the Goudy italic ampersand, a prominent feature in several company logos. Both use the same flush right copy that focuses attention on the key bold items along the margin. (Note the rebus — an ancient forerunner and stand-in for type.)

Bookman bold, set tight and minus leaded, was used to express this **desktop lament.**

CHAPTER 8

High-Res Raster

Artist

Jack Davis worked in advertising art direction and graphic design using traditional media prior to coming to the Macintosh in 1984. After working on an MFA in Computer Imagery and Design at San Diego State University, he originated the Computer Graphics department at Platt College in San Diego and became its first director. He is currently graphics editor of *Verbum* magazine, art director of The Gosney Company and an international speaker on computer graphics.

Project

A local rock band requested a design for a cassette album, *Revealer.* It was to be a J-card, the folded insert that fits in a cassette box. I had pretty much free rein, so I created roughs in two separate directions. One idea portrayed a medieval scribe working on an illuminated manuscript which, through the subject matter and the light source, suggested divine illumination. The second idea was purely a type treatment with various shadows and filters, all created in Adobe Photoshop. The band preferred the type design rather than the more literal depiction.

I used a Macintosh IIci with 8 MB of RAM and a 200 MB hard disk. After creating the image, I placed it in Aldus Page-Maker, added the credits and output negatives on a Linotronic L-300 at 2540 dpi.

PROJECT OVERVIEW

Illuminating type

A mysterious and mystical atmosphere was what I tried to project with the two disparate ideas that I first showed Bill Randall's band. The medieval scribe was scanned (from a copy of a medieval manuscript) into Photoshop, but it proved to be too narrow a scope for the band and they preferred just the word "Revealer" with a shadow behind it. I played with various filters and shadow effects until I found the combination that suited both me and the band. This time I showed them five or six comps based on the type idea. I did some limited shadow studies, but I decided that I wanted the shadow to be something not found in nature. I didn't want an obvious direction for the light source — I wanted it to be unexplainable.

Taking size into consideration

Because I was using a raster program — the image is formed by pixels — rather than vector software, which uses mathematical algorithms to create objects, I knew that I would have to create the picture two to four times larger than the finished size. I created my image at 72 dpi so that shrinking it to 25 percent would result in an approximately 300 dpi file, more than sufficient for a screen ruling of 150 lpi (see "Determining a sampling ratio" on page 116). Scaling a scanned photo to 50 percent (to produce 150 dpi) can be sufficient depending upon the content of the image. For example, if there are few graduated fills in the image, if it has geometrical objects or rough textures, pixeling (jagged edges) won't be seen. Type, especially letters with subtle curves or diagonals, is best reproduced at a higher resolution to make the edges smoother.

A local rock band needed a cassette cover for their album, *Revealer*. A medieval scribe poring over an illuminated manuscript was one of the first ideas submitted to the band.

Another rough comp was presented (below), this time a type treatment created in Adobe Photoshop, a program best known for its image-altering capabilities on scanned continuous-tone photographs. Photoshop, likened to a "low-end Scitex," has the ability to create special effects that aren't limited to scanned images but can be applied to images created within the program as well.

a

Raster vs. vector

The blurring feature in Photoshop provides a good way to achieve a realistic shadow. You could never create that effect in a vector drawing program. However, in a vector program you could change a shadow at the last minute, because each form is a discrete object or a set of discrete objects. A raster program has no discrete objects. So as soon as another image (perhaps type, or something copied from another picture) is placed on top of the background, the background pixels it "covers" are replaced by the new pixels and can often be retrieved only if the previous version of the image has been saved in some form (on the clipboard, in the scrapbook or in a separate file, for example). This lack of flexibility forces a designer to plan very carefully. The benefits of the medium, however, make up for the extra planning and other limitations of working in a raster environment. For example, the variability of contrast, brightness, distortion, blurring and a variety of other special effects in Photoshop is impressive. Raster images tend to be much more realistic than vector illustrations.

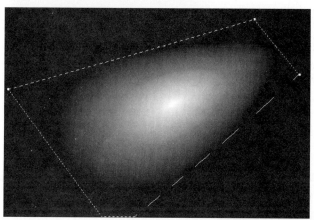

b

c

The spotlight and shadow for the Revealer logo started with a sphere created with the blend tool set for a radial blend (a). The sphere and the area around it were then selected and distorted to produce the spotlight efect (b). Finally, selected text was also distorted and then blurred to form the shadow (c).

The twisted shadow coupled with graduated Bodoni type creates an impossible illusion. The distorted and blurred spotlight would be very difficult, if not impossible, to attain in a vector drawing program.

To begin the type logo for the *Revealer* cassette cover, I opened Photoshop and selected New to open the New dialog box. I specified the width to be 1300 pixels and the height to be 800; I left the resolution at the default 72 dpi. I also chose Gray Scale mode and clicked OK (Figure 1). When my page opened, I changed the foreground color to white by touching on the inner square at the bottom of the tool palette and then, when the Photoshop Color Picker dialog box opened, entering 0 in every process color field. I changed the background color to black by touching on the outer square and entering 100 in the black process color field. Once I had my beginning and ending colors selected, I double-clicked on the Blend tool to access the Blend Tool Options dialog box (Figure 2). I chose a Radial fill with a midpoint skew of 50 percent.

The midpoint skew is the point at which the color is an even mix of the foreground and background colors. The parameters range from 13 percent to 87 percent, with 13 percent compressing the starting-color-to-midpoint range into a relatively small band and giving the midpoint-to-ending-color range a broad area. A setting of 87 percent does the opposite, and 50 percent puts the midpoint in the middle of the gradation.

Radial Offset determines the distance from the starting point that the radial fill displays the foreground color before any gradations of color begin. The value is a percentage of the total distance from the starting point to the ending point of the drag line and ranges from 1 percent to 99 percent. Entering 99 percent will give you no gradation at all, only your starting color. Entering nothing gives you a complete graduation, so I left that field blank.

The Color Space option defines the colors the radial fill will cycle through before reaching the background color. I left RGB because I wanted only intermediate gray levels — rather than additional colors — as the transition

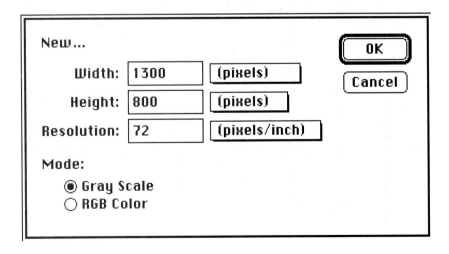

Figure 1. Establishing a new Photoshop file. The width and height pulldown menus offered a choice of pixels, points, picas or inches for the units of measurement. Width also includes an additional unit (columns), which can be set in the Preferences dialog box under the Edit menu.

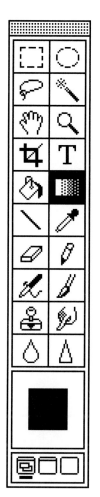

progressed from foreground to background. ▎ *To cycle through other hues, select the HSB (Hue, Saturation, Brightness) model for either a clockwise or counterclockwise transition around the color wheel.* ▎ *To see colors, you must be in the RGB mode.*

Having set all my parameters, I clicked OK. Then I clicked on a point near the mid-right of my page and dragged the blend line out about 6 inches in order to create a graduated sphere (Figure 3).

Tool specs

I double-clicked on the elliptical marquee in the tool box, which brought up the Elliptical Marquee Options dialog box. In the dialog box I chose Constrained Aspect Ratio and entered 1 for the height and 1 for the width, which would constrain my marquee to a perfect circle (Figure 4). ▎ *Double-clicking on many of the tools will bring up an Options dialog box for that tool. Double-*

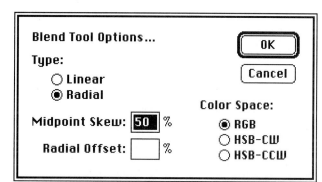

Figure 2. Controlling a blend. Double-clicking on the blend tool brought up the Blend Tool Options dialog box, where a radial blend (as well as exactly how the blend was to be executed) could be specified.

Figure 3. Creating a graduated sphere. The blend tool can create linear or radial fills that use the foreground and background colors as beginning and ending points. Other parameters control how quickly each half of the gradation takes place and how much of the starting or ending color is present.

clicking on the grabber changes the view of your image to a 1:2 ratio. Double-clicking on the magnifying glass changes the view of your image to a 1:1 ratio. Double-clicking on the eyedropper changes the foreground color to black and the background color to white. Double-clicking on the eraser erases the entire image.

Then, while holding down the Option key so that the marquee would expand from its center, I dragged the marquee around the radial fill that I had created until it encompassed the whole sphere. While the marquee was still activated (the dotted line was moving around the selection — this is called the "marching ants" in some circles), I chose Effects, Distort under the Image menu (Figure 5). This gave me a square box, the handles of which I pulled and maneuvered until I got the spotlight-looking effect that I wanted (Figure 6). ▌ *When applying this sort of distortion, make sure that the background*

Figure 4. Constraining the marquee. The Constrained Aspect Ratio forces the marquee to select an area with the specified proportions.

Antialiasing

Vector type, which includes type created in any PostScript program, is created by mathematical algorithms that describe the curves and lines as relationships in space. Bitmapped type, on the other hand, uses pixels on a grid to exactly map the letters point for point. Bitmapping can create stairstepping on curved strokes. To avoid stairstepping, many raster (bitmapped) programs apply antialiasing. As you can see from this example, the black at the edge of the antialiased left half of the *O* falls away to gray, whereas the bitmapped right edges hold the black color, creating a much harsher, stairstepped outline.

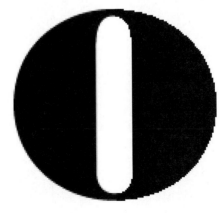

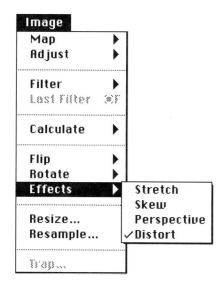

color chosen matches the background of the image so that dragging the selected section doesn't leave white holes.

Adding noise

After a graduated fill was applied to the background, I selected the Add Noise filter from the Image menu and entered a Uniform factor of 2 (Figure 7). Adding noise uniformly causes random switching of pixels from 0 to plus or minus the factor entered, in this case 2. This means that if an image were all black (represented in the color picker as R-0, G-0, B-0 and meaning the absence of all color), a noise factor of 2 would randomly convert the color values of some of the black pixels to R-1, G-1, B-1 and others to R-2, G-2, B-2, for example. All the colors created this way are close to black but not quite black. The Gaussian model uses a bell curve instead of a simple plus or minus factor. It not only lightens the dark areas but also darkens the light areas, which wasn't what I wanted. I added this slight amount of noise because when a ramp of 256 gray shades is printed, even with high resolution, subtle banding can result. Adding noise, in effect dithers the pixels slightly, which somewhat intermixes the bands and softens the lines between them. Unless you're looking at the image at 800 percent magnification, you can't notice the individual pixels colored by the application of Add Noise. Instead you perceive a smooth gradation.

Figure 5. Image distortion. Once an area is selected with the marquee, choosing Effects, Distort under the Image menu allows continued manipulation of the image by means of four corner handles until the user clicks outside of the marqueed area.

Figure 6. Creating a spotlight. When Effects, Distort is applied, the four corner handles determine the angle and amount of distortion. The gradations remain smooth throughout the process.

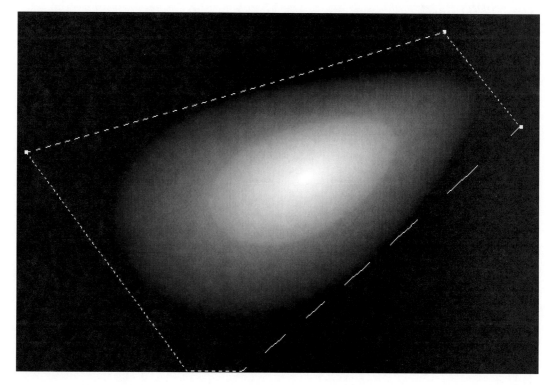

Setting type

With the background and spotlight completed, I began to set type. Clicking the text tool near the right, where I wanted the text to begin, brought up the Type dialog box, and I specified Bodoni Poster, 170 points, –10 Spacing, Left alignment and Anti-aliased (Figure 8). Choosing Anti-aliased creates cleaner-looking type because the program smooths the edges of the letters where the "jaggies" would otherwise occur because the type is bitmapped (see "Anti-aliasing" on page 110).

I chose Bodoni because it's a bold but elegant typeface, and I didn't want the text to look too strange, even with the special effects. I wanted the design to be compelling and at the same time mysterious.

Having chosen my type specifications and typed in the word "REVEALER" in the lower text box, I then hit the Return key to enter the parameters I had set. ❚ *In Macintosh software, anytime a selection button has a heavy black line around it, it represents the default choice and hitting the Return or Enter key is the same as clicking on the button.*

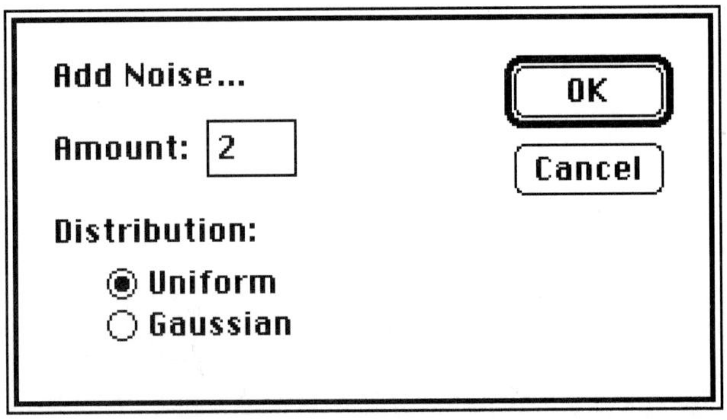

Figure 7. Adding noise to smooth banding. A small amount of Noise works as a very subtle dither that softens banding but is not discernible as a pattern to the naked eye.

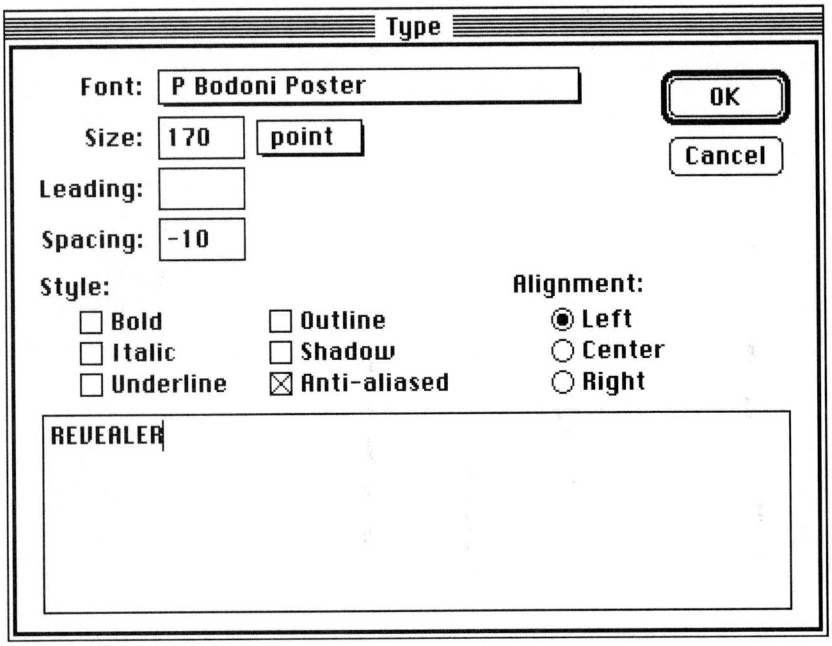

Figure 8. Entering text. Photoshop's straightforward Type dialog box lets the user specify the basic type styles as well as a parameter for anti-aliasing text, which smooths type.

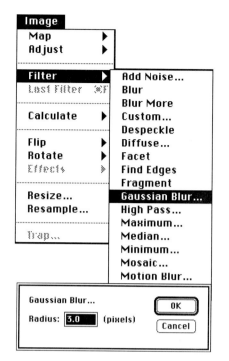

Figure 9. Adding a Gaussian blur. Gaussian blur is the filter to use if a very blurred image is desired.

The word "REVEALER" was now selected and lying across my distorted spotlight. I copied it to the clipboard (Command-C) because I knew I would want the original after I had created a distorted shadow of the type.

Shadow twisting

With my text still selected, I chose Effects, Distort under the Image menu and pulled on the four corner handles of the text, twisting it similarly to the way I had twisted the spotlight. Once I had it to my liking (at about a –50-degree angle with the left end slightly wider than the right), I clicked outside the selected area so that it became part of the image underneath and was no longer manipulable. I then went to the Image menu again, but this time I chose the Gaussian Blur filter, which is similar in effect to choosing Blur or Blur More several times. A dialog box appeared for me to enter the radius in pixels (Figure 9). The radius value determines how much information is used from neighboring pixels in the blur calculations. The wider the radius, the more blurred the image becomes. I typed in 3 and hit the Return key. In a few seconds I had my twisted, muted shadow (Figure 10). You can continue to apply the same filter to an image by typing Command-F, but I thought mine looked fine, so I left it as it was.

Blending into the fringe

Having created my shadow, I needed the uncontorted "REVEALER" in front of it, so I pasted the original type back into the picture (Command-V). With the type again selected, I chose Fringe from the Select menu (Figure 11). A Fringe dialog box appeared and I entered 4 pixels as the width of my fringe. I hit Return, and now I had a double line of marching ants. I double-clicked

Figure 10. Completing the glows. A Gaussian blur added to the entire image gives both the spotlight and the shadow a soft glow characteristic of a distant light source.

on the blend tool and chose Linear fill. With black as the foreground color and white as the background color, I clicked the blend tool on the top left of the first *R* and then dragged the blend line to the bottom right of the last *R*. The 4-pixel-wide rim now had a ramp from black at top left to white at bottom right (Figure 12). With the fringed type still selected, I pasted the word "REVEALER" again and this time clicked the blend tool on the bottom right of the last *R* and dragged the direction line to the top left of the first *R*. This created a ramp in the opposite direction (Figure 13).

On each step of this illustration, contrast and brightness were optimized by eye for the greatest detail (Figure 14). I could control the size of the spotlight this way as well as how much of the shadow fell away into the darkness.

Finishing the cassette cover

I didn't need to create any alpha channels for this project (see "Designating alpha channels" on page 117). I prefer to use the more intuitive controls in Photoshop. Had I done this in other leading raster image-editing software, I probably would have had to define masks. But I prefer a less complicated approach for a fast project like this. The total production time was less than half a day. Once I finished the image in Photoshop, I saved it as a TIFF file and placed it in PageMaker (Command-D), where I added the credits.

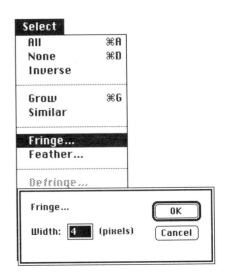

Figure 11. Fringing the letters. Pasting the letters onto the image leaves them selected so that operations can still be performed on them. Without clicking outside the letters, Fringe was selected and "4" was entered in the Fringe dialog box to create a 4-pixel-wide fringe.

Figure 12. Giving text an unearthly glow. With the Fringe command, varied "halo" effects can be created around text or objects.

Figure 13. Graduated type. With the text selected, the blend tool was used to place a graduated fill selectively inside the letters. Selected objects do not need to be connected to each other in order to share the same blend effect.

TIFF vs. PICT

Grayscale raster images are better saved in the TIFF format, especially if they're to be placed in PageMaker. TIFF is a more robust format, and PageMaker allows changes to the image through the Image Control dialog box found under the Element menu (Figure 15). ■ *When you place a raster image in PageMaker, it's important to specify the printer that the file will eventually be sent to because that specification can affect the scaling of a raster image, especially an image that has patterns in it (such as a MacPaint file). Once the image is placed in PageMaker and the printer is chosen with the Print command (found under the File menu), holding down the Command and Shift keys will not only proportionally constrain the image (which is the function of the Shift key), but will also make the image snap to sizes that look good at the printer's resolution. With files that have no discernible pattern to them, this snapping to optimal sizes is not as important as with files that are filled with patterns.*

Figure 14. Controlling brightness and contrast. Controls for brightness and contrast are accessible under the Image menu. The dialog box consists of simple slider bars that allow the user to alter the brightness and contrast and then preview the effect of these changes.

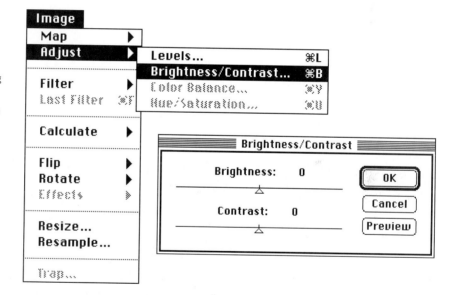

Figure 15. Using Image Control. With the image selected, choosing Image Control from PageMaker's Element menu brings up this dialog box where screen ruling and angle, as well as the gray map, can be changed. To make a MacPaint image opaque, simply click on Gray. To make a grayscale image transparent, click on Black And White.

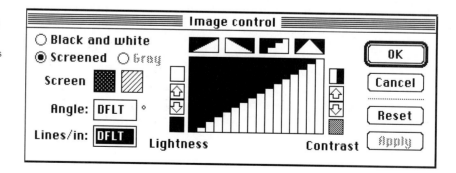

In retrospect

For so many reasons, Photoshop is a great environment to work in. The fact that when you enter type, it comes in selected is a boon to a designer. This way you can paste anything into it or fill it with ramps or distort it or do any of a multitude of other things.

The ability to create a fringe that exactly follows the line of the text and can be a defined width adds many design opportunities. Without that function,

---

**Determining a
sampling ratio**

Knowing the screen ruling that will be used in the printed piece is the first step in determining a sampling or scanning ratio (so called because the scanner is taking samples of the picture at a prescribed rate). The screen ruling should be determined before any scanning is done, because the scan has to record enough information to print a photograph at the required ruling. Not enough information results in a pixelated, or mosaic, look.

The equation below represents a commonly used formula to determine the final resolution needed:

$$1.25 \times lpi = dpi.$$

That is, 1.25 multiplied by the lines per inch (or screen ruling) — a number that can be obtained by asking your printer — equals the dots per inch (resolution) needed to adequately print that photograph.

Some software manufacturers and graphic designers suggest a ratio as high as 2:1 (meaning 2 pixels per halftone dot rather than 1.25 per halftone dot). Beyond a 2:1 ratio, more information is present than the imagesetter can use. The additional information is worthless for improving picture quality, but it still takes up storage space and increases file-handling time for screen refresh and printing.

Once you've multiplied the screen ruling by a number between 1.25 and 2 to get the final resolution, the scan resolution can be calculated by comparing the size of the original you're scanning to the size of the printed image. For example, if the original is 8 inches across and the printed image will be 2 inches across, the scan resolution can be ¼ of the final resolution.

This scan resolution or sampling resolution represents the smallest possible rate at which the photograph can be sampled to ensure that there is enough information to adequately print the image. However, some artists suggest scanning at twice the calculated sampling resolution and then re-sampling within the image-editing program to eliminate "graininess" that can be introduced by scanners (especially low-cost) models.

Creating raster images
When Photoshop's tools are used to create an image "from scratch," the ratio between final resolution and screen ruling needs to be taken into account even if no actual scanning is to be done. There still needs to be enough information to hold a particular line screen without the loss of smooth gradations and other symptoms of too little information. For example, working at the typical 72 dpi screen resolution, you have to create an image four times as large as it will be printed in order to get approximately 300 dpi final resolution, which is approximately two times a 150 lpi screen ruling.

Type is especially resolution-sensitive, because if curves are to be seen as completely round, rather than as built of pixels as they really are, the density of information has to be sufficient to smooth out the corners.

$$\text{Scan resolution} = \frac{\text{Size of printed image} \times \text{final resolution}}{\text{Size of original}}$$

to get a fringe effect one would have to scale a copy and align it precisely. A fringe can be used to create several different looks. For example, it can create a chiseled effect, a glint of light or a halo. There's a whole unexplored realm of photo-realistic typography that can be accessed by using raster image-editing programs like Adobe Photoshop. Effects can be created here that are unavailable in object-oriented programs.

Designating an alpha channel

Photoshop's alpha channels provide a way to store selected elements of an image with the ability to return a selection to the screen in precisely the same place each time. Use the following method to create and use an alpha channel.
1. Using one of the selection tools (marquee, lasso or magic wand), select an area (a).
2. The area can be added to by holding down the Shift key or subtracted from by holding down the Command key (b).
3. Once the selection is defined, choose Selection→Alpha under the Select menu (c).
4. Here the masking is shown in a grayscale format (d). Pure black is completely masked, protected from effects of painted or pasted images. Pure white is completely alterable. Any other gray levels are partially alterable, according to their percentage of white.
5. The selection can still be altered at this point by using any of the editing tools (e).
6. Once the mask has been refined, choose Alpha→Selection to use it. Again, on the screen the selection marquee (marching ants) will appear. In this example, a simple black-to-white blend was masked (f).
7. The difference between a simple selection and one that has been converted into an alpha channel is that the alpha channel is a permanent selection and can be reused by choosing Channel under the Mode menu and then selecting the appropriate channel number (g).

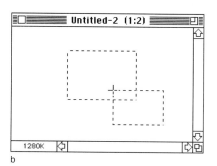
b

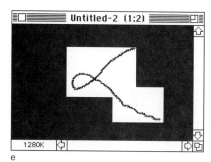
e

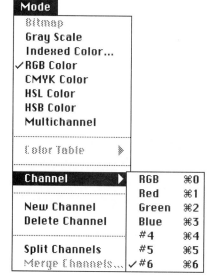
f

c

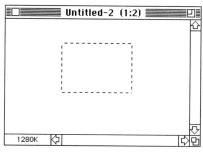
a

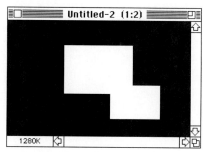
d

g

Jack Davis

"Play Doh type, Play Doh photography, Play Doh tech-pens, Play Doh compositions . . . It's the totally pliable nature of design within the digital environment that keeps me awake more nights than I care to think — usually with smiles on my face and exclamations of 'Wow!' on my lips. And it's these two factors — the 'wow' and 'fun' factors that I expect will greatly increase for motivated designers who explore the new visual communication capabilities of the computer, not only for the print media but for hypermedia and interactive publishing."

The San Diego chapter of the American Institute of Graphic Artists enlisted Davis to design the **cover** for its education directory. The task required developing imagery that would echo the existing style of the accent graphics and text already in place in the interior of the directory.

Below are a few of the **logos** that Davis has designed for *Verbum* magazine, the Verbum Gallery of Digital Art and *Verbum Interactive*, a CD-ROM–based multimedia magazine.

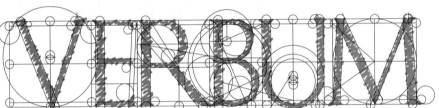

Each of these type treatments was created in Adobe Photoshop with filters and scans of water. **A Painted Face** is part of the title screen for a how-to article in *Verbum Interactive,* a CD-ROM magazine. The Zigzag filter was used to create the ripple effect.

    Clear Water Products, a logo for a New Zealand pool chemical company, was developed with Photoshop's Minimum and Zigzag filters to create the beveled type and ripple effect respectively.

    Aqua and **Water** are test images Davis developed while working on A Painted Face and Clear Water Products.

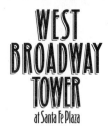

Space for Science, developed for the planned expansion of the Reuben H. Fleet Space Theater and Science Center, combines elements from Swivel 3D (the ball and molecule in the form of TIFF files) with line work and type in FreeHand.

The typeface in the **West Broadway Tower logo,** was drawn in Illustrator from scans Davis made of Binner Gothic, an Art Deco typeface.

The **Bradford Pharmaceuticals logo** plays off of the company's use of silicon wafers to create the *B* from a graduated fill of dots.

These two **logo comps,** developed in Photoshop, make use of filters to create type effects. The chrome initials were created with a plug-in filter from Aldus Gallery Effects by Silicon Beach Software.

    For the ball, Photoshop's Spherize filter was used to mimic a texture map on a 3D surface.

C H A P T E R   9

Sportswear Typography

Artist

Mike Uriss studied graphic arts at both the American Academy of Art at Chicago and the School of the Art Institute of Chicago and then went on to receive a diploma from the Platt College Computer Graphics program. He is currently employed as a computer graphics designer at NTN Communications, Inc., a broadcast company for interactive television with clients primarily in the hospitality industry (hotels, bars and so on). NTN Communications is also involved in educational uses of closed-system television at colleges and other educational institutions.

Uriss's work has been published in *MacUser, Desktop, Verbum* and *Publish* magazines, and has been shown in *Verbum's* Imagine Exhibit in Tokyo, Boston, Newport Beach and San Diego. Besides working for NTN, he also does freelance illustration, design and production (using both traditional and modern design techniques) for advertising agencies and design studios.

Project

The "1991 Spring Break San Diego" typographic illustration was produced for Pacific Sportswear of San Diego, California, a manufacturer of custom active apparel with a national client base. This particular design was to be used in a series of clothing articles aimed at the college market. I was provided with the typed copy and told to "Go to work!"

Corel Draw 1.2 from Corel Systems of Ontario, Canada was the software that I used. This program ran in Microsoft Windows 2.0., a screen-display shell that creates an interface very similar to that of the Macintosh computer. A Logitech mouse served as the pointing device.

My hardware consists of an Everex 386 PC with a 40 MB internal hard drive and 1 MB of RAM. A VGA color monitor was also used. The illustration was proofed on a Hewlett-Packard LaserJet Series II printer that had been enhanced with a PostScript-emulation cartridge from Pacific Data Products. The file was then output as a single film positive on the Linotronic at 1270 dpi using a RIP 4. The silkscreeners masked the positive in order to create the separations.

CRAIG McCLAIN

PROJECT OVERVIEW

Design constraints

I knew that I had to create art that would look good and be readable within the limits of the silkscreening and embroidery processes. I'd designed art before for these kinds of applications, and I knew, for example, that extremely thin line weights tend to get lost and can interfere with an accurate reproduction of the art. Also, very complex designs for embroidery can cause the manufacturing to be uneconomical.

Though silkscreeners can use dot screens (usually not higher than 60 lpi) in producing art, I've found that solid areas of color are more effective and carry the art better. In a method called a "fountain" or "rainbow," two (or sometimes even more) inks are used on one screen. This produces a smooth blend between the colors. Two inks can also be used to produce two separate colors per screen if the items being colored are separated by enough nonprinted space so that the printing process doesn't mix the colors.

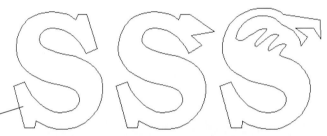

In the "1991 Spring Break San Diego" typographic illustration, the dolphins enliven the *S* and also playfully illustrate a beachy environment, suggesting the resort setting where the clothing items were to be sold.

A flamingo provided another treatment for the *S*, and served as the basis for another design.

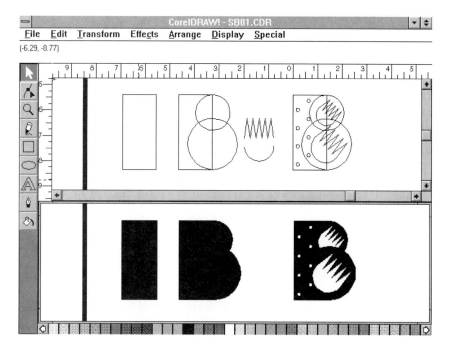

Resort motifs

For this illustration, I thought certain typographic characters might be enhanced with the introduction of some illustrative elements. I experimented with a motif of dolphins and waves to suggest a resort setting. I wanted to try something with a flamingo, too, just because it's a popular motif. I also wanted to incorporate a few geometric shapes, as in the *B* of "Break," in order to liven up the design.

Because I had a pretty clear idea of what I wanted to do, I began the illustration right on the computer. I often skip the preliminary penciled thumbnails when I can envision a fairly logical direction to take.

Departing from the beach motif and incorporating geometric designs in the *B* livened up the illustration and gave the character a different twist.

The sun element for the word "Spring" was assembled from a circle and a triangle element that was copied in 30-degree steps around its perimeter.

Starting with the rectangle tool (which simply draws rectangles), I established the parameters of the "live area" (the maximum area that an image can occupy for manufacturing purposes) by clicking and dragging an outline. To use the box for what I had in mind required converting it to Bezier curves. This function allows an outline to be combined with other outlines. When applied to typographic characters, the function allows the letters to become graphic elements, which gives the artist control of their shapes. Converting type to outlines is a one-way street, however, because once type has been converted, it can no longer be edited as text.

I clicked on the rectangle once to select it and then chose Convert To Curves from the Arrange pull-down menu (Figure 1). I double-clicked on one vertical side of the box to select it. At this point the Node-editing pop-up menu offered an option to add a node in the middle of the selected line. (Nodes are equivalent to the anchor points of Adobe Illustrator and Aldus FreeHand, for example.) After the node was added (and while it was still selected), I chose Break Apart from the Arrange menu. This command allowed me to break the vertical line in half while keeping a node on each end. I did the same to the other vertical side (Figure 2).

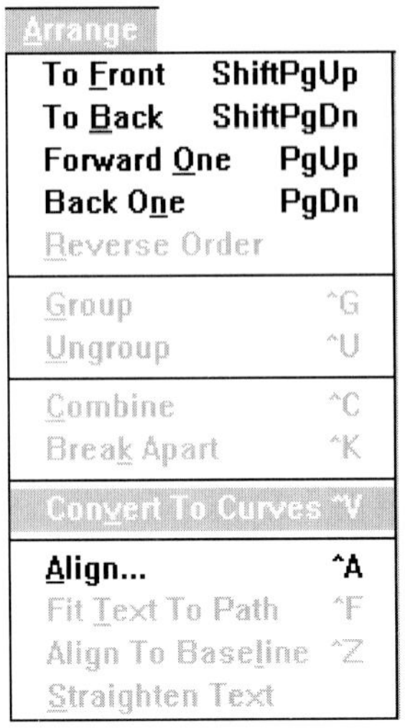

Making waves

I shortened the vertical sides so that they were quite close to the horizontal top and bottom, respectively. With the pencil tool, I then drew one curve with a node on each end. Clicking on a curve's node causes control bars to appear that allow the user to edit the shape of the curve (Figure 3). Using the magnifying tool — by selecting the magnifying tool and then clicking and

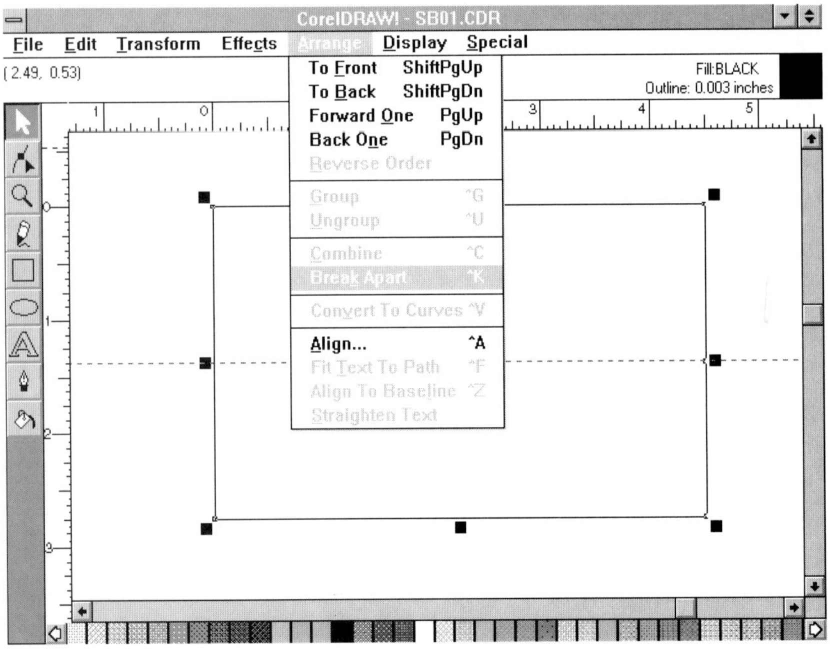

Figure 1. Converting curves. With an object selected (even type), Convert To Curves from the Arrange menu produces an outline that can be edited.

Figure 2. Splitting sides. A rectangle was drawn and converted to editable curves. While the node that had been added to the converted rectangle was still selected, Break Apart was chosen from the Arrange menu, which separated the line into two pieces.

dragging a marquee around the area you wish to magnify — helps in adjusting a curve's shape (Figure 4).

When I had magnified the curve and moved the control bars until I was happy with the shape of the first wave, I used the duplicating feature to step-and-repeat as many curves as I thought would be needed to suggest an ocean. By drawing a marquee around them with the arrow tool, I selected all of the individual waves. Then I clicked on the Combine command under the Arrange menu; a prerequisite for joining paths together. The nodes at either

Figure 3. Controlling the curve. Clicking on a curve's node causes control bars to appear that allow the user to edit the shape of the curve.

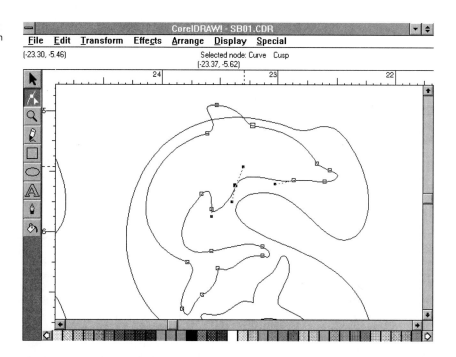

Figure 4. Zooming in for a better view. Selecting the magnifying tool and then clicking and dragging a marquee around an area enlarges that particular area.

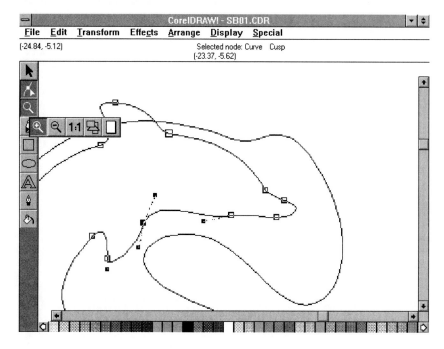

end of each curve had to be joined. With the node-editing tool, I double-clicked on the overlapping nodes in order to select them and then used the Join option in the Node-Editing dialog box. When the wavy line was one path, I duplicated it for the bottom set of waves by clicking and dragging while holding down the Control key and the + key on the 10-key pad. Both wavy lines were joined to each of the top and bottom pieces of the original rectangle. Then a second set of wavy lines was placed over the edge of the first set. Within the Pen Attributes dialog box (accessed by double-clicking on the pen icon in the toolbox) I assigned a 1-point white stroke to the overlapping wavy lines. This created the illusion of multiple waves and also added more interest to the line (Figure 5).

Drawing the dolphins

The dolphin *S* was drawn with the pencil tool over a TIFF (tagged image file format) image that was a scanned pencil sketch I did of the mammal. Corel Draw offers an autotrace feature but it usually assigns too many nodes, some of which must then be deleted. ∎ *The fewer nodes a curve has, the smoother it will be. Fewer nodes also make for a smaller file and faster printing.*

Once one of the dolphins was drawn, the drawing was flipped with the Mirror option from the Transform menu (Control-Q). The copy was modified by cutting the head and fin areas from the rest of the outline and flipping them again to match the vertical orientation of the first dolphin. From the resident fonts in Corel Draw, a large capital *S* was set in Cupertino (similar to ITC Cooper Black), converted to curves and edited by clicking and dragging on its nodes in order to contain the two dolphins (Figure 6).

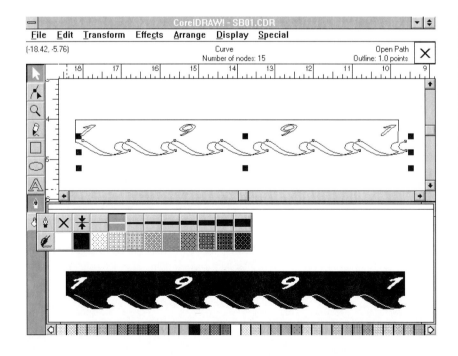

Figure 5. Drawing white-crested waves. Within the Pen Attributes dialog box (accessed by double-clicking on the pen icon in the toolbox) I assigned a 1-point white stroke to the overlapping wavy lines in order to make the waves look more interesting.

Finishing "Spring"

The "pring" text of the word "Spring" was set in Switzerland Black (similar to Helvetica Black) and wrapped around a circle that had no fill and no stroke. The Sun shape in the center of "pring" was created by drawing a triangle and then duplicating and rotating it 30 degrees 12 times around a smaller circle concentric with the one used for the "pring." The rotation is automatic with the Repeat function under the Edit menu (Figure 7). Curved heat waves were then added to fill out the circle where the text ended. The first one was drawn with the pencil tool, and then duplicated and rotated.

Playing with geometry

The outline of the *B* was drawn as a rectangle joined with two halved circles and created as a sans serif character in contrast to the serifed *S*. ▌ *Corel Draw offers an easy way to edit the circumference of a circle. You just click on its node with the node edit tool and drag it to where you wish it to be. Releasing the mouse*

Figure 6. Duplicating dolphins. Once one of the dolphins was drawn, the drawing was flipped with the Mirror option. The copy was then modified to match the vertical orientation of the first dolphin. A large *S* (shown here as a screen dump) was set in Cupertino and edited by clicking and dragging on its nodes until it could contain the two dolphins.

Figure 7. Creating sun rays. Rotation is automatic with the Repeat function under the Edit menu. The Sun shape was created by drawing a triangle and then duplicating and rotating it 30 degrees 12 times.

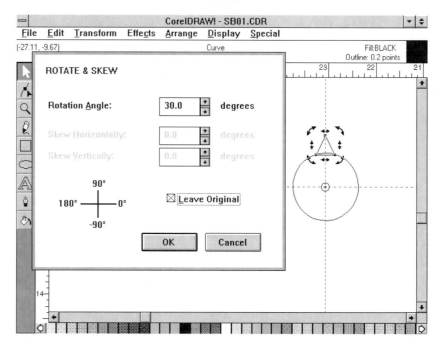

button outside the outline creates an open partial circle. Releasing the mouse button inside the outline creates a pie-shaped piece or a shape resembling a pie with a piece missing, depending upon where the mouse is released.

The toothed shapes within the *B* were formed using the Snap To Grid feature, an option that constrains the drawing to an invisible grid that can be adjusted in the Preference dialog box accessed through the Display menu. Using the pencil tool, I drew straight lines with the grid turned on to ensure even spaces between the teeth. These were then joined to a half section of a circle, duplicated and reduced (Figure 8). ∎ *To reduce an object and maintain its correct aspect ratio, click on any of its corner points (different from nodes) and drag to whatever size you wish. To resize an object horizontally or vertically, click on one of the left, right, top or bottom center points and drag.*

Finishing touches

The "reak" part of the word "Break" is a playful arrangement of various modified type styles. "San Diego," placed on the bottom section of waves, was set in Freeport (similar to Letraset's Freestyle). Extra letterspace was added using the node edit tool directly on the text string, a click-and-drag technique. The same effect can also be attained with a numerical setting in the Spacing dialog box accessible via the Type Specification dialog box (Figure 9). The characters were then stretched horizontally with the arrow tool by clicking and dragging on the side of the selected text block. "1991" was easily modified to the same width as "San Diego" with the Copy Style From option under the Edit menu. This command assigns selected attributes from one object (text or graphic) to another by overwriting its original attributes. Once the type was all set, the design was printed on a LaserJet printer for proofing (Figure 10).

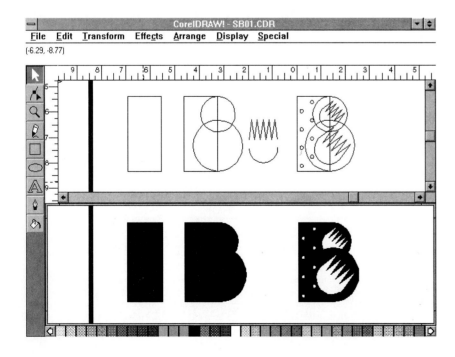

Figure 8. Building teeth on a grid. With the pencil tool, straight lines were drawn with Snap To Grid turned on to ensure even spaces between the teeth.

In retrospect

Plans are to test market this and other new merchandise, and then (pending the results) offer more custom applications in which various resort names are dropped in. Once a prototype is created, custom orders are fairly easy to provide using the tools available in Corel Draw. Because this design was drawn on the computer, variations on a theme can be created in record time. This gives the client many options to choose from, without the designer having to spend a lot of time designing.

Figure 9. Adding letterspace. Extra letterspace can be added using the node edit tool directly on the text string. Or, as shown here, the extra space can be entered numerically in the Text Spacing dialog box accessible via the Text Specification dialog box.

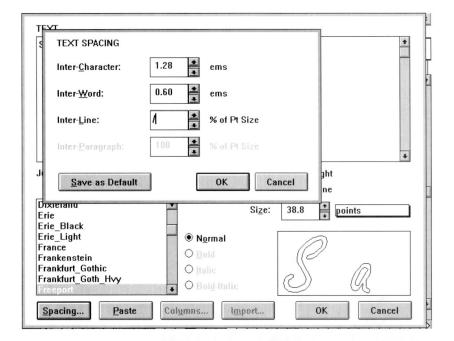

Figure 10. Proofing the final design. Once all the elements were in place, a final proof was made on the LaserJet printer to ensure that all design elements were correct and visually pleasing.

Mike Uriss

"I have learned to regard good typography as an interesting marriage between fine art and geometry. Type can be highly expressive. It has the ability to communicate ideas and emotions while at the same time conforming to strict guidelines that often employ the use of involved mathematical formulas. Take a close look at any font and you'll see that each typeface has it's own unique characteristics. Different typefaces can evoke very different feelings and attitudes.

"Thousands of typefaces are now available to the graphic designer and more are becoming available due to recent developments in personal computer software and the skills of talented programmers. Now the designer can render many variations on a theme with a precision that would take at least two or three times the amount of work using traditional methods."

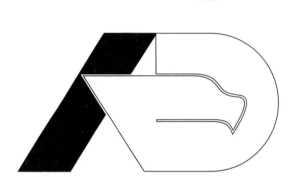

Carolyn's is a small business that conducts ceramics classes. Personalized instruction is offered so the look of the mark has to be one of warmth. In Aldus Free-Hand 2.0, shapes made with the drawing tools were combined with PostScript fonts exported from Letraset's FontStudio.

AD (for American Design) was rendered in Corel Draw by skewing a rectangle, then converting it to curves, and finally combining a circle with hand-drawn elements to form the eagle/D motif.

The 1991 **Broadcast Schedule** mark is used as a masthead for monthly calendars, one of the services offered to customers of the NTN Interactive Television Network. After the *1991* was fit to a path in Corel Draw, the numerals were given the illusion of perspective with the extrude function.

Simple text treatments give **All New Bonus Rounds 7 Days A Week** a much livelier look than setting it as just a headline. This illustration was used in the NTN broadcast calendar and newsletter for the month of January 1991.

© 1991 NTN COMMUNICATIONS, INC.

UnderCover is the mark for a trivia game played on the NTN Interactive Television Network. The use of the skewed *Cover* as the shadow of *Under* lends a feeling of mystery to the look of the mark.

Three Guise seen here are a bit of pun: We all don guises from time to time. Created in Aldus FreeHand, the illustration combines hand-drawn forms with skewed and rotated characters set in Caslon 3.

Agassi vs Sampras, produced for Pacific Sportswear of San Diego, California for a series of souvenir specialty items, is a good example of the use of the extrude function in Corel Draw to give a look of perspective to text set with the program's resident font.

C H A P T E R   1 0

Modern
Movement

Artist

Paul Sych, an accomplished jazz guitarist as well as a leading Toronto graphic designer, attended the York University and the Ontario College of Art in Toronto, Canada. Prior to opening his own design studio, called Faith, he worked at Reactor, a Toronto design firm known for its "industrial-strength art." Reactor owner and creative director Louis Fishauf introduced Sych to the Macintosh computer. Now Sych designs at least 90 percent of his work on the Macintosh. His computer design has been seen on specialty Coke cans, various McDonald's commercials, and a Canadian version of *MTV* called *New Music*.

Project

General Motors wanted a new, innovative look for their 1991 Pontiac brochure. They were targeting younger buyers, so they wanted the brochure to be upbeat and modern. GM contacted their Canadian advertising firm, MacLaren:Lintas. The Canadian firm was to modify a brochure that had been designed in the United States by D'arcy Masius Benton & Bowles, Inc. Editing the text, choosing visuals supplied by the American firm, and creating a new cover, MacLaren:Lintas would redesign the brochure for the Canadian market. MacLaren's vice president and creative director, Ray Fry, contacted Reactor, and we began the project.

For the brochure cover, I used a Sharp JX-300 scanner and Chromascan software to scan in a Pontiac wheel rim. The scan was color-corrected and filtered in Adobe's Photoshop and then placed into Illustrator 3.0, where type and graphics were added. The scan, by itself, was output to Du Pont's 4CAST Digital Color Imager. The graphics and type were printed as positive film on the Linotronic L-300 imagesetter at 2540 dpi.

Additional hardware included a Mac IIci with 5 MB of RAM, a 100 MB hard disk, an Apple 13-inch color monitor and a 45 MB removable cartridge drive.

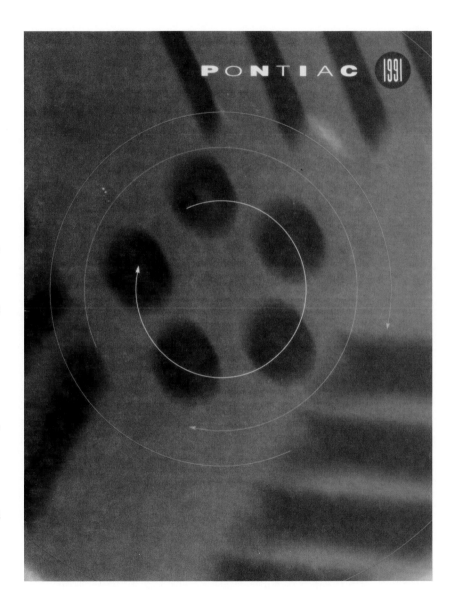

**PROJECT
OVERVIEW**

Playing on the rim

When I first met with MacLaren's creative director, Ray Fry, we noted that one thing Pontiacs have in common is the wheel rim. We had been looking through the previous year's Pontiac brochure and realized that all the Pontiac rims were very similar. The rim design seemed to characterize the car. So we came up with the idea of using a big photo of the rim for the cover and then adding type and graphics that suggested movement.

Pontiac is GM's performance car. We wanted the brochure, and especially the cover, which might be the first contact the company has with a potential buyer, to evoke performance also.

As soon as we settled on the wheel as the basis for the design, I saw circular lines with arrows on them following the movement of the wheel. But I just had regular, run-of-the mill arrowheads in mind. Fry was the one who noticed that the arrowheads were similar to the Pontiac emblem. Why not play that up? So I gave a suggestion of the Pontiac emblem by rounding the back of the arrow and adding a small, white four-point star on top. This became a motif that we used throughout the brochure.

The backward-and-forward movement used in the word "Pontiac" on the cover of the brochure was repeated on the opening page of each model's section.

After looking at a previous year's Pontiac brochure, we realized that one consistent feature on all the Pontiacs was the wheel rim. We decided to play up this consistency by enlarging a picture of the rim for the cover of the 1991 brochure.

A Cibachrome print was made of a transparency of a car, with the wheel enlarged and isolated. Movement was the feeling we were trying to evoke with both the graphics and the type.

GRAND AM

36

Here are two personal styling machines. The SE Coupe is an affordable point midway between the muscular GT and the base LE Coupe. It has Rally instrumentation, rear spoiler, GT-type front fascia, 14″ aluminum wheels and Touring tires. For some sun on your face, just push the buttons that open the LE Convertible's power-operating top and electric tinted windows. For dedicated sun worshippers, the '91 model is available with a white exterior, white cast aluminum wheels and an all-white vinyl interior with seating surfaces perforated to help keep you cool. Both SE and LE come with either the standard fuel efficient 2.0L overhead cam engine with Electronic Fuel Injection or the optional 140 HP 3.1L V6 – 5-speed manual or 3-speed automatic transmission for either. And that's just the beginning.

Sans serif type was used for brochure headers, text and captions. The type was sometimes expanded, sometimes condensed, but was always given wide leading.

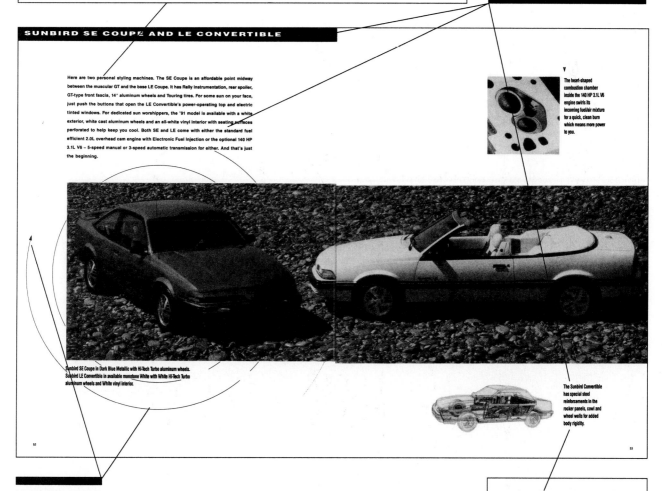

SUNBIRD SE COUPE AND LE CONVERTIBLE

Here are two personal styling machines. The SE Coupe is an affordable point midway between the muscular GT and the base LE Coupe. It has Rally instrumentation, rear spoiler, GT-type front fascia, 14″ aluminum wheels and Touring tires. For some sun on your face, just push the buttons that open the LE Convertible's power-operating top and electric tinted windows. For dedicated sun worshippers, the '91 model is available with a white exterior, white cast aluminum wheels and an all-white vinyl interior with seating surfaces perforated to help keep you cool. Both SE and LE come with either the standard fuel efficient 2.0L overhead cam engine with Electronic Fuel Injection or the optional 140 HP 3.1L V6 – 5-speed manual or 3-speed automatic transmission for either. And that's just the beginning.

The heart-shaped combustion chamber inside the 140 HP 3.1L V6 engine swirls its incoming fuel/air mixture for a quick, clean burn which means more power to you.

Sunbird SE Coupe in Dark Blue Metallic with Hi-Tech Turbo aluminum wheels. Sunbird LE Convertible in available monotone White with White Hi-Tech Turbo aluminum wheels and White vinyl interior.

The Sunbird Convertible has special steel reinforcements in the rocker panels, cowl and wheel wells for added body rigidity.

52

53

Motion is conveyed by the use of circular lines of varying radii. The custom arrow-heads suggest the Pontiac emblem.

The Sunbird Convertible has special steel reinforcements in the rocker panels, cowl and wheel wells for added body rigidity.

My assistant, Kim Dolan, and I scanned a Cibachrome print of the photo of the wheel rim at 200 dots per inch (dpi), which created a file of around 10 MB. We brought this file into Adobe Photoshop, where we increased the Red value in the Color Balance window. (This window is accessed by choosing Adjust and then Color Balance under the Image menu.)

We then selected the rim: First we double-clicked on the elliptical marquee tool and chose an Aspect ratio of 1 to 1 so that the marquee would be constrained to a perfect circle. Holding down the Option key while dragging the marquee made it draw from the center, and this way we were able to select just the rim accurately. Next, we chose the Motion Blur filter from the Image menu. We left the default (0°) angle but changed the Pixels setting to 20. However, we continued to apply the Motion Blur filter with these settings until we got the look we wanted, which was one of a wheel in motion. We sent this file to a service bureau to get a QMS print of it, but the file kept bombing. Had we realized then that we could have simply resampled the file to shrink its size, we would have saved ourselves a lot of trouble; but at the time Photoshop was new to us. Instead, we got an 11 x 17-inch 4CAST print (Figure 1), which was about six times as expensive. (See "Continuous-tone color printers" on page 139.) Eventually we did resample the file to 72 dpi, which reduced it to an easier-to-manage 3 MB.

Figure 1. Setting the wheel in motion. A 4CAST print of a Pontiac rim was made from a scan of a Cibachrome print, color-corrected and filtered to blur the image in Photoshop. 4CAST uses a continuous-tone method to produce the image, making it appear more like a photograph than most digital prints, even at its relatively low resolution of 300 dpi.

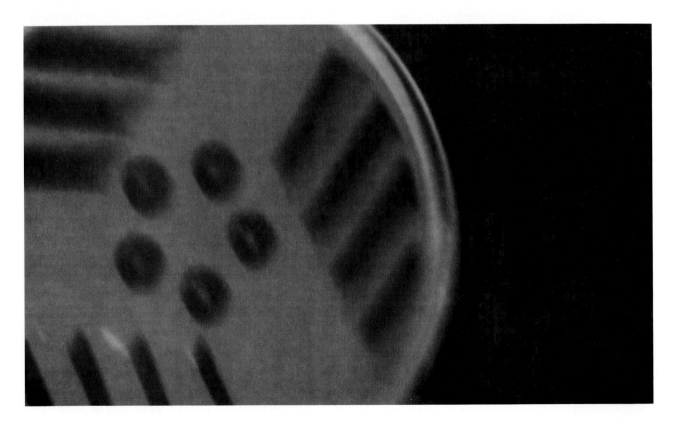

Illustrator 3.0

The Reactor studio was a beta test site for Illustrator 3.0. This gave us the opportunity to do some things that couldn't be done in Illustrator 88, such as importing color images from Photoshop (saved in an EPS format) and actually seeing them in color. ∎ *Although Illustrator 88 and 3.0 can import TIFFs, they can only be used as templates or guides for tracing; they can't be incorporated into the illustrations. However, TIFFs can be converted to EPS format in Photoshop and then incorporated in Illustrator files.*

In Photoshop we saved the EPS with an 8-bit PICT color preview so that we could see the image on-screen in color. Saving the EPS with a 1-bit preview allows you to see the file in black-and-white only, and there's virtually no difference in file size between the two (Figure 2). We also saved the file as Binary. A Binary EPS is half the size of an ASCII EPS, and we found that the file imported into Illustrator 3.0 was just fine. ∎ *Certain programs, such as Aldus FreeHand and PageMaker, do not support Binary EPS files.*

Opening Illustrator and choosing New (and no template) brought up the document window. We then selected Place Art under the File menu, found the image of the rim and double-clicked on it. Any EPS image comes in as a rectangle with an x through it while you are in the Artwork Only mode. The only way to see the image is to choose Preview Illustration under the View menu. But Louis Fishauf showed me how to open a file in two windows at once so that I could work and preview at the same time. ∎ *Open the file in the Artwork Only mode and then to go to Windows and choose New Window. That will open an exact copy of the window that you have before you. Choose Preview Illustration for this window and then make both windows half the size of the screen by dragging on their bottom right corners. Drag one of the windows by its title bar until the two are side-by-side. Then whatever you do in the Artwork Only window will be reflected in the Preview window. This works only if you open the window from New Window, however, not if you simply open the file twice.*

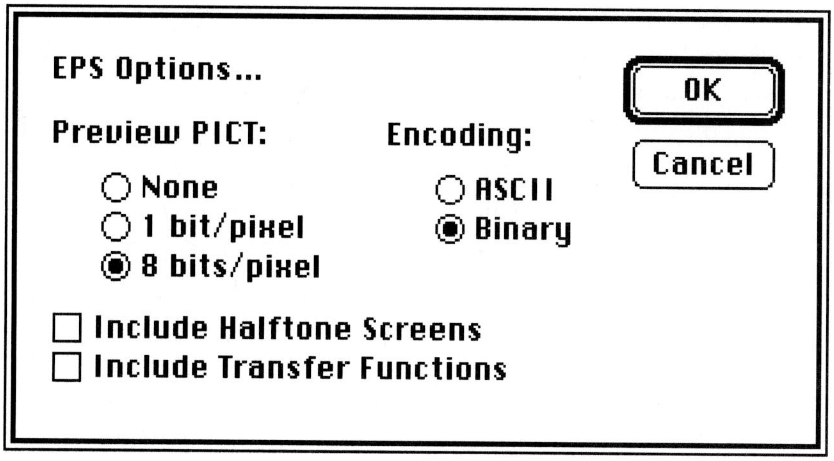

Figure 2. Converting an image to EPS. Choosing 1 bit/pixel and 8 bits/pixel will end up giving you the same file size. One bit is only black-and-white, whereas 8 bits will give you a color preview.

Once we had the EPS file of the rim imported into Illustrator, I began drawing the colored circles. First I selected the oval tool. In Illustrator 3.0 most of the tools, if you click and drag to the right, will show you more choices (Figure 3). I slid the pointer to the right to choose centered-oval. A reference box at the bottom left of the window has a brief description of your tool choice or, if you're in the middle of a procedure, it will tell you what to do next.

Centered-oval means that the oval will draw from the center. I held down the Shift key to constrain the oval to a perfect circle. Once I had the first circle in the right position, I used the scaling tool and, using the center of the rim as the point of origin, I made scaled copies of the original circle but preserved the line weight and the position of the wheel's center. I then selected each circle and gave its outline a color. While I was coloring the circles, I continued to watch the window set to Preview Illustration to make sure that I liked the colors. Conceptually, I wanted to represent the colors of the spectrum with the circles.

When I had finished drawing the circles, I ungrouped them and cut them at random places with the scissors tool. At this point, I scanned in the Pontiac emblem and, using it as a template, drew an arrowhead. I scaled it down and added it to the end of each arc with all the arrowheads pointing in a clockwise direction. I wanted the arrowheads to accentuate the movement of the rim.

Giving type the illusion of movement

Now it was time to deal with the type. From the moment I started drawing the circles, I knew what I wanted to do with the type — to make it move, but in a different way from the wheel and its arcs. So I chose to make every other letter bold, as if it were in the foreground, and the alternate letters lighter in weight, as if they were farther away. Using the Type tool, I clicked and typed a *P*. I highlighted the *P* and then chose Style from the Type menu (Figure 4).
▌ *In Illustrator 3.0 you can start typing as soon as you select the Type tool. You no longer use a text box to enter text. More letters can be added simply by clicking the Type tool next to an already typed letter.*

I selected Helvetica Black, 24 points and clicked OK. Using the scale tool, I clicked on the bottom left of the selected *P* and then dragged to the right, enlarging the *P* horizontally by about 150 percent. I then typed an *O* next to the *P* so that it was in the same text block. Highlighting the *O*, I selected Helvetica Light, left everything else the same (including the horizontal scaling) and clicked OK. I then had the first two letters and the type specifications set for the word.

I highlighted the first two letters, copied them and inserted them three more times in the same text block. I then selected each letter separately and typed in the appropriate letter for the word "Pontiac." Each letter took on the correct type specs. There was one extra letter at the end of the word, so I deleted it (Figure 5). The type now looked animated to me, moving near to far. I decided that the only word I didn't want to animate was "1991." I

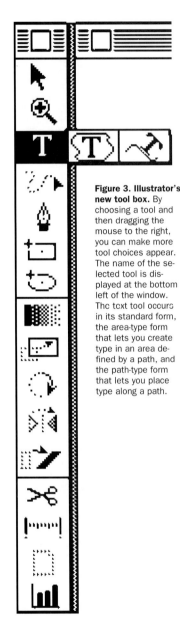

Figure 3. Illustrator's new tool box. By choosing a tool and then dragging the mouse to the right, you can make more tool choices appear. The name of the selected tool is displayed at the bottom left of the window. The text tool occurs in its standard form, the area-type form that lets you create type in an area defined by a path, and the path-type form that lets you place type along a path.

P

Figure 4. Editing text. Text can be typed directly into the document without using a text box. Highlighting text selects it and then you can type Command-T to access the Type Style window, where the specifications of the highlighted letter(s) are shown.

```
═══════════════ Type Style ═══════════════

─Character────────────────────────────      OK

Font:  Helvetica-Black                      Cancel

Size:    24   pt     Horiz. scale: 100  %   Apply

Leading: 29   pt     ☒ Auto leading         Revert

Tracking: 0   em/1000 ☐ Auto kerning

Vert. shift: 0  pt

─Paragraph────────────────────────────

─Indentation─    ─Alignment─      ☐ Hanging
Left:   0  pt    ◉ ▤  ○ ▤            punctuation
Right:  0  pt    ○ ▤  ○ ▤          Leading
First line: 0 pt ☐ Justify last line before ¶: 0  pt

                                 Spacing Options...
```

Continuous-tone color printers

Continuous-tone color printers can provide hard copy to serve as tight comps. In some cases these prints can also be used as mechanical art for more traditional prepress preparation. But because the color separation and reproduction processes used in these printers are quite different from those used in prepress and printing operations, they can't effectively be substituted for proofs such as Matchprints and Chromalins.

Du Pont's 4CAST
Du Pont's 4CAST Digital Color Imager produces consistent color hard-copy output directly from the Apple Macintosh, Unix-based workstations, IBM-compatible PCs and color electronic prepress systems (Scitex, Hell and Crosfield). The technology that 4CAST uses is dye sublimation, a dry process that employs heat to turn solid dyes to gas and to fuse those colors to a special receiver paper. The dyes are transferred to the paper first in yellow, then in magenta, cyan and black. There are 256 levels for each of the four process colors. Resolution is 300 dpi. Output of a full 11.9 x 17.3-inch image takes about seven minutes.

The Macintosh interface kit for the 4CAST includes software, written by Adobe Systems, Inc., and an interface module to be installed on the host computer. A minimum of 80 MB of free hard disk space (preferably on an external drive) is required to allow the 4CAST to create its separations.

Canon's Color Laser Copier 500
The CLC500 is both an input and an output device. It can scan reflective art (up to 11 x 17 inches) at 400 dpi, as well as transparencies, and produce output with over 16.7 million colors. The CLC500 can also take input from live video, still video disks and NTSC signals. Third-party software is required to drive the color copier from a host computer. An IEEE-488 (GPIB) interface is also required. Zooming, color conversion, texture and more advanced graphic functions can be accessed with the CLC500.

Kodak's XL 7700 Digital Continuous-tone Color Printer
Offering photographic-quality output at a maximum image area of 10 x 10 inches, the XL 7700 includes a 12 MB image buffer. Picture information is downloaded to the printer from the user's PC, workstation or network. Either the GPIB or SCSI interface is provided. Over 16.7 million colors are available at a resolution of 200 dpi. The printer also has built-in commands that include scaling, rotating and sharpness filters for edge enhancement.

wanted that to be static. The typeface I used for "1991" was the first typeface that I had ever designed (Figure 6). I call it "Oleo."

Once I had the type worked out, I continued to layout the rest of the brochure in Illustrator, using the continued motif of the circles, arrowheads and animated text on nearly every page (Figure 7). I designed the whole brochure and set the type for the text on the computer, but the production agency that MacLaren:Lintas worked with didn't have Macintoshes, so they had to reset all the type, matching the copy in the laser prints I provided as proofs.

Getting output

When we went to output the file (the graphic rim images), the service bureau simply couldn't get it out of the Lino. I think that the scan, saved as an EPS, was just too big for the imagesetters and RIPs (raster image processors) they had available at the time. So the film separator at MacLaren scanned the 4CAST print we had made of the rim, took it just slightly out of focus to get rid of a moiré pattern that had cropped up, and separated it in the traditional way. Because the rim already had a motion blur on it, taking it slightly out of focus didn't create a problem. The graphic elements were output on positive film at 2540 dpi and positioned on the 4CAST print with registration marks. (We output about 10 circles of varying size and just picked which ones we wanted for each page.) We indicated all the colors on the film positives and also made a final comp on the 4CAST with all the graphics in place so that the production people could see what was intended. (This couldn't be shot for the

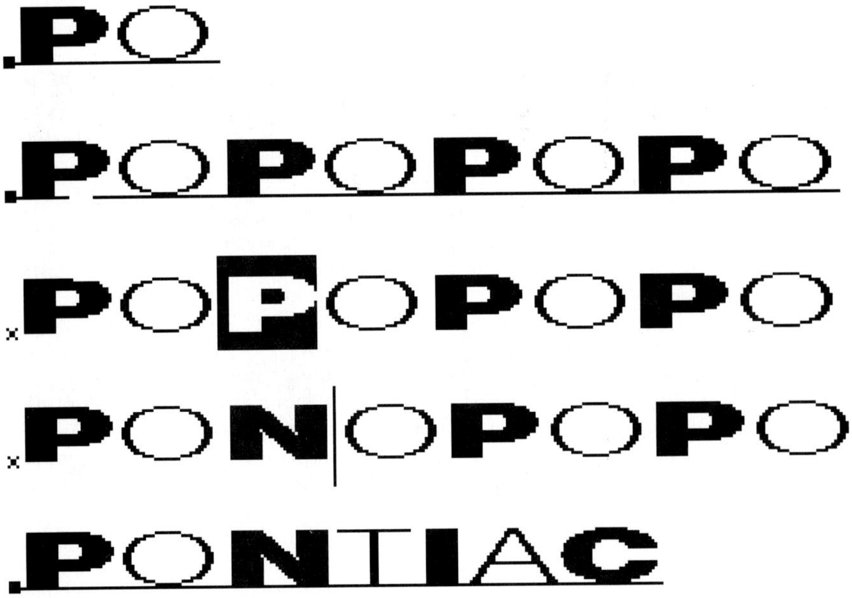

Figure 5. Setting alternating type. The first two letters were entered, and type specs were set for each of them. These letters were highlighted, copied and pasted three times in the same text block. Next, letters were highlighted, one at a time, and changed to spell the word "Pontiac." Finally the extra *O* at the end was deleted.

Figure 6. Using a custom typeface. The "1991," found on the Pontiac brochure cover, was set in a modified version of Oleo, a custom typeface.

cover because taking the picture out of focus would have blurred the graphics and type.)

In retrospect

Generally, when I work, I come up with an idea on a sketchpad and then scan it and bring it into Illustrator. I feel more "hands on" that way, like there's a balance between head and hand, or between intellect and feeling. Once the scan is in the computer, I can draw over and "finesse" it. And the computer gives you so much speed. I can change colors in an instant. A client can come and proof the job right on the computer. If the client doesn't like yellow, or wants it warmed up a bit, I can immediately add more red. How tedious it would be to make 10 color combinations on the same job if I were doing it the conventional way. The Macintosh makes multiple options a beautiful opportunity rather than a headache.

Louis Fishauf used to say when I was learning the computer, "Even if it takes you an extra week, do it on the Mac." Now I can do a job in a quarter of the time.

Figure 7. Using the type. A typical two-page spread in the Pontiac 1991 brochure demonstrates the continued use of thick and thin type, the Pontiac emblem and colored circles with arrowheads to show movement.

PORTFOLIO

MICHAEL RAFELSON

Paul Sych

"I want the work that I create to be emotionally beautiful rather than a static thing. That's the whole premise for my company, Faith. I try to create art that's emotionally sound. Sometimes you see stuff that's good, but there's something missing. I liken it to a musician who is technically together, but is lacking one element, and that element is emotion.

"I'm heavily influenced by Lester Beall, a graphic designer from the 1940s who is known for magazine cover design (Scope, Fortune and so on) among other things. He was influenced by the European Avant-Garde movement. When I look at Beall's work, I sense a lot of emotion. He used icons, which is a motif I like. I'm also influenced by Bradbury Thompson, a designer who revolutionized the term "talking typography" or narrative typography. Thompson's marriage of typography and imagery from the late 1940s to the early 1970s was truly lovely. Sometimes I find it hard to capture my own voice because when I look at my stuff, all I see are the forces that have influenced me. When I show my work to my friends and clients, however, they don't see those influences — they see me.

"When I design, I often relate processes to my music background. It's almost like I'm improvising on paper. If I'm working on a design problem, I think about how I would resolve that problem if I were playing the guitar. I bounce ideas back and forth between music and design constantly."

An invitation to the company's opening party incorporates the **Faith logo** and a border made up of 8s. The logo uses Sych's soon-to-be-released typeface Dig.

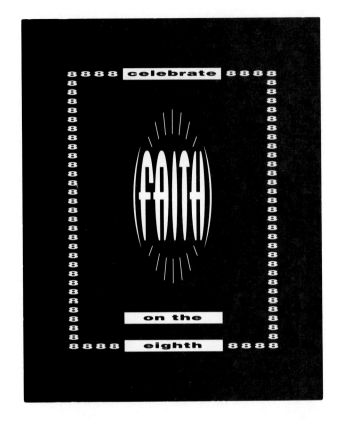

Camille Bouchard, a sales representative for the Buntin Reid Paper Company in Toronto, uses this **notecard** as a calling card/thank you note for his clients. Sych juxtaposed Adobe Systems' Helvetica Black, Goudy and Linoscript fonts in an unusual and pleasing design.

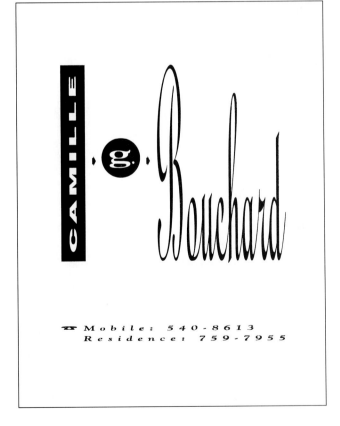

Bingo Bongo, in Sych's soon-to-be-released typeface Stardust, was developed for a gallery show.

The New Music is a mark for *City TV,* a Canadian television serial about music.

Face 90 was developed for Letraset's 1990 promotional materials.

Hip to the Scene is one of a series of t-shirt designs for Reactor Artwear.

Diet Sprite is a custom wordmark developed by Sych for the soft drink's Canadian advertising.

Cité Mag was created for a Montreal magazine store of the same name.

Can't Beat the Real Thing was developed for Coca Cola for all of its Canadian advertising. The custom typeface, Oleo, was also used for the "1991" on the cover of the Pontiac brochure.

The **S** symbol is the mark developed by Sych for Floria Sigismondi, a world-renowned fashion photographer.

Dig That Beat is another of the t-shirt designs for Reactor Artwear.

For its 1990 television campaign featuring Big Macs for 90¢, McDonald's restaurants of Canada hired Sych to create **90!**

In the Groove is another of the t-shirt designs for Reactor Artwear.

A Glimmer of Hope, in Sych's own typeface Equinox, was developed for the Canadian Committee on Acid Rain.

CHAPTER 11

Tackling a Non-Roman Font

Artist

Cleo Huggins received a master's degree in digital typography from Stanford University. For her thesis project she designed an 800-character hieroglyphic font. She also worked for five years at Adobe, and while there designed a music notation font called Sonata. Currently, Huggins is an independent designer working on type and graphic design. She designs the covers for Apple's technical journal and for the Apple Developer Group's CD ROMS. She is also involved in developing type for the Macintosh and NeXT computers.

Project

There are very few presses in the world that have Egyptian hieroglyphs and fewer with the skill to set them. A press that is a favorite of many Egyptologists is England's Oxford University Press. But sending manuscripts there to be printed is very expensive for the typically underfunded scholar. Consequently, Egyptologists often draw their hieroglyphs by hand, a laborious process that can result in an illegible sentence or a page that looks unprofessional.

With the recent trend toward desktop publishing in most schools, Macintosh computers are fairly accessible. I decided that a hieroglyphic font that could be set on a Macintosh would ease the economic and time constraints generally faced by students of Egyptology. Bitmapped hieroglyphs already existed for the Mac but this still was not a solution for publication-quality pages. So I converted an existing hieroglyphic font (the Gardiner font used at Oxford) to an outline PostScript font.

I used an Abaton scanner and Microtek software to scan enlarged photocopies of the Gardiner hieroglyphic font and saved the scans as MacPaint files. I then used Adobe Illustrator 88 to create curve-fitting outlines. I uploaded the Illustrator files to a SUN-3/50 workstation running UNIX, where the files were converted to PostScript fonts with a program I wrote called mkAIfont.

Digital type, new rules

An old type designer came to speak in one of my classes. He was demonstrating tricks that typographers use to make a face dynamic. For example, he advised tilting a character 1 degree forward in order to make it more active. On the computer, that's the last thing you want to do. As an angle approaches any 90-degree increment, the jaggedness of the line increases until it reaches a perfectly vertical or horizontal orientation. A grid doesn't lend itself to 1 degree increments.

Because a jagged line distracts from the character shape, in converting the hieroglyphs to outline fonts, I took artistic license and straightened angles that were close to horizontal or vertical. Even though the design character of the original metal font was altered, this seemed preferable to a rough appearance. The higher the resolution, the closer the angle can get to 90 degrees without perceivable stair-stepping, but on a laser printer, that's still not very close. Even at 1270 dpi, the eye can see the unevenness.

In the "old" computer days, when I worked at Adobe, if a type design caused distracting jaggies, we created two versions of the font: a 300 dpi with no tapers, and a higher-res version with its slight tapers. Optima is a perfect example. It's a beautiful face that looks terrible on the laser printer. With most final output being produced at higher resolution, fonts like Optima can be organic again, with the understanding that the laser printer is just a proofing tool.

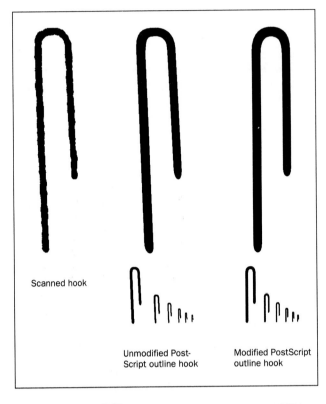

Scanned hook

Unmodified Post-
Script outline hook

Modified PostScript
outline hook

In re-creating the hieroglyphs as outline fonts, slightly tilted characters, which are easily reproduced with metal type, have problems with jaggies when reproduced on a digital system. This is most often seen at small point sizes. Because hieroglyphs are normally set at 12, 14 and 18 points, tilted characters were straightened so that when the font was rasterized (for example, when it was sent to a laser printer), undesirable jaggedness would be avoided.

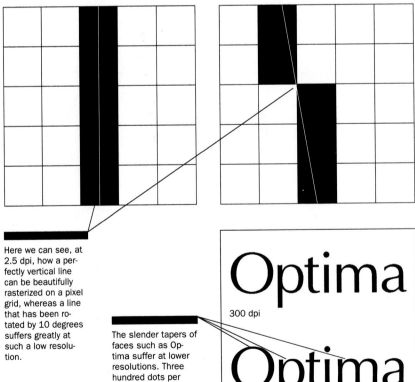

Here we can see, at 2.5 dpi, how a perfectly vertical line can be beautifully rasterized on a pixel grid, whereas a line that has been rotated by 10 degrees suffers greatly at such a low resolution.

The slender tapers of faces such as Optima suffer at lower resolutions. Three hundred dots per inch is just not fine enough to accurately reproduce the subtle curves that mark the Optima typeface.

Optima

300 dpi

Optima

2540 dpi

Large character sets

I saw this project as a problem-solving model for other unusual non-Roman fonts. Large character sets are necessary for recording many Eastern languages. For example, the Kanji font, a Chinese alphabet, has over 7000 characters. Two bytes are used to describe each character in the character set. The first byte points to the particular font group the character is in, and the second byte then specifies the character in that font group. This is one way to handle huge character sets.

Large character sets are no big deal for the computer itself; the limiting factor is the keyboard. How do you devise a method that allows the user to choose characters that can't be seen? One solution would be to access the characters phonetically. For example, the sound *ka* might have several possible combinations. A word-processing program with its search function, could show the user all the possible characters that would represent that sound and the user could pick the applicable character. Another solution could be for the user to draw the characters on an electronic tablet and have the computer match the handwriting with the appropriate font characters.

In converting the hieroglyphs to outlines, I had to decide how I was going to make the font accessible to the user. The biggest problem was the keyboard arrangement. I broke the font down into sub-units, smaller character sets based upon the 26 Gardiner categories. Font A is designated "Man and His Occupations"; font B, "Woman"; C, "Gods" and so on. The characters in each font were arranged in their Gardiner sequence.

Although it's fairly easy to find the characters this way, it's a cumbersome solution. You end up selecting a few char-acters from each of many fonts just to set a sentence. Unfortunately, having a lot of fonts in a document can often cause a printer to crash. The ease of printing large character sets is definitely affected by the size of the printer's or imagesetter's memory.

A soon-to-be released program called MacScribe, which is being developed in Paris and is sponsored by Institut d'Orient, has a solution to the problems created by large character sets. Instead of memorizing the keyboard layout, the user can bring up windows for each font and select the characters visually. There is also a scratch pad available where the user can arrange the hieroglyphs, manipulate them and place cartouches (an oval enclosing characters that represent the name of a sovereign) around them before actually pasting the glyphs into the document.

The first laser printers available could only process font files with a size of 200K or less. Typically, fonts use between 30 and 60K of memory and are a problem only when many are used at once. The entire hieroglyphic set reached 1500K, several times over the maximum limit. To solve this problem, the font was broken down into 26 categories of several characters each. Here the bitmapped subgroup "Gods" can be seen.

The term *hieroglyphs* was coined around A.D. 150 to refer to the sacred images carved on temple walls in Egypt. In Greek, *hieros* means sacred and *glyphé* means carving. Hieroglyphs are small graphic representations that were arranged in either columns or lines. They were used in Egypt for three to four thousand years. At first they only represented the object that they depicted, but later the hieroglyphs were used to convey abstract thought.

Rather than redevelop a whole set of new hieroglyphs, I used an already existing font as my template and converted those shapes into outline form. The Gardiner font, designed in England in 1927, is the most popular metal hieroglyphic font and is the one used at Oxford (Figure 1). In 1983 Oxford University scanned the font in fixed sizes to use for their publications and for outside works. Hieroglyphic screen fonts arrived on the scene in 1986 (Figure 2). They were available and useful but were not suited for high-quality publishing. Most Egyptologists still added handwritten characters to their typeset documents. It was clear that an affordable, scalable outline font for

Figure 1. Starting with the Gardiner font. The most popular font used by Egyptologists was designed in 1927 from the drawings of Norman and Nina de Garis Davies, Egyptological artists working with Sir Alan Gardiner at Oxford.

Figure 2. Using a hieroglyphic screen font. A screen font can never print at a higher resolution than its 72 dpi because, as a bitmap, it has a set resolution. Printing a character at a size larger than the screen font was designed for simply enlarges the "blocks" of which it's constructed.

personal computers was needed. This font would give students of Egyptology access to a publication-quality product.

Trying out Metafont

I had intended to use a program called Metafont, which was designed by Donald Knuth at Stanford University. Knuth had developed this program because he hated the way his mathematical equations looked when printed. With Metafont, he could set his own equations. My first step in translating the Gardiner font into outlines was to take 18-point printed hieroglyphics and enlarge them so that Metafont could be applied to determine a path structure. But it quickly became apparent that, due to the complexity of the hieroglyphs, specifically the lack of repeatable shapes and the frequent occurrence of crossing pieces, Metafont was not the program to use.

Metafont allowed the user to give the computer a formula describing the structures of a set of shapes (letterforms). Once the computer had the formula for each shape, the user could instruct it to apply overall characteristics, like making all the strokes thicker, taller or wider. Doing this generated many styles. But in reality, there are many typefaces that don't adapt well to such a perfect model. For example, the strokes of some letters are purposefully thinned where they join so that they don't appear too heavy or cause ink traps (Figure 3). These exceptions or inconsistencies are introduced to make a font optically consistent.

If I had been designing a new hieroglyphic character set, I could have made the shapes work with Metafont. However, I was working from an existing font that didn't have the proper characteristics for conversion in the Metafont

Figure 3. Accounting for aesthetics. The thickness of the stem stroke of lower-case letters must be slightly thinner than the thickness of the stem stroke of capitals, otherwise the capitals' stems look too thin. Also, diagonal strokes of letters must be thinner than vertical strokes, or the diagonals will appear too heavy. Such variations are difficult for a program like Metafont to take into account.

program, so I decided to find another route for converting the hieroglyphs into outlines.

Experimenting with Fontographer

With a program like Altsys's Fontographer, a type designer uses a scan of existing artwork as a template and can then place key points around the image or use the autotrace function (Figure 4). Once the outlines for the font are completed, the Generate Font command can be used to convert the file into the predefined font format required by PostScript. Although producing a finished font is relatively easy in Fontographer, detail was hard to obtain with the large circles that were used to indicate points. ▋ *In current versions of Fontographer, points can be specified in any of three sizes.*

Perhaps the biggest problem with using Fontographer was that the resulting font format was restrictive. Once a font had been generated, it was no longer an editable graphic element. ▋ *More recent versions of Fontographer allow the font to be reopened in the program and also saved as an EPS that can then be edited in Illustrator or FreeHand.*

It was important to be able to edit the hieroglyphs because I felt that Egyptologists would desire the flexibility of using the fonts as graphic elements and even modifying or adding to them on occasion. Many programs can now convert fonts to outlines — Altsys's Metamorphosis, Taylored Graphics's Fontliner and Adobe's Illustrator 3.0 — but when I started this work, these programs weren't available.

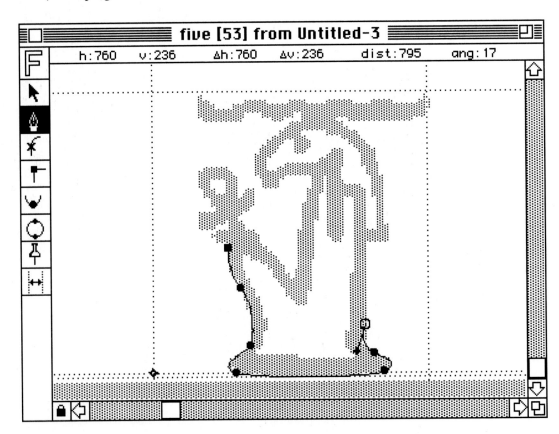

Figure 4. Using a hieroglyphic template. With a scanned image as a template, Fontographer allows you to outline the image. The outline can then be converted into a font character by the command Generate Font.

Working with Adobe Illustrator

I much preferred the drawing interface of Illustrator over that of Fontographer and decided that I would have more control in this program over the resultant shapes. Illustrator drawings could also be imported into such programs as Aldus PageMaker and Letraset's Ready,Set,Go. Illustrator, however, does not produce a printer font. Because this was several years ago, when not as many programs were available for the Macintosh, my only option for getting exactly the program I wanted was to write my own which I called mkAIfont. This still wasn't a completely satisfying solution because my program didn't generate screen fonts for my printer fonts.

If my fonts were to be used on the NeXT machine, with Display PostScript, it didn't matter that there were no screen fonts because the screen can use the printer information. However, my real goal was to make the font available to Egyptologists, and this meant making it usable on the Macintosh. More recently I considered using a program called KeyMaster (now called Art Importer, see "Using Art Importer" on this page), which converts EPS or PICT graphics into characters accessible from the keyboard. On-screen one sees bitmapped representations of the characters, but the PostScript code is sent to the printer, enabling it to produce the letters or artwork at the printer's particular resolution.

At the time I was developing the hieroglyph fonts, there were two problems with this plan of attack: First, KeyMaster allowed only 16 characters per font, far fewer than I had planned. (Art Importer allows 256 characters per font —

Using Art Importer

Art Importer allows EPS or vector PICT files to be converted into font characters. This means that you can turn logos, drop caps or anything you wish to access with a keystroke into Art Importer fonts.

To begin converting artwork, select New under the file menu and this window will appear showing you 256 slots for placing your artwork. Highlight the slot where you want your first selection to go (a). Choose Import from the file menu. Find your EPS or PICT file and open it. You'll see a message indicating that Art Importer is generating the character. When it's done, a figure will appear in the selected slot.

Double-clicking on that slot will open up a bitmap-editing window where you can clean up the screen font and adjust the side bearings (the space around the character) (b). For especially fine detail, you can choose a higher magnification from the Special menu. When you've finished with all the characters you want to include in this font,

Save the file. Then place the printer font in your System folder (c), install your screen font (d), and save the AFM (Adobe Font Metrics) file if you want to re-edit the font later (e). (The AFM contains character widths, kerning pairs and bounding boxes. Certain text-handling programs use this file, but generally you can ignore it.)

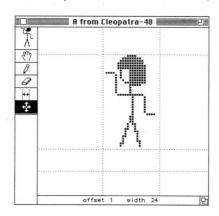

a

Cleop

c

Cleopatra.bmap

d

Cleopatra

e

b

a number dictated by Macintosh and Adobe standards for character sets.) But more critical, I found that when I placed my graphics in KeyMaster, the bounding box (the exact rectangular area in which the image falls) was scaled to the same height for every character, whether the characters were originally the same height or not. This caused relative shapes (such as a man lying down and a man standing up) to be inconsistent (Figure 5). I realized that I could create invisible (no fill, no line), identical rectangles and place them around every Illustrator drawing, but at this point I had already completed most of the illustrations and I multiplied the time that it would take me to do that and decided that it wasn't worth it.

Making design decisions

I had to decide early in the conversion process whether I would convert the Gardiner font "as is" or make some aesthetic alterations. The Gardiner font was already a derivation of the original hieroglyphs and the forms had been, in the interest of consistency, simplified due to the limitations of a metal typeface. A digital medium is not restricted by the same limitations, and so I looked to the original hieroglyphs for features that had been left off the metal font. For example, the lips and eyebrows of men were present on the original hieroglyphs, but absent on the Gardiner font (Figure 6). I began putting back the missing features, but after making these enhancements and then running tests on the Linotronic L-300 at medium resolution (1270 dpi), I realized that this extra detail was lost at smaller point sizes; more important, it required more memory from the already stressed LaserWriter (Figure 7).

Another consideration was whether to round shapes that met at corners or to make them sharp. Many of the Gardiner shapes appear rounded, but this is perhaps because foundry tools are inexact at such small sizes or because the ink spread when the impression was printed. It seemed to me that the intent was to produce a perfect corner, but the characteristics of the medium

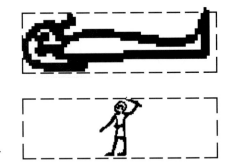

Figure 5. Making bounding boxes. In creating a font set with KeyMaster (now updated and called Art Importer), one of the biggest drawbacks was that the bounding boxes of all the characters were automatically scaled to be the same height, and, consequently, sizes and weights of horizontal characters couldn't be made consistent with those of vertical characters. (Art Importer will not import shapes with bounding boxes that are inconsistent with other already imported art.)

Figure 6. Noting missing features. Due to the limitations of a metal font, the lips and eyebrows of men on the original hieroglyphs (left) were absent from the Gardiner font (right).

prevented that from occurring. Having removed those limitations by way of a digital medium, it made sense to change the soft corners back to sharp ones in the font conversion. However, after I had created a few characters with these perfect corners, the resultant shapes seemed inconsistent with the more natural forms (Figure 8). I decided that even if the intent had been to create a perfect corner, the accuracy of the computer proved to alter the style of the characters and that it was perhaps better to follow the idiosyncrasies of the Gardiner font in order to retain consistency.

Using Cleo

"Cleo," as I named the Egyptian hieroglyphics that I had converted from scans of the Gardiner font, is a series of outline fonts available for use on laser printers and imagesetters supporting PostScript. Intended to address the printing need of students and scholars of Egyptology as a high-quality, versatile font, Cleo (with approximately 800 characters) is organized as a series of subfonts following the categorization scheme laid out by Gardiner. Key position charts are supplied with the Cleo hieroglyphic fonts or you can use the Key Caps desk accessory (Figure 9). Accompanying screen fonts are provided. The sizes of the printer subfonts range from 9 to 216K. These printer fonts may be stored to disk on disk-based printers or stored as needed in the memory (RAM) of the laser printer. To use Cleo most efficiently, the

Figure 7. Losing detail at smaller sizes. Even at 1270 dpi, the man's features begin to get lost at sizes of 24 points and smaller and the features themselves can even be distracting. The details also require additional printer memory, even at the smaller sizes at which they don't show clearly.

150 pts   72 pts   48 pts   24 pts   12 pts

Figure 8. Comparing metal and digital styles. Rounded corners (left) seemed to be more in keeping with the rest of the Gardiner characters, even though it appeared that Gardiner's intent was to make sharp corners and that it was the inherent characteristics of the printing press that softened them.

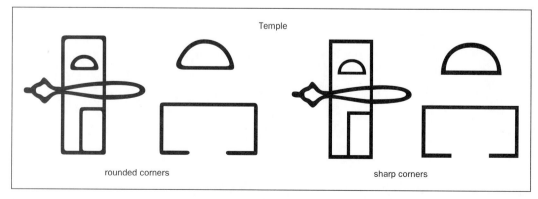

Temple

rounded corners   sharp corners

screen fonts for all the subfonts should be installed using either the Font/DA Mover or a program such as Suitcase (see "A look at Suitcase II" on page 155). Given the large size of the entire Cleo font — over 1500K — and the wide range of characters necessary in many hieroglyphic transcriptions, it's most practical to store the entire font on a laser printer disk. The alternative is to download the fonts as needed using FontDownloader, which is included with Cleo. This method will work as long as the total number of fonts needed by one document does not exceed the printer's memory.

In retrospect

The invention of the printing press so dramatically affected our concept of type that it dictated the eventual shapes of letters, allowing people to forget the origins of those shapes. The fluidity of the letterforms got lost in the transition between scribes painstakingly recording documents in beautiful calligraphic script and the casting of lead typefaces that unified the letterform but froze it into static pieces whose individuality could be provided only by kerning.

There are languages in which the angle of the baseline changes depending upon the length of the word. This is a problem that could never be addressed on a traditional printing press. In some cultures the shapes of the characters change depending upon context and position. "Ligature-like," they are

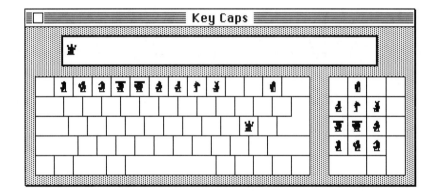

Figure 9. Using Key Caps. Pulling down the Apple menu provides access to the desk accessory Key Caps, which displays the keyboard arrangement of any installed or Suitcase-linked font selected from the Key Caps menu.

Figure 10. Making ligatures. A ligature is the fusion of two characters. Originally instituted by scribes, ligatures were space-saving devices. Later they were preferred for aesthetic reasons because an adjoining *f* and *i*, for example, looked much better tied together than placed at their normal distance.

affected by the characters next to them (Figure 10). We need to design new software to tackle these very individual problems. Professor R. K. Joshi of Stanford University has an idea of creating a dynamic font, one in which each character has its own mini-program that, depending upon a variety of factors, dictates its shape. These could be considered "context-dependent shapes" — their context defines their form.

In order to meet all the needs of people who use electronic type, I think font development will soon have to embrace these concepts. The computer may even challenge the traditional notion of what a font is, adding capabilities that were never before possible, such as incorporating symbols scanned from photographs. This would be useful for languages that are still being deciphered, such as the Mayan hieroglyphs, because reproducing these hieroglyphs as faithfully as possible is extremely important, both to minimize assumptions made about a character and to provide an actual representation for cataloging the various symbols. Through font development the computer provides an accessibility to preserving and studying ancient languages that affects the way we currently think about language, again allowing written language to more accurately reflect spoken thought.

A look at Suitcase II

The purpose of the desk accessory Suitcase II is to decrease the size of your Macintosh System file and allow you to turn font and desk accessory files on or off as you prefer.

To use Suitcase II, place the application in your System folder and then restart the computer. Selecting Suitcase II under the Apple menu opens the program's main window (a). By clicking on the appropriate button you can see which DAs, fonts, function keys and sounds are installed.

To install a new suitcase — for example, a font — click on the Suitcases button (Command-C). This brings you to a screen that shows you the names of the suitcases that are currently installed (b). (Several fonts could be inside one suitcase.) Clicking on the Open Files button takes you to the next screen, which allows you to look anywhere on your hard disk (or even on a floppy) to find the suitcase you wish to open (c). If you can't find the name of the file you want in the list, try clicking on Show All Types.

Once you find the file, click on Open. This opens the file but leaves you at the same screen (unless the maximum number of suitcase files are open, in which case it takes you back to the first screen). You must then click Cancel. This seems a little confusing because it seems as if you're cancelling your last action, but in fact, that action has already been completed and you are only cancelling from this screen, which takes you back to the first screen, where you can then Quit.

a

b

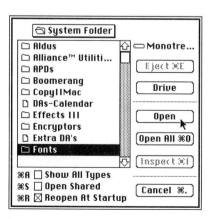

c

Cleo Huggins

"While working on the design of Sonata (a music notation font), I realized that some languages, such as music, don't adapt well to the printing technologies we've been perfecting since Gutenberg. We can easily print text on a line using only letters and punctuation, but to compose a score, for instance, musicians use symbols for pitch, rhythm and duration in an overlapping and intertwining arrangement. Music notation does not conform to the linear nature of the printing press, and this has resulted in odd or incomplete character sets for the press.

"There are many languages whose beauty has been compromised because they've been simplified for printing purposes. Hebrew, Arabic and Hindi are richer languages than you would expect from looking over the standard character sets that are available today. In some cases, languages that did not conform to the rigidity of lead were completely ignored.

"All this could change with the popularity and availability of the computer. Through computers, our method of documentation can evolve beyond the old metaphors of printing presses, typewriters and typesetters. We can command computers to create letterforms and other notations as elegantly as the best scribes. All this is exciting to me. I get to be an archaeologist, digging around in the origins of written languages and making their beauty available through the computer."

Sonata, part of the Adobe Type Library, is a music notation font whose character set has more than 170 symbols, including many composites. Sonata can be used with an appropriate music-setting application to produce elegant printed music, or with any Macintosh program that uses the font menu since it's in the standard font format.

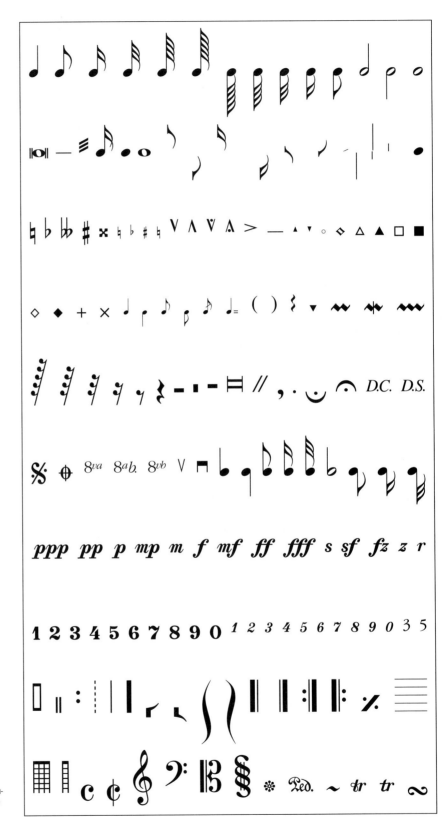

Although we are now very used to seeing dis torted type, in 1984, when this 8 x 5¾-inch, 12-page accordion-fold **calendar** was produced for Adobe, it was the first time that the ability to distort and overlap type was available. The story behind the calendar, which won a Type Directors Club 31 award in 1985, is as follows:

It was actually a continuation of a project I did at Rhode Island School of Design. I distorted letters on a grid to form a cube and then sand-blasted them on sheets of glass. It was a cool effect — the letters seemed to float together and form an invisible cube. When I discovered that I could easily distort letters with PostScript, I duplicated the glass project. It evolved into a calendar as I started creating spinning cubes that reminded me of tornados and other weather patterns. At the time there was no Macintosh to play with the PostScript. I used Emacs, a text editor in UNIX on a monitor connected to a main-frame. I learned enough PostScript to do what I wanted to do and asked programmers to help with the rest. There was no way to see what I would get until I printed it. By the end of the project, I had memorized the positions of every PostScript coordinate on the page and could tell ahead of time what the changes I made to the code would look like. It amazed me how you just learn to adapt to what you have and how little it bothered me that I had to write code to move an object rather than dragging it visually across the screen. Finally, when the Linotronic came out, it was like Christmas — I saw the same file output at 1270 dpi and it was so much more precise.

Gallery

The following pages showcase examples of digital typography from leading artists and designers. In some cases the artwork consists of display type alone. In other instances the type is an integral part of a larger electronic composition.

Nathan Weedmark

is a San Diego artist who has been using the Macintosh computer since it came out in 1984. Before using computer, Weedmark used pen and ink, watercolors and acrylics in his art, much of which has demonstrated his concern for the environment and related politics. Weedmark says he likes using the computer because it allows him to "combine words and images quickly."

You've Seen One is an example of concrete poetry that Weedmark produced on the computer in 1986. The artist used the words of Ronald Reagan, quoted at the time he was governor of California, "You've seen one redwood, you've seen them all." He used the cut, paste and rotate functions of Silicon Beach's SuperPaint to create the effect of trees. A quote from Wordsworth creates a contrapuntal border at the top.

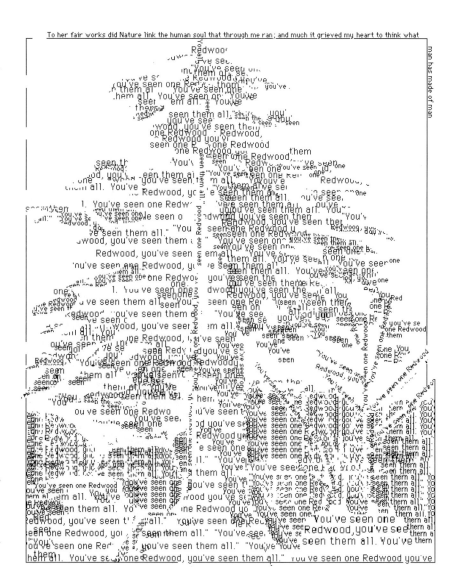

Donald Gambino
is director of the undergraduate computer department of the School of Visual Arts in New York City. He has taught there since 1983, and continues to teach computer graphics and consult. Using both IBM and Macintosh personal computers, Gambino stresses creativity in his teaching, showing his students that computers can be pushed well beyond the uses even the software designers imagined.

These mandala-like designs were created in FreeHand using **Palatino 5s** and **Garamond 3s.**

Stacked Numbers and **Stacked Alphabet** were created on a Mac Plus using FreeHand. The Cheltenham characters were created at 500-point size, outlined and stacked.

The images on this page were created using only Adobe's Carta typeface. Clockwise from the top are **Why Bother?** (a PageMaker 4.0 document) and **Earth Day 1990** and **Leaf Us Alone,** both done in FreeHand.

Studio MD

of Seattle produces most of its work on Macintosh computers, though each of the partners in the firm has eight to ten years' experience in "traditional design." Firm principals are Glenn Mitsui, Jesse Doquilo and Randy Lim. Mitsui says that their "most rewarding" jobs are the ones that give them creative leeway to innovate, and that frequently have very small budgets attached. Hence, Studio MD's guiding business principle is "Caution — Low Overhead."

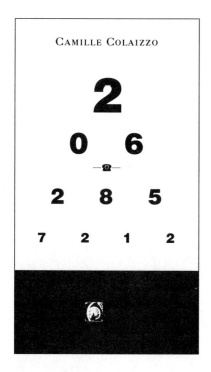

Colaizzo is a corporate identity package for an optician. It incorporates classical Italian-style clip art and contemporary type treatment. The clever "eye chart" business card is folded and glued to form a collapsing box with die-cut holes revealing eyes peering out. The numbers of the phone number are arranged like the letters on an optician's wall chart. The whimsical logotype design (which contains three TIFF files and one EPS file) blends science, art and a warm sense of humor.

The **Leonhardt Group** of Seattle commissioned Studio MD to illustrate **Talk'n Trash** for the Washington State Department of Ecology, Waste Reduction and Litter Control. The colorful and witty 24 x 36-inch poster promoting conservation was designed by Leonhardt principal **Rick Hess,** who describes his firm as committed to "the unexpected in design solutions."

TIFF files of crumpled newspapers appear through the headline typography, which was drawn as masking objects on the computer. Scanned typeset copy is used to fill each of the whimsical trash objects on the poster, adding texture and originality to the piece. A sidebar of copy warns us that we each will "throw away" 600 times our weight in garbage over a lifetime — and thus pollute the environment as well as waste valuable recyclable energy — if we do not conserve and recycle now.

GALLERY

Studio MD

These **illustrations for Litho Development Research** in Portland, Oregon were drawn in Free-Hand 3.0. The typography adds to the sophistication of the combined TIFF files, simplified halftones and drawn elements.

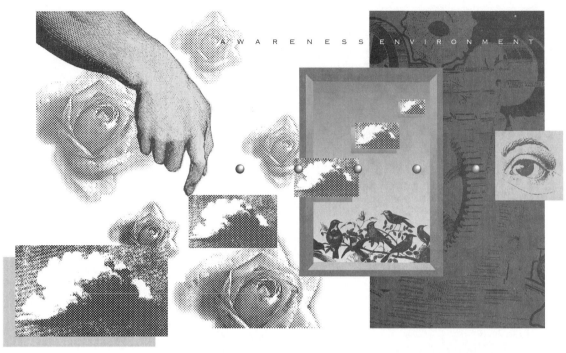

Mitsui . Studio M D . 91 ©

T H E   L D R   E L I T E   F A M I L Y   O F   P R O D U C T S

T H E   F U T U R E   O F   L D R   I N T E R N A T I O N A L

...ng is an assembly procedure.
...gatives, halftones, color
...ons and any other components
...positioned. This includes line
...the paste-up and its overlays
...created to allow certain colors to
...be blocked out); the assembly
...nal cyan, magenta, yellow and
...egatives; and the exposure of line
...negatives to create the final
...film. Becoming a

...uding the
...(and in some cases the
...tion) of mechanical pre-press
...es such as stripping and multiple
...ots. Electronic stripping accuracy
...precise positioning the same
...sed to produce the final output.
...ectronic files can be edited
...A standard page template
...s a new page by "pouring" new
...ements into it, and electronic
...ages can be edited in ways that
...ossible through non-electronic
...s. Another major advantage of
...nic pre-press is that PostScript
...n be produced on relatively
...sive Macs and printed on a
...of machines, ranging from low

John Weber

is a self-taught graphic designer in Columbus, Ohio who describes his work as "an eclectic assemblage of whatever is at hand — the ultimate in recycling." Approaching his work with a sense of humor and an aversion to guidelines, Weber typically designs work that incorporates the casual look of randomly assembled images with the clean, precise look generated by a computer. Weber seeks an ephemeral, emotional quality in his work.

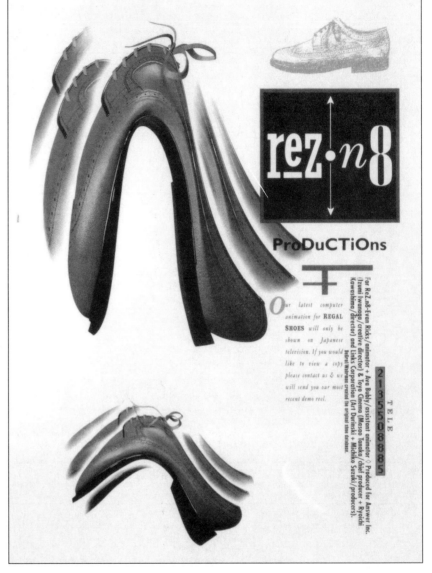

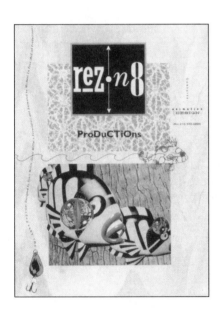

Rez.n8 Productions is a video animation company that commissioned Weber to design its advertising. Weber sought to create an art piece and at the same time make the readers of video trade publications aware of the company's presence.

Fish Bark is a visual pun describing a new "sampler" of the company's work. The designer created an environment on the printed page by combining video stills of the fish with scanned images of tree bark, his own TV screen distorted and colorized in the background, and other art drawn and assembled in FreeHand on a Macintosh.

Regal Shoes incorporates video stills from a TV spot produced for Japanese viewers.

design: (for the Holidays) Weber

Laser Sound & Vision is a letterhead combining scanned images rendered in Photoshop with computer drawn lines and computer-shaped text assembled in Free-Hand.

V'ice Sycle is a holiday greeting card incorporating scanned found art images with type and art produced in Photoshop and FreeHand.

Thrilla At Willa is an invitation to a golf tournament. It incorporates scanned found art with typography, some set and some custom-drawn in FreeHand.

Reactor
Louis Fishauf is the creative director and founding partner of Reactor Art and Design, Ltd. of Toronto, Canada, a graphic design studio which is also an illustration agency and art gallery. Fishauf started the firm in 1982 after spending 15 years as a magazine art director, during which time he won 11 international magazine awards. His preferred graphic design software is Illustrator 3.0.

Satellite Services was designed as a trade magazine ad for a postproduction video and sound recording studio. The ad appeared in *Backstage* and *Millimeter* magazines. Production was done in Adobe Illustrator 3.0.

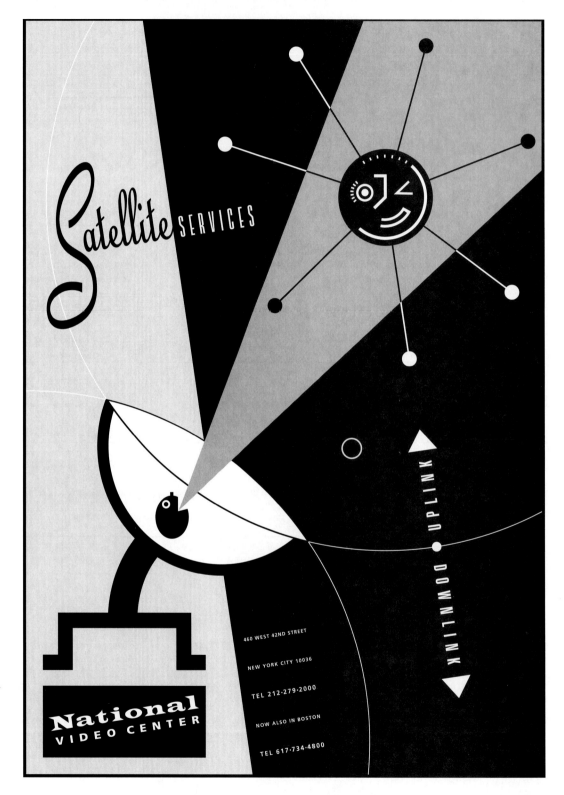

Reactor Xmas Show & Party was a post-card invitation for Reactor Gallery created in Adobe Illustrator.

Club Monaco is a design for labels and hang tags for a clothing line. The cut paper illustration was created by Paula Munck, and later scanned and redrawn in Illustrator.

Reactor Type Style is the cover for a promotional book of Reactor typographic and logo design.

The Radiant City Story is a hand-drawn logo (produced in Adobe Illustrator) for a comic book series published by Vortex Comics.

Hammer is a logo hand-drawn in Illustrator for labels and hang tags for a line of men's sheepskin jackets.

State O' The Art is a poster advertising computer seminars sponsored by Blumer Levan Inc., a retailer of art supplies and computer software and hardware. Production was done with an early version of Adobe Illustrator, with some of the lettering created with FontLiner and the curved type set with TypeAlign. Most of the special effects provided by these specialized programs are now incorporated in Adobe Illustrator.

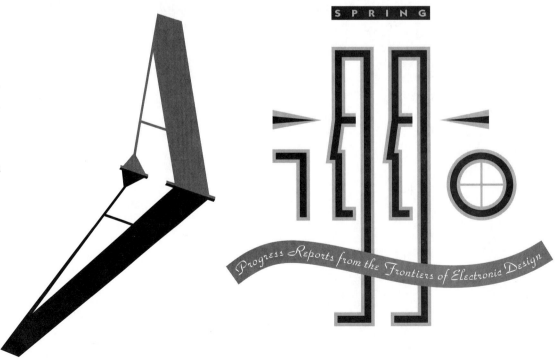

Reactor

Adventures in the 4th Dimension combines scanned images rendered in Photoshop with Illustrator 3.0–rendered type, set on a circle, rotated and skewed. The "fish" in the corner is the artist's signature.

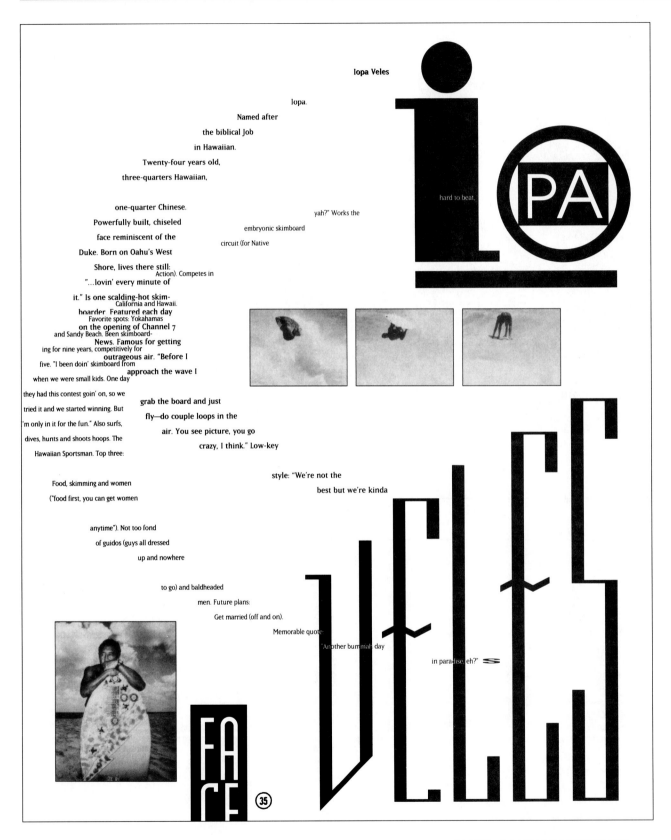

Iopa Veles

Iopa. Named after the biblical Job in Hawaiian. Twenty-four years old, three-quarters Hawaiian, one-quarter Chinese. Powerfully built, chiseled face reminiscent of the Duke. Born on Oahu's West Shore, lives there still: "...lovin' every minute of it." Is one scalding-hot skim-boarder. Featured each day on the opening of Channel 7 News. Famous for getting outrageous air. "Before I approach the wave I grab the board and just fly—do couple loops in the air. You see picture, you go crazy, I think." Low-key style: "We're not the best but we're kinda hard to beat, yah?" Works the embryonic skimboard circuit (for Native Action). Competes in California and Hawaii. Favorite spots: Yokahamas and Sandy Beach. Been skimboard-ing for nine years, competitively for five. "I been doin' skimboard from when we were small kids. One day they had this contest goin' on, so we tried it and we started winning. But I'm only in it for the fun." Also surfs, dives, hunts and shoots hoops. The Hawaiian Sportsman. Top three: Food, skimming and women ("food first, you can get women anytime"). Not too fond of guidos (guys all dressed up and nowhere to go) and baldheaded men. Future plans: Get married (off and on). Memorable quote: "Another bummah day in paradise, eh?"

FACE (35)

Iopa Veles is a spread on a champion skim boarder. The typeface for "Veles" was hand-drawn and then traced in Adobe Illustrator. Other typefaces are "off the shelf."

David Carson

In mid-1989 David Carson became art director of the new magazine Beach Culture, *a publication that would be heavily influenced by Carson's art direction experience with* Skate Boarding *(3½ years) and* Musician *(1½ years). While design and production of the magazine remains a hybrid of manual paste-up and computer production, Carson now reserves his manual production techniques for "special effects." However he produces it, Carson has managed to win 60 international awards for* Beach Culture, *including 1990 Best Overall Design and a Gold Medal for Best Cover from the Society of Publication Design.*

The **Vince Klyn** spread features hand calligraphy which was scanned and redrawn in Illustrator.

John Odam,
art director of Verbum *and* Step-By-Step
Electronic Design, *is a publications and*
book designer who was among the first to
"dabble" in typography design on the
Macintosh. His own incursions into type
design gave him enough insight to have
tremendous respect for the people who
dedicate their careers to this "exacting
craft." When Fontographer was first intro-
duced, Odam experimented to produce
customized fonts to meet the specialized
requirements of some of his clients. Odam
also used the program to re-create fonts
no longer available through type houses.
Before starting his own studio in 1975,
Odam was a staff designer with CRM Book
Publishers (then also publisher of Psychology Today), *and the London division of*
Bantam Books.

Choices is a text-
book cover featuring
a typeface called
Onyx, which Odam
drew in preparation
for a review he was
writing for *Verbum*
magazine on the Fon-
tographer software.

Zane Grey is a book
cover utilizing
Egyptian Bold Con-
densed, a font of
capitals and numer-
als Odam re-created
with Fontographer
software. As a test
of how quickly a
complete alphabet
could be generated
using Fontographer,
Odam re-created this
display font spending
an average of only
15 minutes per
character.

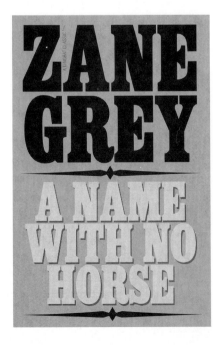

Luft Werken is a design displaying a typeface Odam resurrected from a few characters he found on a 1913 German poster. He calls his new version of this "found" typeface Drucker (German for "printer"). The book title for the mock cover, Odam adds, is "mangled German" and means nothing.

Esoteric Philosophy is a book cover utilizing John Odam's Drucker typeface for the title and author, and decorated with typographic ornaments used directly from the Adobe Illustrator Collector's Edition software.

Carol Twombly,
a type designer at Adobe Systems, Inc., studied graphic design at the Rhode Island School of Design and received an MS from Stanford University in the Digital Typography program under Charles Bigelow. In 1984 Twombly won first prize in the Morisawa Typeface Design Competition for a roman design which has been licensed and released as Mirarae.

GEOMETRIC   FUNKY   FINAL LITHOS

Three stages in the development of **Lithos,** one of the first three display typefaces — Trajan, Charlemagne and Lithos — in the Adobe Originals library.

THE CLEAN MONOLINE SHAPES OF THE LITHOS FAMILY ARE REMINISCENT OF GREEK INSCRIPTIONAL LETTERING. BY WORKING DIRECTLY ON A COMPUTER, I WAS ABLE TO EXPERIMENT WITH MANY DESIGNS **BEFORE SETTLING ON THE FINAL SHAPES. LITHOS WAS DESIGNED ESPECIALLY FOR DISPLAY USE.**

This sample text is set in Lithos ExtraLight, Light, Regular, Bold and Black.

Adobe Caslon, is a revival of the letters cut by William Caslon I in the early 18th century. Weight fluctuations and idiosyncratic shapes in individual characters were retained to capture the vitality of Caslon's original designs. It has also been adjusted so that it won't look too light when printed on a digital typesetter, or too heavy when printed on a laser printer.

Examples of the letter *a* from each of the text sizes (14- at the top, 12-, 11- 10- and 9-point) of a Caslon Foundry specimen are enlarged to the same x-height with sketches overlying the enlargements to show the shape of the letter at each size (a). Twombly's sketches were scanned into the computer (b). The *a* and *b* from Adobe Caslon show the final PostScript result (c). Part of a book page set in Adobe Caslon shows regular and italic type with swash capitals and small capitals (d).

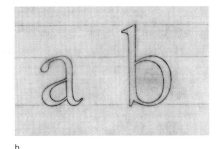

b

c

a   d

Miss Bridget Allworthy
CHAPTER I

Though we have properly enough entitled this our work, a history, and not a life; nor an apology for a life, as is more in fashion; yet we intend in it rather to pursue the method of those writers, who profess to disclose the revolutions of countries, than to imitate the

1990

MINION

A new book face from Adobe

ADOBE SYSTEMS INC. INTRODUCES MINION,™ a new font software package in the growing library of Adobe Originals™ typefaces. Created by Adobe designer Robert Slimbach, Minion is an integrated digital typeface family, inspired by classic old style typefaces of the late Renaissance. Designed primarily for text-setting, Minion combines the æsthetic and functional qualities that make text type easy to read, with the clarity of digital technology. Although inspired by the past, Minion is contemporary in detail and function, and reflects both the designer's personal tastes and the ever-changing demands of modern typography and graphic design. Named after one of the sizes used in the early days of typefounding, Minion is defined as "a beloved servant," which reflects the typeface's useful and unobtrusive qualities. Together, Minion and Minion Expert Collection contain a wide range of weights and expanded character sets, designed to address the needs of fine book designers and typographers.

The following text specimens were set using common font combinations. Point size and leading are designated by number.

Old style roman typefaces form the core of text types used today, and remain a standard because of their visual appeal and readability. Throughout *Old style roman typefaces form the core of text types used today, and remain a standard because of their*

Old style roman typefaces form the core of text types used today, and continue to *Old style roman typefaces form the core of text types used today, and continue to be*

ABCDEFGHIJKLMNOPQRSTUVWXY&Z1234567890abcdef
ghijklmnopqrstuvwxyz1234567890ABCDEFGHIJKLMNOPQRSTUV
*ABCDEFGHIJKLMNOPQRSTUVWXY&Z1234567890abcdefg
hijklmnopqrstuvwxyz1234567890ABCDEFGHIJKLMNOPQRSTUVWX*

Alvin Birgit Carol David Esther Fred Ginger Herb Isabelle Julian Kevin Laurie Margery Ned Olivia Pauline Quinlan Rachel Sumner Terry Ursula Vaughan Wesley Xenia Yvonne Zabrina

Regular · *Italic* · **Semibold** · ***Semibold Italic*** · **Bold** · ***Bold Italic*** · **Black** · Display Regular · *Display Italic* · *Swash Display Italic* · *Swash Italic* · *Swash Semibold Italic* · EXPERT REGULAR
EXPERT ITALIC · EXPERT SEMIBOLD · EXPERT SEMIBOLD ITALIC · Expert Bold · Expert Bold Italic · Expert Black · EXPERT DISPLAY REGULAR · EXPERT DISPLAY ITALIC · Ornaments

Robert Slimbach, *who joined Adobe Systems, Inc. in 1987, had begun working on type and calligraphy in 1983 in the type-drawing department of Autologic in Newbury Park, California. He has focused primarily on text typefaces geared to digital technology. Slimbach has designed typefaces for International Typeface Corporation as well as several Adobe Originals typeface families, including Adobe Garamond and Utopia.*

Minion is a contemporary family of digital typefaces inspired by the classic, old-style typefaces of the late Renaissance. It was designed primarily for text-setting, combining the aesthetic and functional qualities that make text type inviting to read with the clarity of digital technology. Named after one of the type sizes used in the early days of typefounding, Minion means "a beloved servant," reflecting the typeface family's useful and unobtrusive qualities.

Jeff Girard

flunked high school art class because he spent most of the class time drawing cartoons out of Surfer *magazine. After graduating from Cal Poly San Luis Obispo (California) with a degree in graphic communications, Girard went on to become art director of* Surfer. *Girard now produces freelance projects through his own business, Victoria Street Graphic Design in San Clemente, California.*

ASP EUROPE
CONTINENTAL
BY DEREK HYND
COLLISION

Human Vehicle Water Energy, Girard's definition of the term *surfing*, was used as a title for a *Surfer* magazine photo page. All characters were drawn in Adobe Illustrator, outlined in white with no fill. Letters *a*, *e* and *g* all utilize the same letterform.

Continental Collision was created with Adobe's TypeAlign software.

THE NEED FOR SPEED

The Need For Speed displays an original typeface by Girard called Airstream. Airstream exists in several weights, from light to ultra-black, and is based on a 1930s typeface called Huxley. Adobe Illustrator was used in drawing the characters.

Invitation Only is an example of existing type that has been "tuned." The initial caps have been outlined, the finials rounded and type composed in Adobe Illustrator.

Gotcha Change is a special effect that can be created in either PixelPaint (using the Warp function) or Photoshop (using the Twirl function). Adobe Illustrator was used to trace the modified letter shapes and clean up the jagged edges.

Max Seabaugh, a San Francisco–based illustrator and designer, has translated his cut-paper style of artwork to the opaque layers of the PostScript illustration environment.

Font Wars, produced with Adobe Illustrator, was drawn for *Verbum* magazine to illustrater an article about the new page-description languages being developed by Microsoft and Hewlett-Packard to compete with Adobe's PostScript.

Adobe Type Manager (ATM) — a program for both Macintosh and Windows that creates screen fonts as needed from *outline fonts*. This saves on the space required to store fonts and makes more sizes available for better display or for output to printers that use bitmaps.

Adobe Type Reunion — a program for the Macintosh that groups all *styles* and *weights* of each *typeface* in the same menu entry and arranges the menu entries in alphabetical order. The styles and weights can be reached via submenus.

aligning figures — numerals that line up at the *baseline* and rise to equal heights, rather than the *oldstyle* or *hanging* figures, some of which extended below the *baseline*. Also called *lining figures.*

all caps — type set in capital letters only.

antialiased fonts — said of type fonts on screens and dot-based printers that have had their edges adjusted or shaded to smooth what would otherwise have been jagged portions caused by the limited number of possible dot positions.

apex — a part of a character where two lines meet at the top, such as the point on the letter *A*.

arm — a part of a letter that extends horizontally or diagonally up, as the two top parts of a capital *Y* or the top stroke in a *T*.

ascender — the part of a character that reaches up from a distinct main body of the letter towards the top of the line. For example, the upper half of the left vertical line making up the small letter *b* is the ascender.

ascender line — an imaginary line connecting the tops of any *ascenders* in a particular type *font*. Depending on the *typeface* design, it may or may not be equal to the *cap height*.

ASCII —(pronounced ASS kee) acronym for *American Standard Code for Information Interchange,* a standard code established by the American National Standards Institute to achieve compatibility between various types of data processing and data communications equipment.

ASCII character set — a standard set of characters used on most computers and printers.

ATM — see *Adobe Type Manager.*

attribute — a characteristic such as *style, weight, size* and so on of a block of type or a single character.

autoleading — a setting on many typesetting systems that picks the normally-appropriate spacing (*leading*) between lines of text based on *type size* and *style*.

automatic font downloading — a feature on some laser printers that loads any *fonts* (sets of characters) needed by a document being sent from the computer to the printer without requiring the user to load the needed fonts manually.

automatic hyphenation — in computer *typesetting,* a paragraph specification that directs a word processing program to *hyphenate* text automatically by applying a set of standard rules followed by a check against an *exception dictionary.*

autotrace — a mode on some drawing programs that creates a set of curves to represent outlines corresponding to a *bitmap* (array of dots) image. It is sometimes used to capture the shape of existing type samples in typeface-creation programs.

backslanting — referring to characters and graphics, *oblique* (at an angle) but leaning top to the left.

bad break — the proofreader's expression for word *hyphenation* done at an inappropriate location (such as in the middle of a syllable).

banner — a large headline or title. Originally, it meant a headline that extended across the full page, but it is now used to indicate any large head.

bar — a horizontal line comprising part of a character, as in the central line in the *H*.

base — referring to *film* and *papers,* the underlying material, in many cases now a form of Mylar or other similar plastic.

base alignment — on a *typesetter* or printer, a setting or mode that specifies that the normal lower reference edge of all letters should be lined up horizontally even in a line of mixed sizes or styles where the top edges might be uneven. This mode is also called *baseline alignment.*

baseline — **1.** a reference line used for the vertical alignment of characters. Except for characters with *descenders* (such as *y*), the baseline is normally the line crossing the bottom-most part of the character. **2.** the invisible reference line upon which characters of type are placed.

baseline alignment — see *base alignment.*

baseline deflection — in typesetting, a change in the vertical alignment of characters. Not all systems can do this in the middle of a line.

baseline to baseline (b-b) — the distance between lines of type. With *cold type*, it is often referred to as the *leading*, but on the older *hot type* systems, the baseline-to-baseline distance includes leading plus the type *body size*.

b-b — see *baseline-to-baseline*.

Bezier — a type of curve often used for specifying type outlines and in some computer-aided design (CAD) and drawing programs. A Bezier curve is defined by specifying four control points that set the shape of the curve, but the points do not necessarily lie directly on the curve itself.

bf — an abbreviation for *boldface*. The abbreviation is seen in type specifications and as a proofreader's mark.

bitmap — a type of graphic format in which the image is made up of a large number of tiny dots arranged on a closely spaced *grid*.

block — as a style for text layout, set with no indentations (but usually with extra spacing between paragraphs).

block letter — a letter created with equal *stroke weights* (widths of the lines) and simple curves.

body — **1.** in typesetting, the unit that carries each character of type. While on traditional *hot type* (metal type) this was the actual piece of lead alloy, for *cold type* (photographic type) this is an imaginary box surrounding the character image. **2.** the main text on a page or on a spread of several pages.

body height — **1.** the height of the main part of the average lowercase letter in a particular font, not counting any *ascenders* or *descenders*. Also called the *x-height*. **2.** the baseline-to-baseline distance for a font of type without any added spacing. In older *hot type* (metal type), it was the size of the actual metal pieces on which the type was cast.

body size — **1.** *body height*. **2.** the total height reserved for each line of a particular *typeface*. For *cold type* (photographic type), it is the size of an imaginary reference box around each letter, while for *hot type* (metal type) it is the size of the actual piece of metal. Body size is normally measured in *points* (the printer's measure of size equal to approximately ½₂ inch).

body type — **1.** the type used for the main text of a piece of typeset material. Some *typefaces* are designed for this use and are more readable for longer runs of text. **2.** a type that is commonly used for text. Generally, this means type up to 14 *points* in size.

bold — short for *boldface*.

boldface — printing done in a similar style to standard letters, but made to appear darker, with thicker, more pronounced strokes. Most *typestyles* have a companion bold face. Boldface is used for emphasis and for adding visual mass to a section of type. Sometimes written as "bold face."

boldline — a text format that puts the first line of each paragraph in *boldface*, often in *all caps* (capital letters).

border — a line or repeating ornamental element used to edge or outline a section of type or artwork.

bounding box — in photographic or electronic composition, the imaginary rectangle around each letter or graphic element, used to set the spacing and align the characters.

bowl — a circular part of a letter, such as the rounded bottom of the letter *b*.

bracketed serif — a *serif* (perpendicular or angled line ending) that meets the main stroke in a curve.

broken rule — **1.** a dashed line. **2.** a border made up of short parallel lines running at right angles to the direction of the border. Also called *coin edge*.

bullet — **1.** the round dot (•). It is used in typeset material mainly to introduce items in a list. **2.** because a true bullet character is not available on standard typewriters and many computer printers, a small letter *o* or asterisk is sometimes used in place of a bullet.

calligraphic letters — letters that are meant to look like handwritten script or fancy hand lettering.

camera-ready — referring especially to the output of word processing programs, text formatters, *typesetters* and other devices, pages that are output in a form ready for reproduction.

cap height — the distance from the *baseline* to the imaginary line connecting the tops of the capital letters in a particular type *font*.

cap line — the imaginary line connecting the tops of the capital letters in a particular type *font*. Depending on the *typeface* design, it may or may not be equal to the *ascender line* connecting the top of the *ascenders*.

caps and small caps — a style of lettering that shows capital letters in their normal form, and what would ordinarily be lowercase letters as capital letters of a slightly smaller size. Also called *c&sc*.

card — to add small amounts of vertical space between the lines of typeset material.

case — as applied to the letters of the alphabet, whether the letters are capital (upper case) or small letters (lower case). The term comes from where the letters were stored in the past when typesetting was done with cases of individual pieces of metal type. The upper case, in one of the more common arrangements, held the capital letters, the lower case the small ones.

casting off — the calculation of the expected length of material when it is to be set in type. It is usually done either by actually counting words or characters or by counting a sample and then using that as a multiplier for estimating the total.

center — in *markup* (instruction to the person setting type) and proofreading, the instruction to center type or other design elements.

character count — **1.** the number of characters on a line. It is used to estimate the total number of lines or pages that will be occupied by text of a given number of characters. **2.** referring to a specific *typeface*, the average number of characters per *pica* (⅙ inch).

character set — the set of letters, punctuation marks and other symbols that can be displayed by a monitor, printer, phototypesetter or other device. Different *fonts* may have different character sets.

cicero — a European unit measurement for type and layout. At 4.55 mm, a cicero is slightly larger than a *pica*.

c&lc — short for *caps* and *lower case*, an instruction for how material should be formatted. In this style, which is commonly used for headlines, the initial letter of each important word is set in caps, the rest in lower case.

close up — (pronounced cloze up) the proofreader's instruction to reduce the amount of space between words, either in general (to "tighten up the line") or at a specific marked point.

code — referring to automated typesetting, an instruction that tells the typesetting system what size and style of letters to use and how to format the output. Different brands of equipment use different codes.

coin edge — a *broken rule*.

cold type — type produced by photographic, xerographic, *strike-on* (impact) or similar methods rather than by arranging strings of metal characters (which are formed by metal casting and are therefore called *hot type*).

column rule — a vertical line, usually rather thin, used to separate columns of type.

compositor — a person, company or machine that sets type.

condensed — a style of type that occupies less than the normal width. Traditionally, *typefaces* have been designed as families, including a normal and a condensed style (and in some cases an *expanded* style that uses more space than normal). Many recent electronic systems do not use separate condensed faces, but instead produce them by squeezing the corresponding normal type.

copy — in publishing and typesetting, text that is to appear in the piece being produced.

cross stroke — **1.** a smaller line segment of a character or other graphic figure that meets a main segment at close to a right angle. **2.** a horizontal part of a character or other graphic figure.

c&sc — an abbreviation for *caps and small caps*.

cursive — *typefaces* that resemble script handwriting, with connected strokes and curved lines. Cursive faces are used to add a touch of formality or artistry to printed pieces such as invitations and announcements. But since many of the characters must come in several forms to connect their beginning and end strokes with adjacent characters, they are more difficult to use.

cut-in head — a headline, subhead or other title element in text that is placed within the normal text area. Cut-in heads are normally *left-aligned*, larger and often bolder than normal text.

cut-in letter — a much larger letter used to start a block of text, and placed within the top corner of the text block area. It is also called an *initial* or *drop cap*.

GLOSSARY

descender — **1.** a part of a letter that extends below the main *body*, as in the tails of the small *y, g* and *j*. **2.** a letter that extends below the *baseline*, such as the *y*.

diacritic or diacritical mark — an accent or other element added above, below or occasionally alongside a letter to indicate a difference in pronunciation. These include the umlaut (ü), ague (é) and cedilla (ç).

dictionary — **1.** a list of exceptions to the rule set used for the *hyphenation* or spelling-checking routines in a typesetting system. **2.** for a spelling-checking program, a list of words that are to be considered acceptable. Dictionaries may be stored in compressed form, which saves space but causes occasional mistaken matches, or in literal form.

dingbat — a small, decorative icon or symbol, such as a star or *bullet*.

discretionary hyphen — a special hyphen character placed in word processing and typesetting files that marks where the word may be broken with a hyphen at the end of a line. If the word doesn't need to be broken there, the hyphen is not printed. Also called *ghost hyphen*.

display type — larger type than used for the text of a piece of work. Depending on the circumstances, this would typically be type of 18 points (¼ inch) or larger.

double up — to set a block of type in two sections to be placed side by side. This method is sometimes used when a block is too wide for the capabilities of a particular typesetting system.

downloadable fonts — *typefaces* supplied in software form that are loaded into a computer system, and then sent to a printer, *typesetter* or other output device as needed.

downstyle — using lower case, particularly for material that is normally set in upper and lower case or all upper case.

dummy — **1.** a mock-up of a project, made either for planning and approval purposes or to serve as instructions to the *typesetter*. **2.** especially in the newspaper industry, a rough or semi-rough layout of a page used for planning.

em — **1.** a square unit with a width equal to the current *point* size (height of the line of type). It gets its name from the letter *M*, which is usually about as wide as the type size. Em measures are most often seen as specifying the width of a column or the size of an indentation. **2.** a space character with a width equal to the height of a capital letter of type. Also called *em quad*.

embedded — **1.** referring to output formatting commands, commands for the printer or ones that are included within the regular text, rather than specified in a separate file or by direct keyboard commands. **2.** referring to interfaces for disk and tape drives, built into the device rather than supplied as an add-on or separate card.

em dash — a dash that is one em long (equal in length to the type size, or about the same width as a letter *M*). Also called an *em rule*.

em quad — see *em*.

em rule — see *em dash*.

en — **1.** the printer's unit of measurement half as wide as the current line size. It gets its name from the width of the letter *N*, which is commonly about half as wide as a capital letter is high. En measures are most frequently seen in specifications for the length of dashes and *rules* (lines), and for spacing. **2.** a space character with a width half the current *point* size. Also called *en quad* or *en space*.

en quad — see *en*.

en space — see *en*.

exception dictionary — in *automatic hyphenation*, a list of words that do not follow the rules the system uses for breaking words and inserting hyphens.

expanded — a style of type that takes more than the normal amount of width. The style may be used for emphasis or for fitting copy to larger spaces. Many recent electronic systems do not use separate expanded faces, but instead produce them by elongating the corresponding normal type characters. Also called *extended*.

extended — see *expanded*.

extended character set — a typeface or set of characters that includes additional characters beyond the *ASCII character set* used on most computers and printers.

extra bold — type that uses even heavier and darker strokes than *boldface*, and therefore is much darker than the normal medium type. Some *typefaces* are designed with extra bold *weights*, but many electronic composition systems can create a synthetic one on request.

face — short for *typeface*, a collection of letters and other characters in a given style.

family — a group of variations on the same basic *typeface*, such as *fonts* with a range of *weights* (character thicknesses, such as normal *medium* face, *boldface, light*), *posture* (slant, such as *roman* and *italic*) and various other parameters. Some electronic composition systems can create an entire family from a single basic pattern, but purists insist that each must be designed individually for best appearance.

fifth generation — for typesetting equipment, a unit with direct electronic formation of the image, such as a laser printer.

figure — **1.** a numeral (character symbol for a digit). **2.** an illustration or chart, particularly one identified by number or sequence from within the text.

figure alignment — the way the bottom of a series of numbers line up. The two most common are *lining*, which keeps a common baseline, and *oldstyle*, which allows some digits to have descenders.

figure space — a space equal in width to a numeric figure (usually an *en*, which is half the *point* size in width). It is used to line up columns of figures.

fillet — a round corner connecting a *serif* (ornamental cross stroke) to a letter on *oldstyle* types.

film — as applied to typographic output, a special photosensitive material used to create an image on transparent material.

fl or FL — an abbreviation for *flush left*, the *markup* instruction to align a block of text along the left margin.

flag — the stylized name of a newspaper or publication shown on page one. The masthead, however, is the listing of the personnel and business information often given on the editorial page, the table of contents or some other inside page. Also called the nameplate.

floret — an ornamental typographic element resembling a flower.

flush — **1.** referring to the formatting of text and illustrations, to align with a specific reference line. Unless otherwise stated, the line is the left margin. **2.** to clean out buffers (temporary holding areas) or memory in preparation for a program halt or switch.

flush left (fl) — material aligned along the left margin, or an instruction to align material that way. Flush left is the normal style for handwriting and typewriting, and is often used for typeset material with either *ragged* (uneven) or *justified* (equal length) lines.

flush paragraph — a paragraph that starts with no additional indentation. Sometimes called *block* style.

flush right — material aligned along a right margin, or an instruction to line up material that way. Occasionally, lines of text will be set flush right for ornamental use, but in this culture it is considered harder to read.

font — **1.** traditionally, a complete set of the characters in one *typeface, style* and *size*. **2.** in many electronic systems that can create derivative images (such as different *sizes* and *weights*) from a single set of stored characters, an overall family of letter designs (which, traditionally, is called a *family*).

font cartridge — for a printer or other output device, a plug-in shell containing memory chips that hold outlines for a *font* or *family* of fonts.

font metric — a series of numbers describing the width and proper spacing for each character in a font. These metrics are used by the layout program for planning the page and by the printer for executing it.

font substitution — during output of a page, the replacement of a specified *font* (*typeface*) by a similar available font.

footline — **1.** the last line on a page, often used for a page number or running title. **2.** a repeating line at the bottom of a series of pages, often containing the publication name and date or issue.

foundry type — metal type that has been cast in individual pieces meant for reuse. It is made of harder material than the lead alloy used for *linecast* ("Linotype") type.

fractional kerning — a feature on some page layout programs that allows the user to specify the spacing between characters in portions of the basic *units* used for character widths.

full flush — material formatted to be even with both margins (left- and right-*justified*).

full measure — in typesetting, a line set to the entire line length.

galley — **1.** a copy of typeset material, arranged in columns instead of made up into pages. Galleys are the normal output of typesetting systems that do not allow page makeup during typesetting, and of *hot-type* (metal type). **2.** traditionally, the first round of proofreading is done on galleys, so any preliminary copy of typeset material furnished for proofing is sometimes called a galley.

generation — the number of reproduction steps that an image is removed from the original (which is the first generation). In general, higher generation images are likely to be less sharp.

ghost hyphen — another term for a *discretionary hyphen*.

gimcrack — a small decorative typographic symbol.

glossary — in some typesetting programs, a list of phrases or blocks of text that can be called up and inserted in text using shorter abbreviations or special key sequences.

gothic — **1.** a group of *typefaces* with no *serifs* and broad, even strokes. News Gothic is perhaps the best-known. **2.** particularly in Britain, a type classification of ornate letters based on medieval forms that here would be called black-letter or Old English.

greek — **1.** to show placeholder patterns instead of letters at small typesizes during layout, preview or even *dummy* output. **2.** to use a symbol, outline or box in place of a picture as a placeholder during layout, preview or even *dummy* output. *Picture greeking* is offered as an option to speed display on some page layout programs. **3.** to place nonsense text (or sometimes greek letters that simulate text) in a design as a placeholder for text that will be added later.

grid — **1.** a set of reference lines and points used to specify where dots can be placed to make up *bitmap* characters for display on-screen or on a printer. **2.** in page layout, a reference pattern of lines or boxes used as the underlying framework for the page design, but that is not printed in the final copy. **3.** on a phototypesetting machine, the reference copy of each character the machine uses to expose the *film*.

hairline — **1.** the thinnest *rule* (line) available on a system or in a *font*. **2.** a thin defect in a letter, often noticed only as a sense of fuzzy type rather than as a specific break. **3.** in a type style with various width strokes, the thinnest of the strokes.

hair space — in *hot type* (metal type), an extremely thin space used to make fine adjustments. Now, generally used for fine spaces added to typeset material.

hanging figures — a style of numerals often used with older *typestyles* that had parts of certain digits extending below the *baseline*. More modern typefaces instead use *lining figures*, which look cleaner because they all line up at the baseline. Also called *oldstyle*.

hanging indent — a style for setting text paragraphs where the first line is set to the full column width but succeeding lines are indented — the reverse of the normal procedure that indents the first line. Hanging indents are commonly used for lists, dictionaries and bibliographies. Also called *outdent*.

hanging punctuation — punctuation that carries over into the normal margins instead of staying entirely within the edges of the type area. Hanging punctuation, if done well, is often considered more elegant because it keeps a more even visual edge on blocks of text.

hard hyphen — a hyphen that is meant to be shown whether it would fall in the middle of a line or at the line end.

hard return — a carriage return (end of line character) that is always used to break a block of text, rather than one used to end a line only at the current text width.

hard space — **1.** a space that is always shown as indicated, rather than expanded or contracted to make lines fit the space. **2.** a space that is treated as a printing character rather than a break between words. Most systems will not end a line at a hard space. Sometimes called a *nonbreaking space*.

hint — as applied to digital *typefaces,* additional information encoded with an *outline font* to guide the placement of dots when the outline is turned into a *bitmap*. Hints are especially needed at small sizes, where there are few available dot positions and simple rounding may not produce very good-looking characters.

h&j — see *hyphenation and justification*.

hot type — metal type. (It is called hot type because it is produced by melting the metal and then casting it into characters). Increasingly, hot type technologies have been replaced by *cold type* methods, which use photographic or electronic processes to create an image.

hot zone — in typesetting and word-processing programs, a range of characters where the system will look for a place to break a line between words.

hyphenation — in speaking of a computerized *typesetting* or word-processing system, the process of breaking up words that are too long to fit on a line by adding hyphens at the correct spot. On the simplest system, the word that must be broken is displayed, and the user must supply the hyphen. On more sophisticated systems, hyphenation is done automatically by applying a set of standard rules followed by a check against an exception dictionary. While a good hyphenation program with a large *exception dictionary* can correctly hyphenate in most instances, it will still miss a small proportion of words.

hyphenation and justification (h&j) — the process of setting text into lines and adding any needed codes and hyphens to make the words fit.

imagesetter — a high-resolution system for creating page images on *paper, film* or other material.

imaging area — the area in which an output device can place a mark, most often expressed as the bounds of a rectangle. On most electronic printing and imaging devices, this is smaller than the full sheet of paper, resulting in a "live area" or print area smaller than the page size.

initial — a letter larger than the normal text size, used to start a paragraph, chapter or section. Initials may be plain or ornate, and extending above the line (raised) or below (dropped).

italic — **1.** a typestyle designed to reflect some of the elements of handwritten script. Italic *typefaces* slope top to the right and have rounded lines (but not all tilted typefaces are italic). Material that would be set in italic in printed material is underlined in typewritten material (and similarly, the proofreader's mark indicating text to be set in italics is a single underline). **2.** on many electronic *typesetting* systems, a mathematically-synthesized *oblique* (slanted) version of a standard *font* used as the italic equivalent.

jaggies — a colloquial term for the jagged edges formed on the normal (*raster scan*) screen display or low-resolution printer when diagonal lines are displayed. The effect can be minimized with various antialiasing strategies.

jump — **1.** in typesetting, a change in *baseline* (horizontal reference line for character alignment). **2.** in page layout, to break a story and continue it on another page.

justify — **1.** to align text or other page elements along a margin, or along two margins. In normal practice, text is always left justified (lined up evenly at the left margin), but typeset material is often both left and right justified. Typewritten materials and letters and other informal documents are usually left justified, but ragged (nonjustified) on the right. When neither side is specified, justification usually refers to full justification (both left and right sides).

kern — **1.** the process of decreasing the space in certain letter combinations (such as *Ta*) that look better when part of one letter sticks out into the other letter's space. Most computerized *typesetting* systems can kern letters on command, and many automatically kern specified letter combinations. **2.** the part of a letter that hangs over beyond the space normally given to that character (for example, in some *typestyles* the tail of the *y* reaches back under the previous character). **3.** more informally, to decrease the amount of space between all characters, which more properly is called *tracking*.

kerning pair — two characters for which the inter-character spacing should be reduced below the standard amount.

key — **1.** a drawing or tracing showing where the different colors should be used on a multicolor printing job. **2.** to identify specific sections to be typeset by tagging them with a letter or number.

leader — connecting lines made up of dots, dashes or some other character used to tie together parts of a composite element. One commonly-seen use is in the phone book, where a dot leader is often used to connect the subscriber name or address to the phone number.

lead-in — **1.** the beginning words of a section of text or a caption. The words are often set in a larger *type size* or in bold to attract the reader's eye. **2.** a style of text formatting that emphasizes the first words of a block of text with larger characters, *boldface* or other special treatment.

leading — (from the name of the metal, so pronounced "led"). **1.** originally, with metal type, extra spacing between lines provided by inserting strips of lead in standard sizes (certain *point sizes*). **2.** often used for the extra space added between lines on electronic and photographic typesetting. **3.** although strictly speaking, leading is the amount added on top of the *body size* of the type, with phototypesetting systems the term is often used for the total *baseline-to-baseline* distance, including the spacing used by the type.

left align — to line up characters, blocks of text or other graphic elements on the left side.

letterspacing — the addition of small spaces between letters within words to make the total line length come out to a desired value.

ligature — **1.** a combination of two (or more) letters, treated as a single unit for typesetting. Many *fonts* support ligatures for *fi, fl* and other similar overhanging combinations. **2.** strictly speaking, the ligature is the actual connection between two characters, but common usage applies it to the character combinations rather than the added connecting lines, which are now often omitted.

light or lightface — *typestyles* that use strokes that are thinner or not as dark as the standard (medium) *typeface*. Light types are not as frequently used as mediums or bolds, but many electronic typesetting systems can produce a synthesized light face on request.

linecaster — a machine that casts lines of type into *slugs* (lines) of metal. The best known brand is the Linotype.

line length — the horizontal size of a line of type, usually specified in *picas* (6 picas to an inch).

lining figures — see *aligning figures*.

logo or logotype — **1.** a drawing, symbol or icon used as if it were a single element of type. **2.** commonly used as a synonym for a trademark, especially one made up of a stylized collection of letters.

lowercase — letters other than capitals.

marking engine — the part of a printer that actually puts the dots or lines on the paper.

markup — adding of directions, formats or control codes needed by a particular typographic or page layout program or system.

matrix — **1.** referring to *hot* (metal) *type*, a mold used to form characters. **2.** the array of possible dot positions used to form characters on a video display or printer. **3.** on a phototypesetting system, a set of photographic images containing the character set or font being used.

medium — a standard *weight* (darkness or line thickness), rather than a *light* or *bold* style.

metal type — printing type formed out of case metal characters. The two principal varieties are *foundry type*, which is cast as individual characters and then combined to make lines and pages; and *linecaster* type, which is molded into complete lines or *slugs* containing the desired text, used and then melted down again.

modern — in speaking of *typestyles*, refers not to our current age but to what was modern in the early nineteenth century. Modern *typefaces* are some of the most commonly used text faces, including such well-known styles as Times Roman and Bodoni. Typically, modern faces have good contrast between thick and thin strokes, and thin, straight *serifs*.

monopitch — see *monospaced*.

monospaced — referring to type, a style in which all characters take up the same amount of horizontal space. For example, an *M* takes the same space as an *i*. Although most typewritten material is monospaced, almost all typeset material uses *proportional spacing*. Also called *monopitched*.

mutt — a typesetter's term for the *em space*. It's claimed that *mutt* and *nut* are easier to distinguish than *em* and *en*.

negative — as applied to typographic images, showing white or transparent images on a black background.

nonbreaking space — a *hard space*.

nut — the printer's term for the *en space*. See *mutt*.

oblique — referring to type, styles that have their principal axis at an angle to the vertical. *Italics* are the most commonly seen oblique variety, but not all oblique *typefaces* are italics.

OCR — short for *optical character recognition*, the process of reading typed or printed characters. The data is read by an optical scanner as it passes under a photoelectric device and is recorded on a magnetic tape or disk.

OCR-B — a printing *typeface* designed both for machine reading and for easy human readability.

oldstyle — **1.** a broad family of *typefaces* characterized by wide, round letters, fairly even line widths and sloping *serifs*. Some of the better known oldstyle faces include Caslon and Garamond. **2.** referring to numerals, a style that allows some digits to have *descenders* or variations in body height (in contrast to *lining figures*, which are all the same height and sit on the *baseline*).

on — in typography, the size of the total space from one line to the next, including the type and any additional *leading* (spacing). For example, 10 point type with 2 points of extra leading is referred to as "10 on 12."

open — **1.** a noticeably large amount of space between letters, words or other typographic elements. **2.** too much space between elements. **3.** as applied to *font* and typographic systems, built around published specifications available to any manufacturer who chooses to compete.

outdent — a *hanging indent*.

orphan — a *widow*.

outline font — a *font* (collection of characters) in which the character forms are described as geometric shapes or paths rather than as *bitmaps* (collections of individual points). When the characters are needed for screen display or printing, they are converted to the most appropriate bitmaps for each display device.

pack — to encode characters into other characters or bit patterns so they will occupy less space, or to make them compatible with a particular communications link.

page description language (PDL) — a computer language for describing how text and graphics should be placed on a page for display or printing. Most are meant to be generated by computer programs and read by printers, without direct human intervention. The best-known example is the *PostScript* language.

page layout — a class of computer programs that help the user arrange text and graphic images on pages.

paper — as applied to typographic output, the special photosensitive material used in most *imagesetter* systems. In most cases, the output is black on white (*positive* image) on opaque material. This is in contrast to *film*, for which the image is usually *negative* and the background transparent.

PCL — short for *Printer Control Language*, a standard printer language developed by Hewlett-Packard for sending information to their printers.

phototype — **1.** character images produced by photographic processes. **2.** specifically, type created by flashing light through photographic negatives of the desired characters.

pica — a printer's measure approximately equal to ⅙ inch.

pi characters — special characters that are not part of the normal character set or font, but that are added for special text. Typical examples include mathematical symbols or special accents.

point — **1.** a printer's measure, particularly of vertical distance on a page. One point is equal to 1/12 *pica* and approximately equal to 1/72 inch. It is most often used to indicate the size of type. **2.** for paper thickness, 1/1000 inch.

positive — as applied to typographic images, showing dark characters on a white or transparent background.

PostScript — **1.** a trademark of Adobe Systems, Inc. for the firm's *page description language (PDL)* used to describe images and type in a machine-independent form. **2.** used loosely to refer to the interpreter program that translates PostScript language files to the actual sequences of machine operations needed to produce the output image.

PostScript-compatible — the term for printers, fonts or output products that work with *PostScript* language files but are not licensed by Adobe Systems, Inc.

PostScript interpreter — a program built into a printer or run as a utility that converts page descriptions in the *PostScript* language to the actual dots needed for printing or display on-screen.

PostScript printer — a printer that includes a built-in interpreter (translator) for the *PostScript* page description language (PDL).

PostScript Type 1 — an outline font format specified by Adobe Systems, Inc. It includes both compression (to make the files smaller) and *hinting* (to provide better dot placement at small type sizes). Originally, Adobe considered this format proprietary and encrypted the information as well.

PostScript Type 3 — an outline font format specified by Adobe Systems, Inc. that includes the character shapes but no additional *hinting* or compression.

posture — referring to the style of type, whether upright (such as *roman* styles) or *oblique* (such as *italics*).

proportional characters, proportional spacing — characters designed so that some characters, such as *m*, take up more horizontal space than others, such as *i*. Proportional characters pack more information into the same space, are easier to read and look more like traditional typesetting than do constant-width *monospaced* fonts.

ragged — said of type where the successive lines do not all start or end at the same position. When not otherwise specified, ragged lines are only ragged on the right while *flush* (even) on the left.

range — on a typesetting system, the set of sizes available.

raster image processor (RIP) — a device or program that translates the instructions for an output page in a *page description language (PDL)* or graphics output language to the actual pattern of dots supplied to a printing or display system. Also called a *rasterizer*.

rasterizer — a *raster image processor*.

regularize — to smooth the shape of a letterform before converting it into outline format.

resolution — **1.** in typesetting, the size of the smallest change that can be accurately controlled or noted. Used mostly in conjunction with digital *typesetters*, which construct each character from bit patterns in memory. A finer resolution means smoother, sharper characters. **2.** for graphics output particularly, *spatial resolution* (how closely packed are the spots making up an image), measured in dots or lines per inch. **3.** for displays, the output density (in dots or pixels per inch). **4.** the *video resolution* (measured in horizontal lines across the largest square that can be fit on screen). **5.** the *color resolution* (measured in the number of colors in the palette or the number available on screen at any one time).

reverse — **1.** to change the tonal orientation of an image, making the darker elements lighter and the lighter darker. Note that to reverse the spatial orientation of an image is known as flopping or reflecting the image. **2.** short for reverse print, a print that inverts the black and white areas from the image used to make it.

reverse leading — a displacement of a line of type back towards the top of the page to tighten up vertical spaces, for special effects or to start a second column. This type of movement is possible only on electronic or phototypesetting systems.

right-aligned — said of a block or line of type that is lined up even with the right margin.

RIP — (pronounced rip) short for *raster image processor*.

roman — **1.** the style of letters with upright main stems, in contrast to *italics* and other *oblique* letters that have stems set at angles. Roman types are the standard variety in most Western languages. **2.** a class of *typestyles* based on the lettering style used by Roman scribes. These *fonts* have good contrast between strokes and pointed *serifs*. Some of the more popular styles include Garamond and Century.

rules — vertical or horizontal lines on a page.

runaround — the adjustment of the length of successive lines of type so they fit around an illustration. Sometimes called a *wraparound*.

sans serif — *typestyles* that do not have *serifs* (extra lines or embellishments at the end of the main strokes making up the characters). These are often more modern-looking than faces that do have serifs (note that *modern* is used to refer to some older types), but many people find them hard to read in large blocks of text. Also referred to as *gothic*.

scale — **1.** to change in size proportionately. **2.** the amount by which an image should be enlarged or reduced. **3.** as applied to type, to change in size and adjust the resulting character forms to fit the new size.

screen font — a file that tells the computer how to form characters for on-screen display. Screen-font characters are *bitmaps*, formed as patterns of dots at the screen resolution of 72 dots per inch.

series — the complete size range of a *typeface*.

serif — **1.** a small cross-stroke or ornament at the end of the main strokes making up a character. Most older types have serifs, and many people find types with serifs easier to read. **2.** *typestyles* that have these segments.

set — **1.** to produce text in typographic form. **2.** the way a block of text is formatted in type, such as *flush, ragged, solid* or *tight*.

set size — the width of a block of type of a given *typeface, style* and *point* size (height). Types with wider set sizes take up more room for the same content.

set solid — type formatted with no *leading* (extra space) between the lines.

showing — a display of the various type *fonts* and ornamental elements available from a type compositor system.

side bearing — the blank area to each side of a letterform used to set the spacing between characters.

slug — **1.** a line of metal type. **2.** in *hot type, leading* (vertical spacing material) 6 points or more in height. **3.** an identification line showing which story a section of copy or typeset material belongs to. Slugs are usually placed at the top corner of submitted copy, and the top line of any *galleys*.

small caps — a set of specially designed capital letters equal in size to what normally would be the lowercase letters for that *typesize* and *style*. Small caps are normally used in *caps and small caps* formats in place of lowercase letters.

soft font — **1.** a *font* (set of character shapes) distributed in the form of a software program or data file on disk rather than built into a chip, cartridge or printer. **2.** particularly, a software font formatted for loading into one of Hewlett-Packard's LaserJet printers.

soft hyphen — another term for *discretionary hyphen*.

soft return — a line ending used only for that particular column width but not a permanent part of the copy that would indicate the end of a paragraph.

solid — see *set solid*.

sort — a printing character. An old *typesetter's* term.

Sp — proofreader's symbol for "spell out" (as applied to figures and abbreviations).

spaceband — on a Linotype or other *linecaster*, a variable-width space that expands if needed to make a line *flush* (even with both left and right margins).

spec — to determine the format, size and other typographic characteristics for a block of text.

square serif — a group of *typefaces* that have *serifs* of the same thickness as the main strokes. This includes faces such as Barnum and Helleni, as well as many typewriter faces.

squeeze — to set type closer together than normal.

stem — the main vertical stroke (or one of the main vertical strokes) making up a character. For example, the central vertical stroke in the letter *T*.

stereotype — a curved printing plate made by pouring metal or plastic into a mold made from raised type. These types of plates are used on high-speed rotary presses, such as those used to print newspapers and magazines.

straight matter — material to set in type that is only text, with no headlines, tables or other material requiring special formatting.

straight quotes — the characters "and '. They are used in most computer languages to mark the start and end of literal values or strings. However, text material looks better with *typographic quotes* (" and " or ' and '). The double straight quote is also used as an inch mark. The single straight quote is also used as a foot mark.

strike-on — typesetting methods that use impact printing, particularly ones that use fully-formed characters such as those produced by the IBM Selectric family.

stroke weight — in speaking of the lines, curves and shapes that make up graphics and letter forms, the width or darkness of that element.

style — as applied to characters or blocks of type, characteristics that do not alter the basic *font*, including posture (such as *roman* or *italic*) and weight (such as *light*, *medium* or *bold*). **2.** as applied to blocks of type, the case (*upper*, *lower* or *caps and small caps*), justification (*full*, *ragged*) and similar design choices.

swash letter — **1.** an ornamental letterform used particularly at the beginning of chapters or sections. **2.** strictly speaking, an *italic* letter with extra flourishes used for that purpose.

symbol set — the set of characters, numbers and special symbols included in an electronic *font*.

tail — **1.** a downward-sloping part of a letter, such as the lower arm of the *K* or *R*. **2.** a *descender*, particular one with a curve at the end as in the letters *y* or *g*.

text type — *typestyles* and *sizes* used for the main text of written material. Generally, this means type of 14 points or less in size, and in one of the more readable *typefaces*.

thin space — the thinnest space normally used to separate words or other typographic elements (not counting the *hair space*, which is normally used within elements or in combinations). It is usually the same width as the period.

throughput — for typographic systems, the amount of type produced in a specified amount of time. For most electronic and photographic *imagesetters*, it is usually given in inches per second or lines per minute.

tight — said of lines having very little space between words (or other elements). Good typography requires that lines be neither too tight nor too loose.

top alignment — a mode available on some typesetting systems that lines up characters by their top reference points.

tracking — decreasing the amount of space between letters over a selected range of characters.

true color — **1.** systems in which the color information in the image is used directly to create the output color rather than as an index to a table of colors in a palette. **2.** said of color systems that have enough available colors to make the choices seem contiguous to the human eye. In most cases, this is considered to be 24-bit color (about 16 million available colors).

TrueType — the font technology selected by Apple and Microsoft for generating screen and printer fonts from outlines.

Type 1 — see *PostScript Type 1.*

Type 3 — see *PostScript Type 3.*

typeface — a complete set of characters in a particular design or *style*. Typefaces are the basis for families of fonts with different *weights* (such as *light, medium* and *bold*), different *point sizes* and different postures (such as *roman, italic* or other *oblique*).

typesetter — **1.** a machine or computerized system for setting type. **2.** a person or company that sets type.

type size — the height of the area reserved for each letter of type. For *hot type,* it is the size of the type *body,* while for *cold type* it is the height of the imaginary *bounding box* around each letter used to align the type.

typestyle — the particular format or variation on a basic type design, such as *italic* versus *roman* or *bold* versus *medium.*

typographer — **1.** a person who designs or specifies type. **2.** a person or company that sets material in type.

typographic quotes — the characters *"*and *"*or *'*and *'.* They are preferable to the s*traight quotes* (*"*and *'*) when used for text material, but most computer languages only use the straight quotes. The typographic quotes are not included in the normal *ASCII* coding scheme used on most small computers, but most systems offer them as part of their *extended character sets.*

typography — **1.** the art of design with type. **2.** the design of a particular typeset piece.

u&lc — a common abbreviation for *upper and lower case.*

unit — the term many typesetting systems use for their smallest possible increments in the size and width of characters. Typically, this might range from a few dozen to a few thousand *units* per inch.

upper and lower case — the format often used for titles and headlines that starts each significant word with an *uppercase* letter but otherwise uses *lowercase.*

vertex — a point at which two strokes in a character meet to form a point, particularly one at the bottom (such as in the letter *V*).

weight — when applied to type and lettering, the boldness or thickness of a letter or *font*. Many *typestyles* have been designed with special *light, medium* and *bold* forms. However, on most computer systems the various weights can also be created as electronic variations of a single design.

w.f. or wf — an abbreviation for *wrong font.*

widow — a single word on a line or a line split off from its paragraph.

widow and orphan control — a feature of some word-processing and *page layout* programs that automatically moves line breaks to minimize cases where a break creates a *widow* or *orphan* (a single word on a line or a line split off from its paragraph).

word spacing — the practice of putting sufficient space between adjacent words to fill out a line or create an attractively spaced image.

wrong font — the proofreader's marking for one or more characters typeset in the wrong *typestyle* or size. Most commonly seen as the abbreviation *wf* or *w.f.*

WYSIWYG — abbreviation for "what you see is what you get." An expression characterizing computer programs or systems that show you on-screen what you will get as the output on paper, complete with correct line breaks, *typestyles,* pagination and other formatting.

X — a symbol for line length or column width used in marking copy for typesetting. Unless otherwise specified, the number following the X is the desired width in *picas* (the printer's measure approximately equal to ⅙ inch).

x-height — the size of a small letter *x,* which is also normally the height of the main body of the lowercase letters excluding *ascenders* and *descenders.* Also called the *body height.*

Resources

This appendix lists software, hardware and other resources of use to artists working with digital typography. The resources are grouped in categories in the following order:

Fonts

Font Design and Font Manipulation

PostScript Illustration Software

Page Layout Programs

Paint Programs

Image-Processing Software

Draw Programs

3D Programs

Clip Art

Graphics Tablets

Scanners

Storage Systems

Monitors

Color Calibration

Accelerators

Utilities, Desk Accessories and INITs

Prepress Systems

Printers and Imagesetters

Large-Format Output Services

Film Recorders

Periodicals

Books

Bulletin Board Services

Communication Software

Fonts

Adobe Type Library
Adobe Systems, Inc.
PO Box 7900
Mountain View, CA 94039-7900
800-344-8335

**Bitstream fonts and
Fontware Installation Kit**
Bitstream, Inc.
215 First Street
Cambridge, MA 02142
800-522-3668

CG Type
Agfa Compugraphic Corporation
90 Industrial Way
Wilmington, MA 01887
800-424-8973

**Corel Headline, Corel Loader,
Corel Newfont**
Corel Systems Corporation
1600 Carling Avenue, Suite 190
Ottawa, ON K1Z 8R7 Canada
613-728-8200

Em Dash Fonts
Em Dash
PO Box 8256
Northfield, IL 60093
708-441-6699

Fluent Laser Fonts
Casady & Greene, Inc.
22734 Portola Drive
Salinas, CA 93908
800-359-4920

Font Factory Fonts (for LaserJet)
The Font Factory
13601 Preston Road, Suite 500-W
Dallas, TX 75240
214-239-6085

FontGen IV Plus
VS Software
PO Box 165920
Little Rock, AR 72216
501-376-2083

Font Haus
15 Perry Avenue, Suite A8
Norwalk, CT 06850
800-942-9110

Font Solution Pack
SoftCraft, Inc.
16 N. Carroll Street, Suite 500
Madison, WI 53703
608-257-3300

**Hewlett-Packard Soft Fonts
(for LaserJet)**
Hewlett-Packard Company
PO Box 60008
Sunnyvale, CA 94088-60008
800-538-8787

Hot Type
Image Club Graphics Inc.
1902 11th Street S.E., Suite 5
Calgary, AB T2G 3G2 Canada
800-661-9410

**Kingsley/ATF typefaces
(ATF Classic type)**
Type Corporation
2559-2 E. Broadway
Tucson, AZ 85716
800-289-8973

Laser fonts and font utilities
SoftCraft, Inc.
16 N. Carroll Street, Suite 500
Madison, WI 53703
800-351-0500

Laserfonts
Century Software/MacTography
326-D N. Stonestreet Avenue
Rockville, MD 20850
301-424-1357

Monotype fonts
Monotype Typography, Inc.
53 W. Jackson Boulevard, Suite 504
Chicago, IL 60604
800-666-6897

Ornate Typefaces
Ingrimayne Software
PO Box 404
Rensselaer, IN 47978
219-866-6241

Treacyfaces Typeface Collection
Treacyfaces, Inc.
111 Sibley Avenue
Ardmore, PA 19003
215-896-0860

APPENDIX

Typographic Ornaments
The Underground Grammarian
516 Ardmore Avenue
Pitman, NJ 08071
609-589-6477

URW fonts
The Font Company
7850 E. Evans Road, Suite 111
Scottsdale, AZ 85260
800-442-3668

Varityper fonts
Tegra/Varityper
11 Mt. Pleasant Avenue
East Hanover, NJ 07936
201-884-6277

VS Library of Fonts
VS Software
PO Box 165920
Little Rock, AR 72216
501-376-2083

Font Design and Font Manipulation

Art Importer
Altsys Corporation
269 W. Renner Road
Richardson, TX 75080
214-680-2060

FaceLift
Bitstream, Inc.
215 First Street
Cambridge, MA 02142
800-522-3668

Family Builder
Altsys Corporation
269 W. Renner Road
Richardson, TX 75080
214-680-2060

FontLiner
Taylored Graphics
PO Box 1900
Freedom, CA 95019
408-761-2481

FontMaker
The Font Factory
13601 Preston Road, Suite 500-W
Dallas, TX 75240
214-239-6085

Fontographer
Altsys Corporation
269 W. Renner Road
Richardson, TX 75080
214-680-2060

FontSizer
U.S. Microlabs, Inc.
1611 Headway Circle, Bldg. 3
Austin, TX 78754
512-339-0001

FontStudio
Letraset USA
40 Eisenhower Drive
Paramus, NJ 07653
201-845-6100

LetraStudio
LetraFont Library
Letraset USA
40 Eisenhower Drive
Paramus, NJ 07653
201-845-6100

LetrTuck
EDCO Services, Inc.
12410 N. Dale Mabry Hwy., Suite B
Tampa, FL 33618
813-962-7800

Metamorphosis
Altsys Corporation
269 W. Renner Road
Richardson, TX 75080
214-680-2060

Pairs Professional Kerning Editor and Kerning Tables
Pairs Software, Inc.
1315 Lawrence Avenue E., Suite 104
North York, ON M3A 3R3 Canada
416-510-1741

Publisher's Type Foundry
ZSoft Corporation
450 Franklin Road, Suite 100
Marietta, GA 30067
404-428-0008

Type Align
Adobe Systems, Inc.
PO Box 7900
Mountain View, CA 94039-7900
800-344-8335

Type Director
Hewlett-Packard Co.
3000 Hanover Street
Palo Alto, CA 94304-1181
415-857-1501

TypeStyler
Brøderbund Software
17 Paul Drive
San Rafael, CA 94903-2101
415-492-3200

PostScript Illustration Software

Adobe Illustrator
Adobe Streamline
Adobe Systems, Inc.
PO Box 7900
Mountain View, CA 94039-7900
800-344-8335

Aldus FreeHand
Aldus Corporation
411 First Avenue S.
Seattle, WA 98104
206-622-5500

Arts & Letters
Computer Support Corporation
15926 Midway Road
Dallas, TX 75244
214-661-8960

Corel Draw
Corel Systems Corporation
1600 Carling Avenue, Suite 190
Ottawa, ON K1Z 8R7 Canada
613-728-8200

Cricket Draw
Cricket Stylist
Computer Associates International
40 Valley Stream Parkway
Mallvern, PA 19355
215-251-9890

GEM Artline
Digital Research
70 Garden Court
Monterey, CA 93940
408-649-3896

Micrografx Designer
Micrografx
1303 Arapaho Road
Richardson, TX 75081-1769
800-272-3729

Smart Art
Adobe Systems, Inc.
PO Box 7900
Mountain View, CA 94039-7900
800-344-8335

Page Layout Programs

Aldus PageMaker
Aldus Corporation
411 First Avenue S.
Seattle, WA 98104
206-622-5500

DesignStudio
Letraset USA
40 Eisenhower Drive
Paramus, NJ 07653
201-845-6100

FrameMaker
Frame Technology Corporation
1010 Rincon Circle
San Jose, CA 95131
408-433-1928

Interleaf Publisher
Interleaf, Inc.
Prospect Place
9 Hillside Avenue
Walpham, MA 02154
617-290-0710

Personal Press
Silicon Beach Software
9770 Carroll Center Road, Suite J
San Diego, CA 92126
619-695-6956

QuarkXPress
Quark, Inc.
300 S. Jackson Street, Suite 100
Denver, CO 80209
800-543-7711

Ventura Publisher
Xerox Product Support
15175 Innovation Drive
San Diego, CA 92128
800-822-8221

Paint Programs

Color MacCheese
Delta Tao Software
760 Harvard Avenue
Sunnyvale, CA 94087
408-730-9336

DeluxePaint 3.0
Electronic Arts, Inc.
1820 Gateway Drive
San Mateo, CA 94404
415-571-7171

DigiPaint
NewTek
215 S.E. 8th Street
Topeka, KS 66603
800-843-8934

GraphicWorks
MacroMind, Inc.
410 Townsend Street, Suite 408
San Francisco, CA 94107
415-442-0200

LaserPaint
LaserWare
PO Box 668
San Rafael, CA 94915
415-453-9500

Lumena
Time Arts, Inc.
1425 Corporate Center Parkway
Santa Rosa, CA 95407
707-576-7722

MacPaint
Claris Corporation
5201 Patrick Henry Drive
Santa Clara, CA 95052
408-727-8227

PC Paintbrush IV Plus
ZSoft Corporation
450 Franklin Road, Suite 100
Marietta, GA 30067
404-428-0008

PixelPaint 2.0
PixelPaint Professional
SuperMac Technology
485 Potrero Avenue
Sunnyvale, CA 94086
408-245-2202

Studio/8
Studio/32
Electronic Arts, Inc.
1820 Gateway Drive
San Mateo, CA 94404
415-571-7171

SuperPaint 2.0
Silicon Beach Software
9770 Carroll Center Road, Suite J
San Diego, CA 92126
619-695-6956

UltraPaint
Deneba Software
3305 N.W. 74th Avenue
Miami, FL 33122
800-622-6827

VideoPaint
Olduvai Corporation
7520 Red Road, Suite A
South Miami, FL 33143
305-665-4665

Image-Processing Software

Adobe Photoshop
Adobe Systems, Inc.
PO Box 7900
Mountain View, CA 94039-7900
800-344-8335

ColorStudio
Letraset USA
40 Eisenhower Drive
Paramus, NJ 07653
201-845-6100

Digital Darkroom
Silicon Beach Software
9770 Carroll Center Road, Suite J
San Diego, CA 92126
619-695-6956

Enhance
MicroFrontier, Inc.
3401 101st Street, Suite E
Des Moines, IA 50322
800-388-8109

Gray F/X
Xerox Imaging Systems, Inc.
185 Albany Street
Cambridge, MA 02139
617-864-4700

Hercules Art Department
Hercules Computer Technology
921 Parker Street
Berkeley, CA 94710
415-540-6000

ImageStudio
Letraset USA
40 Eisenhower Drive
Paramus, NJ 07653
201-845-6100

PhotoMac
Data Translation
100 Locke Drive
Marlboro, MA 01752
508-481-3700

Picture Publisher
Micrografx
1303 Arapaho Road
Richardson, TX 75081
800-733-3729

Targa TIPS
Truevision
7340 Shadeland Station
Indianapolis, IN 46256-3935
317-841-0332

Draw Programs

Canvas
Deneba Software
3305 N.W. 74th Avenue
Miami, FL 33122
800-622-6827

MacDraw
Claris Corporation
5201 Patrick Henry Drive
Santa Clara, CA 95052
408-727-8227

3D Programs

AutoDesk 3D Studio
AutoDesk
2320 Marinship Way
Sausalito, CA 94965
415-332-2344

MacRenderMan
Pixar
1001 W. Cutting Boulevard
Richmond, CA 94804
415-236-4000

MacroMind 3D
MacroMind, Inc.
410 Townsend Street, Suite 408
San Francisco, CA 94107
415-442-0200

Sculpt 3D
Byte by Byte
9442 Capital of Texas Hwy N., Suite 150
Austin, TX 78759
512-343-4357

StrataVision 3D
Strata, Inc.
2 W. Saint George Boulevard
Ancestor Square, Suite 2100
Saint George, UT 84770
801-628-5218

Super 3D
Silicon Beach Software
9770 Carroll Center Road, Suite J
San Diego, CA 92126
619-695-6956

Swivel 3D
Paracomp, Inc.
1725 Montgomery Street, Second Floor
San Francisco, CA 94111
415-956-4091

Clip Art

Adobe Illustrator Collector's Edition
Adobe Systems, Inc.
PO Box 7900
Mountain View, CA 94039-7900
800-344-8335

Artagenix
Devonian International Software
Company
PO Box 2351
Montclair, CA 91763
714-621-0973

ArtRoom
Image Club Graphics, Inc.
1902 11th Street S.E., Suite 5
Calgary, AB T2G 3G2 Canada
403-262-8008

Arts & Letters
Computer Support Corporation
15926 Midway Road
Dallas, TX 75244
214-661-8960

ClickArt EPS Illustrations
T/Maker Company
1390 Villa Street
Mountain View, CA 94041
415-962-0195

Clip Art Libraries
Stephen & Associates
2168 Balboa Avenue, Suite 3
San Diego, CA 92109
619-270-8800

Clip Charts
MacroMind, Inc.
410 Townsend Street, Suite 408
San Francisco, CA 94107
415-442-0200

Comstock Desktop Photography
Comstock, Inc.
30 Irving Place
New York, NY 10003
212-353-8686

Darkroom CD-ROM
Image Club Graphics
1902 11th Street S.E., Suite 5
Calgary, AB T2G 3G2 Canada
800-661-9410

Designer ClipArt
Micrografx, Inc.
1303 Arapaho Road
Richardson, TX 75081-1769
800-733-3729

DeskTop Art
Dynamic Graphics, Inc.
6000 N. Forest Park Drive
Peoria, IL 61656-1901
800-255-8800

Digiclips
U-Design, Inc.
270 Farmington Avenue
Hartford, CT 06105
203-278-3648

Digit-Art
Image Club Graphics, Inc.
1902 11th Street S.E., Suite 5
Calgary, AB T2G 3G2 Canada
403-262-8008

Illustrated Art Backgrounds
ARTfactory
414 Tennessee Plaza, Suite A
Redlands, CA 92373
714-793-7346

Images with Impact
3G Graphics
11410 N.E. 124th Street, Suite 6155
Kirkland, WA 98034
206-367-9321

PhotoFiles
GoldMind Publishing
4994 Tulsa Avenue
Riverside, CA 92505
714-687-3815

Photo Gallery
NEC Technologies, Inc.
159 Swanson Road
Boxborough, MA 01719
508-264-8000

PicturePak
Islandview/MGI
PO Box 11087
Richmond, VA 23230
804-673-5601

**Pro-Art Professional
    Art Library Trilogy 1, 2, 3, 4**
Multi-Ad Services, Inc.
1720 W. Detweiller Drive
Peoria, IL 61615
309-692-1530

Professional Photography Collection
disc *Imagery*
18 E. 16th Street
New York, NY 10003
212-675-8500

The Right Images
Tsunami Press
275 Route 18
East Brunswick, NJ 08816
800-448-9815

TextArt
Stone Design Corporation
2425 Teodoro N.W.
Albuquerque, NM 87107
505-345-4800

Totem Graphics
Totem Graphics
5109-A Capitol Boulevard
Tumwater, WA 98501
206-352-1851

Type Foundry
U-Design, Inc.
270 Farmington Avenue
Hartford, CT 06105
203-278-3648

Vivid Impressions
Casady & Greene, Inc.
22734 Portola Drive
Salinas, CA 93908
800-359-4920

Graphics Tablets

Kurta
3007 E. Chambers
Phoenix, AZ 85040
602-276-5533

Summagraphics Corporation
325 Heights Road
Houston, TX 77007
713-869-7009

Wacom, Inc.
Park 80 West, Plaza II
Saddlebrook, NJ 07662
201-265-4226

Scanners

Abaton Scan 300/FB and 300/S
Abaton Technology Corporation
48431 Milmont Drive
Fremont, CA 94538
415-683-2226

Apple Scanner
Apple Computer, Inc.
20525 Mariani Avenue
Cupertino, CA 95014
408-996-1010

C1S-3513 35mm Scanning System
Barneyscan Corporation
1125 Atlantic Avenue
Alameda, CA 94501
415-521-3388

ClearScan
NCL America
1753 S. Main Street
Milpitas, CA 95035
408-956-1040

Dest PC Scan 1000 and 2000 series
Dest Corporation
1015 E. Brokaw Road
Sunnyvale, CA 95131
408-436-2700

Eikonix 1435 slide scanner
Atex Magazine Publishing Systems
805 Middlesex Turnpike
Billerica, MA 01821
617-275-8300

Howtek ScanMaster II
Howtek
21 Park Avenue
Hudson, NH 03051
603-882-5200

HP ScanJet Plus
Hewlett-Packard Company
700 71st Avenue
Greeley, CO 80634
303-350-4000

**JX-100, JX-300, JX-450 and JX-600
Color Scanners**
Sharp Electronics Corporation
Sharp Plaza, Box C Systems
Mahwah, NJ 07430
201-529-8200

LightningScan 400
Thunderware, Inc.
21 Orinda Way
Orinda, CA 94563
415-254-6581

LS-3500 slide scanner
Nikon Electronic Imaging
1300 Walt Whitman Road
Melville, NY 11747
516-547-4200

Microtek Scanners
Microtek Lab, Inc.
680 Knox Street
Torrance, CA 90502
213-321-2121

ScanMan Plus hand-held scanner
Logitech
6505 Kaiser Drive
Fremont, CA 94555
415-795-8500

Silverscanner
LaCie
19552 S.W. 90th Court
Tualatin, OR 97062
800-999-0143

Thunderscan
Thunderware, Inc.
21 Orinda Way
Orinda, CA 94563
415-254-6581

Storage Systems

FWB, Inc.
2040 Polk Street, Suite 215
San Francisco, CA 94109
415-474-8055

Iomega Corporation
1821 W. 4000th S.
Roy, UT 84067
800-456-5522

Jasmine Technology, Inc.
1225 Elko Drive
Sunnyvale, CA 94089
408-752-2900

LaCie
19552 S.W. 90th Court
Tualitin, OR 97062
800-999-0143

Mass Microsystems
810 W. Maude Avenue
Sunnyvale, CA 94086
800-522-7979

MicroNet Technology, Inc.
20 Mason
Irvine, CA 92718
714-837-6033

OCEAN Microsystems, Inc.
246 E. Hacienda Avenue
Campbell, CA 95008
800-262-3261

Pinnacle Micro
15265 Alton Parkway
Irvine, CA 92718
714-727-3300

PLI
47421 Bayside Parkway
Fremont, CA 94538
415-657-2211

Storage Dimensions
2145 Hamilton Avenue
San Jose, CA 95125
408-879-0300

Sumo Systems
1580 Old Oakland Road, Suite C103
San Jose, CA 95131
408-453-5744

SuperMac Technology
485 Potrero Avenue
Sunnyvale, CA 94086
408-245-2202

Transitional Technology
5401 E. La Palma Avenue
Anaheim, CA 92807
714-693-1133

Monitors

Apple Computer, Inc.
20525 Mariani Avenue
Cupertino, CA 95014
408-996-1010

E-Machines, Inc.
9305 S.W. Gemini Drive
Beaverton, OR 97005
503-646-6699

MegaGraphics, Inc.
439 Calle San Pablo
Camarillo, CA 93012
805-484-3799

Mitsubishi Electronics
991 Knox Street
Torrance, CA 90502
213-217-5732

Moniterm Corporation
5740 Green Circle Drive
Minnetonka, MN 55343
612-935-4151

Nutmeg Systems, Inc.
25 South Avenue
New Canaan, CT 06840
800-777-8439

Radius, Inc.
1710 Fortune Drive
San Jose, CA 95131
408-434-1010

RasterOps Corporation
2500 Walsh Avenue
Santa Clara, CA 95051
800-468-7600

SuperMac Technology
485 Potrero Avenue
Sunnyvale, CA 94086
408-245-2202

Color Calibration

The Calibrator
Barco Electronics
1000 Cobb Place Boulevard, Suite 100
Kennesaw, GA 30144
404-590-7900

PrecisionColor Calibrator
Radius, Inc.
1710 Fortune Drive
San Jose, CA 95131
408-434-1010

TekColor
Tektronix, Inc.
PO Box 1000, 60-337
Wilsonville, OR 97070-1000
800-547-8949

Accelerators

Daystar Digital
5556 Atlanta Highway
Flowery Branch, GA 30542
404-967-2077

Radius, Inc.
1710 Fortune Drive
San Jose, CA 95131
408-434-1010

RasterOps Corporation
2500 Walsh Avenue
Santa Clara, CA 95051
408-562-4200

Utilities, Desk Accessories and INITs

Adobe Type Align
Adobe Type Manager
Adobe Type Reunion
Adobe Systems, Inc.
PO Box 7900
Mountain View, CA 94039-7900
800-344-8335

After Dark screen saver
Berkeley Systems, Inc.
1700 Shattuck Avenue
Berkeley, CA 94709
415-540-5535

Capture
Mainstay
5311-B Derry Avenue
Agoura Hills, CA 91301
818-991-6540

DaynaFile for Macintosh
Dayna Communications, Inc.
50 S. Main Street, Suite 530
Salt Lake City, UT 84144
800-531-0203

Diskfit
SuperMac Technology
485 Potrero Avenue
Sunnyvale, CA 94086
408-245-2202

DiskTools Plus
Electronic Arts, Inc.
1820 Gateway Drive, Suite 200
San Mateo, CA 94404
800-245-4525

DOS Mounter
Dayna Communications, Inc.
50 S. Main Street, Suite 530
Salt Lake City, UT 84144
800-531-0203

Exposure
Baseline Pulblishing
1770 Moriah Woods Boulevard, Suite 14
Memphis, TN 38117-7118
901-682-9676

Fastback II
Fifth Generation Systems, Inc.
10049 N. Reiger Road
Baton Rouge, LA 70809
800-873-4384

Flowfazer
Utopia Grokware
300 Valley Street, Suite 204
Sausalito, CA 94965
415-331-0714

Font/DA Juggler Plus
Alsoft, Inc.
PO Box 927
Spring, TX 77383-0929
713-353-4090

InitPicker
Microseeds Publishing, Inc.
5801 Benjamin Center Drive, Suite 103
Tampa, FL 33634
813-882-8635

Kodak Colorsqueeze
Kodak
343 State Street
Rochester, NY 14650
800-233-1650

New Fountain
David Blatner, Parallax Productions
5001 Ravenna Avenue N.E., Suite 13
Seattle, WA 98105
206-633-1432

On Cue
Icom Simulations, Inc.
648 S. Wheeling Road
Wheeling, IL 60090
708-520-4440

Overwood 2.0, shareware
Jim Donnelly
5305 Baltimore Avenue
Hyattsville, MD 20781
301-927-3040

Pyro!
Fifth Generation Systems, Inc.
10049 N. Reiger Road
Baton Rouge, LA 70809
800-873-4384

QuickKeys
CE Software
PO Box 65580
W. Des Moines, IA 50265
515-224-1995

Screen-to-PICT, public domain
Educorp
7434 Trade Street
San Diego, CA 92121
800-843-9497

SmartScrap
The Clipper II
Solutions, Incorporated
PO Box 783
Williston, VT 05602
802-865-9220

Suitcase II
Fifth Generation Systems, Inc.
10049 N. Reiger Road
Baton Rouge, LA 70809
800-873-4384

Prepress Systems

Aldus PrePrint
Aldus Corporation
411 First Avenue S.
Seattle, WA 98104
206-622-5500

Crosfield
Du Pont Imaging Systems
65 Harristown Road
Glen Rock, NJ 07452
201-447-5800

Freedom of Press
Custom Applications, Inc.
900 Technology Park Drive, Bldg 8
Billerica, MA 01821
508-667-8585

Lightspeed Color Layout System
Lightspeed
47 Farnsworth Street
Boston, MA 02210
617-338-2173

APPENDIX

Printware 720 IQ Laser Imager
Printware, Inc.
1385 Mendota Heights Road
Saint Paul, MN 55120
800-456-1616

SpectreSeps PM
Pre-Press Technologies, Inc.
2443 Impala Drive
Carlsbad, CA 92008
619-931-2695

Visionary
Scitex America Corporation
8 Oak Park Drive
Bedford, MA 01730
617-275-5150

Printers and Imagesetters

BirmySetter 300 & 400 Imagesetters
Birmy Graphics Corporation
255 East Drive, Suite H
Melbourne, FL 32904
800-752-5306

Canon Color Laser Copier 500
Canon U.S.A., Inc.
One Canon Plaza
Lake Success, NY 11042
516-488-6700

ColorMate PostScript printer
NEC Technologies, Inc.
Printer Marketing Division
1414 Massachusetts Avenue
Boxborough, MA 01719
800-632-4636

ColorPoint
Seiko Instruments
1130 Ringwood Ct.
San Jose, CA 95131
800-873-4561

ColorQuick
Tektronix, Inc.
Graphics Printing & Imaging Division
PO Box 1000
Wilsonville, OR 97070-1000
800-835-6100

Colorsetter 2000
Optronics, An Intergraph Division
7 Stuart Road
Chelmsford, MA 01824
508-256-4511

Compugraphic Imagesetters
Agfa Compugraphic Division
200 Ballardvale Street
Wilmington, MA 01887
508-658-5600

4CAST
Du Pont Electronic Imaging Systems
1007 Market Street
Wilmington, DE 19898
800-654-4567

HP LaserJet Series II
Hewlett-Packard Company
PO Box 60008
Sunnyvale, CA 94088-60008
800-538-8787

HP PaintJet
Hewlett-Packard Company
PO Box 60008
Sunnyvale, CA 94088-60008
800-538-8787

ImageWriter II
Apple Computer, Inc.
20525 Mariani Avenue
Cupertino, CA 95014
408-996-1010

JLaser CR1
Tall Tree Systems
PO Box 50690
Palo Alto, CA 94303
415-493-1980

**Kodak XL 7700
    Digital Continuous Tone Printer**
Eastman Kodak Company
343 State Street
Rochester, NY 14650
800-242-2424

Lasersmith PS-415 Laser Printers
Lasersmith, Inc.
430 Martin Avenue
Santa Clara, CA 95050
408-727-7700

LaserWriter II family of printers
Apple Computer, Inc.
20525 Mariani Avenue
Cupertino, CA 95014
408-996-1010

Linotronic imagesetters
Linotype-Hell Company
425 Oser Avenue
Hauppauge, NY 11788
516-434-2000

LZR Series Laser Printers
Dataproducts Corporation
PO Box 746
Woodland Hills, CA 91365-0746
818-887-8000

**Mitsubishi G330-70
    color thermal printer**
Mitsubishi Electronics
Computer Peripherals Products
991 Knox Street
Torrance, CA 90502
213-515-3993

Omnilaser Series 2000
Texas Instruments Inc.
PO Box 149149
Austin, TX 78714
512-250-7111

Personal LaserWriter
Apple Computer, Inc.
20525 Mariani Avenue
Cupertino, CA 95014
408-996-1010

Phaser Color Image Printer
Tektronix, Inc.
Graphics Printing & Imaging Division
PO Box 1000, M/S 63-583
Wilsonville, OR 97070-1000
800-835-6100

QMS ColorScript printers
QMS-PS Series Laser Printers
QMS, Inc.
PO Box 81250
Mobile, AL 36689
205-633-4300

Series 1000 Imagesetters
Linotype-Hell Company
425 Oser Avenue
Hauppauge, NY 11788
516-434-2000

StyleWriter
Apple Computer, Inc.
20525 Mariani Avenue
Cupertino, CA 95014
408-996-1010

Turbo PS Series Laser Printer
NewGen Systems Corporation
17580 Newhope Street
Fountain Valley, CA 92708
714-641-8600

UltreSetter
Ultre Corporation
145 Pinelawn Road
Melville, NY 11747
516-753-4800

Varityper printers
Tegra/Varityper
11 Mt. Pleasant Avenue
East Hanover, NJ 07936
201-884-6277

Large-Format Output Services

Computer Image Systems
20030 Normandie Avenue
Torrance, CA 90503
800-736-5105

Gamma One
PO Box 566
North Haven, CT 06473
203-234-0440

Film Recorders

Agfa-Matrix Film Recorder
Agfa
1 Ramland Road
Orangeburg, NY 10962
914-365-0190

FilmPrinterPlus
Mirus Industries Corporation
758 Sycamore Drive
Milpitas, CA 95035
800-944-9770

Periodicals

Aldus **magazine**
Aldus Corporation
411 First Avenue S.
Seattle, WA 98104
206-622-5500

Colophon
Font & Function
Adobe Systems, Inc.
PO Box 7900
Mountain View, CA 94039-7900
800-344-8335

Desktop Commucications
International Desktop Communications Ltd.
48 E. 43rd Street
New York, NY 10017
212-867-9650

MacUser
PC **magazine**
Ziff-Davis Publishing Company
1 Park Avenue
New York, NY 10016
800-627-2247

Macworld
PCW Communications, Inc.
501 Second Street
San Francisco, CA 94107
800-234-1038

Personal Publishing
Hitchcock Publishing Company
PO Box 3240
Harlan, IA 51537
800-727-6937

Publish
PCW Communications, Inc.
501 Second Street, Suite 600
San Francisco, CA 94107
800-222-2990

Step-by-Step Electronic Design
Dynamic Graphics, Inc.
6000 N. Forest Park Drive
Peoria, IL 61656-1901
800-255-8800

U&lc
International Typeface Corporation
2 Hammarskjold Plaza
New York, NY 10017
212-371-0699

Verbum **magazine**
Verbum, Inc.
PO Box 12564
San Diego, CA 92112
619-233-9977

Books

The Gray Book
Ventana Press
PO Box 2468
Chapel Hill, NC 27515
919-942-0220

PostScript Type Sampler
MacTography
326D N. Stonestreet Avenue
Rockville, MD 20850
301-424-1357

The Verbum Book of PostScript
  Illustration
The Verbum Book of Electronic Page
  Design
The Verbum Book of Digital Painting
The Verbum Book of Scanned Imagery
M&T Books
501 Galveston Drive
Redwood City, CA 94063
415-366-3600

Bulletin Board Services

CompuServe Information Services, Inc.
5000 Arlington Centre Boulevard
Columbus, OH 43220
800-848-8199

Connect Professional
Information Network
Connect, Inc.
10161 Bubb Road
Cupertino, CA 95014
408-973-0110

Desktop Express
Dow Jones & Company
PO Box 300
Princeton, NJ 08543-0300
609-520-4000

Genie
GE Information Services
401 N. Washington Street
Rockville, MD 20810
800-638-9636

MCI Mail
1111 19th Street N.W., Suite 500
Washington, DC 20036
800-444-6245

Communication Software

Microphone II
Software Ventures
2907 Claremont Avenue, Suite 220
Berkeley, CA 94705
800-336-6477

Red Ryder
Free Soft
150 Hickory Drive
Beaver Falls, PA 15010
412-846-2700

This book was designed and produced primarily on Macintoshes, although several other kinds of computer systems were used. Text was input primarily in Microsoft Word on a Macintosh IIci and a Mac Plus. Other computers used in the design and production of the book included a Mac II, a second Macintosh IIci, a IIcx, an SE and a Plus.

Text files supplied by artists were converted, if necessary, to Microsoft Word format on the Mac. Files were checked with Word's Spelling function; the Change (search-and-replace) function was used to find and eliminate extra spaces and to insert *fi* and *fl* ligatures.

Pages were laid out and styled using PageMaker 4.0. Body text was set in Adobe's Galliard (10/14.5), and captions in Franklin Gothic (7/8). A Zapf Dingbats "z" was used for the "hint" symbol.

Illustrations for the project chapters and Gallery were created as described in the text and in most cases were supplied by the artist as application files. Most artwork for the book was saved in EPS, TIFF or PICT format and placed in the PageMaker files. Screen shots to show software interfaces were made on a Mac II using FKeys such as Command-Shift-7 (screen-to-PICT) or the Camera desk accessory on a Mac Plus.

During final layout and production, files were stored on 45 MB removable cartridge drives. An Apple IINTX laser printer was used for proofing pages. Pages were output by Applied Graphics Technologies of Foster City, California on a Linotronic L-300 imagesetter with a RIP 3. Pages with type and line art only were output as negatives at 1270 dpi; pages with screen tints or grayscale images were output as negatives at 2540 dpi. In some cases artwork was provided to Applied Graphics Technologies as 35mm transparencies or as final printed pieces, which were shot as halftones and stripped into the page negatives.

The cover was laid out in PageMaker and proofed on a Tektronix Phaser color PostScript printer. The front cover illustration, by Jack Davis, was developed with Adobe Illustrator and Adobe Photoshop. Illustrations on the back cover were created in Illustrator by Louis Fishauf, Tom Gould and David Smith. The "Verbum Electronic Art and Design Series" logo was created in Aldus FreeHand, and the "M&T Books" logo was converted to electronic form in Illustrator. The cover was output as negatives at 2540 dpi with Aldus PrePrint for the four-color separations by Central Graphics of San Diego.

INDEX

INDEX

The Verbum Book of Electronic Page Design
by Michael Gosney and Linnea Dayton

This particular volume introduces designers, illustrators, and desktop publishers to the electronic page layout medium and various application programs, such as PageMaker, QuarkXPress, Design Studio, and Ventura Publishing. Each chapter highlights the talents of a top designer who guides readers through the thinking as well as the "mousing" that leads to the creation of various projects. These projects range in complexity from a trifold black and white brochure to a catalog produced with QuarkXPress. More than 100 illustrations, with 32 pages in full-color, are included. 211 pp.

Book only   **Item #088-5**   **$29.95**

The Verbum Book of Digital Painting
by Michael Gosney, Linnea Dayton, and Paul Goethel

Contained herein are a series of entertaining projects that teach readers how to create compelling designs using the myriad of graphics tools available in commercial painting programs. Presented by professional designers, these projects range from a simple greeting card to a complex street scene. This book also includes portfolios of paintings created by the featured artists, plus an extensive gallery of works from other accomplished artists and 64 pages of full-color paintings. 211 pp.

Book only   **Item #090-7**   **$29.95**

The Verbum Book of PostScript Illustration
by Michael Gosney, Linnea Dayton, and Janet Ashford

This is the premier instruction book for designers, illustrators, and desktop publishers using Postscript. Each chapter highlights the talents of top illustrators who demonstrate the electronic artmaking process. The narrative keys readers in to the artist's conceptual vision, providing valuable insight into the creative thought processes that go into a real-world PostScript illustration project. 213 pp.

Book only   **Item #089-3**   **$29.95**

1-800-533-4372 (in CA 1-800-356-2002)

M&T BOOKS

O R D E R   F O R M

To Order: Return this form with your payment to M&T books, 501 Galveston Drive, Redwood City, CA 94063 or **call toll-free 1-800-533-4372 (in California, call 1-800-356-2002).**

ITEM #	DESCRIPTION	DISK	PRICE

Subtotal	
CA residents add sales tax ____%	
Add $3.75 per item for shipping and handling	
TOTAL	

NOTE: **FREE SHIPPING** ON ORDERS OF THREE OR MORE BOOKS.

Charge my:
- ❏ **Visa**
- ❏ **MasterCard**
- ❏ **AmExpress**

- ❏ **Check enclosed, payable to M&T Books.**

CARD NO. _____

SIGNATURE _____   EXP. DATE _____

NAME _____

ADDRESS _____

CITY _____

STATE _____   ZIP _____

M&T GUARANTEE: If your are not satisfied with your order for any reason, return it to us within 25 days of receipt for a full refund. Note: Refunds on disks apply only when returned with book within guarantee period. Disks damaged in transit or defective will be promptly replaced, but cannot be exchanged for a disk from a different title.

8000

1-800-533-4372 (in CA 1-800-356-2002)

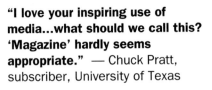

"I love your inspiring use of media...what should we call this? 'Magazine' hardly seems appropriate." — Chuck Pratt, subscriber, University of Texas

VERBUM INTERACTIVE

CD-ROM Multimedia Magazine
Issue 1.0 Macintosh Edition

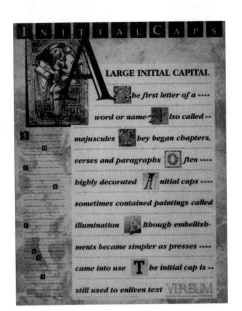

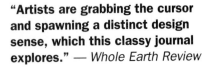

"The emergence of good taste... these guys are very serious about doing things right."— John Dvorak, PC Industry Analyst

"Artists are grabbing the cursor and spawning a distinct design sense, which this classy journal explores." — *Whole Earth Review*

THE JOURNAL OF PERSONAL COMPUTER AESTHETICS

Join the inner circle of electronic art, design and multimedia professionals who've counted on *Verbum* since 1986 to deliver the cutting edge: the Verbum Gallery, regular columns, feature stories, new products, ideas, insights — synergy. *Verbum* is both substance *and* style — each issue uses the latest tools and programs to push the limits of desktop publishing.

Verbum is also pioneering multimedia publishing with **Verbum Interactive 1.0,** a fully integrated CD-ROM "magazine" featuring text (on-screen and for printing), sound, graphics, animations, talking agents, video and music. Columns, features, a Gallery, Source-Bank and more! Includes a tutorial on type effects with Photoshop. Stereo music (playable on regular CD players) from Todd Rundgren, Graham Nash and others. The 2-disc set includes demo versions of Photoshop, Illustrator, ColorStudio, Swivel 3D Professional and TextureSynth. The Verbum Roundtable features an interactive panel discussion on multimedia with six industry leaders. If you don't already have a CD-ROM drive, this is reason alone to get one!

"If I were stranded on a desert island, this is the magazine I'd want with me" — Bob Roberts, *MIPS Journal*